T0373072

THE I TATTI
RENAISSANCE LIBRARY

James Hankins, General Editor

FONZIO
LETTERS TO FRIENDS

ITRL 47

THE I TATTI RENAISSANCE LIBRARY

James Hankins, General Editor
Shane Butler, Associate Editor
Martin Davies, Associate Editor

Editorial Board

Michael J. B. Allen
Brian P. Copenhaver
Vincenzo Fera
Julia Haig Gaisser
†Claudio Leonardi
Walther Ludwig
Nicholas Mann
Silvia Rizzo

Advisory Committee

Lino Pertile, Chairman

Francesco Bausi
Robert Black
Michele Ciliberto
Caroline Elam
Arthur Field
Anthony Grafton
Hanna Gray
Ralph Hexter
Craig Kallendorf
Jill Kraye
Marc Laureys
Francesco Lo Monaco
David Marsh
John Monfasani
John O'Malley
Marianne Pade
David Quint
Christine Smith
Rita Sturlese
Francesco Tateo
Mirko Tavoni
Carlo Vecce
Ronald Witt
Jan Ziolkowski

BARTOLOMEO FONZIO

✦ ✦ ✦

LETTERS TO FRIENDS

EDITED BY

ALESSANDRO DANELONI

TRANSLATED BY

MARTIN DAVIES

THE I TATTI RENAISSANCE LIBRARY
HARVARD UNIVERSITY PRESS
CAMBRIDGE, MASSACHUSETTS
LONDON, ENGLAND
2011

Copyright © 2011 by the President and Fellows of Harvard College
All rights reserved
Printed in the United States of America

Series design by Dean Bornstein

Library of Congress Cataloging-in-Publication Data

Fonte, Bartolommeo, 1445–1513.
[Correspondence. English & Latin]
Letters to friends / Bartolomeo Fonzio ; edited by Alessandro Daneloni ; translated by Martin Davies.
p. cm. — (The I Tatti Renaissance library ; 47)
Latin text with facing English translation.
Includes bibliographical references and indexes.
ISBN 978-0-674-05836-1 (alk. paper)
1. Fonte, Bartolomeo, 1445–1513 — Correspondence.
2. Fonte, Bartolomeo, 1445–1513 — Translations into English.
3. Authors, Latin (Medieval and modern) — Italy — Correspondence.
4. Humanists — Italy — Correspondence. 5. Italy — Intellectual life — 1268–1559 — Sources. I. Daneloni, Alessandro.
II. Davies, Martin, 1951– III. Title. IV. Series.
PA8520.F645Z48 2011
876'.04 — dc22 2010042648

Contents

Introduction

A figure of the first importance in Florentine humanism, Bartolomeo Fonzio (or della Fonte; August 26, 1447–October 1513) was the protagonist of an exceptionally rich and varied life played out from the age of Piero di Cosimo de' Medici and Lorenzo il Magnifico down to the first restoration of the Medici in 1512, thus passing through the disturbed periods dominated by the figures of Girolamo Savonarola and Pier Soderini.[1] Many teachers and literary figures played a significant part, at different times and in different degrees, in his education and mature development: Cristoforo Landino, Bernardo Nuti, and Donato Acciaiuoli, the Greeks Joannes Argyropoulos and Andronicus Callistus, the Ferrarese humanist Battista Guarini, and the Veronese philologist Domizio Calderini. From the time of his literary debut Fonzio showed a wide range of interests, inclining no less to religious and theological subjects than to the study of the pagan *auctores* of antiquity.

His first important work was the *De paenitentia* of 1469, a brief Latin treatise based on a dense web of biblical and patristic sources, but not without originality. In the course of the 1470s, Fonzio prepared a highly successful commentary on the *Satires* of Persius, the *Explanatio in Persii satyras*, first printed at the end of 1477. By the end of that decade he was already an accomplished philologist and scholar securely embedded in the world of humanism. In 1481 he was called to be professor of poetry and rhetoric at the Studio of Florence, a position he held for long periods, though with several interruptions (1481–83, 1484–88, 1494–1504). Arising from his teaching activity were the prolusions, or introductory lectures, to six courses he held at the university (*Oratio in laudem oratoriae facultatis* [Oration in praise of eloquence, 1481], *In historiae laudationem* [In praise of history, 1482], *In bonas artis* [On the humanities,

1484], *In laudem poetices* [In praise of poetry, 1485], *De sapientia* [On wisdom, 1486], *In satyrae et studiorum humanitatis laudationem* [In praise of satire and the humanities, 1487]). Taken together, these give a complete picture of the high conception Fonzio had of the *studia humanitatis* and open up a variety of fruitful approaches to history and culture. To take just a couple of examples, one thinks of his highly original classification of the arts as a whole presented in the *Oratio in bonas artis,* where, however, stress is laid on the role of the *grammaticus,* or philologist, and his importance in laying the critical foundation of every field of knowledge (a proposition taken up again in the *Oratio in satyrae et studiorum humanitatis laudationem*). Especially noteworthy is the syncretism of Platonism and Christianity that pervades the *Oratio de sapientia,* the most speculative and philosophical of Fonzio's orations and a singular novelty in what is, as a rule, a tiresomely repetitive genre, the academic prolusion.

Fonzio's lengthy tenure at the Studio of Florence was conducted alongside, and sometimes interacted with, a sustained and intensive preoccupation with philological criticism of a range of Latin texts. These included Valerius Flaccus, whose *Argonautica* was a lifelong passion on which he lectured several times at the university; Livy's *History of Rome,* some passages of which were critically discussed in his *Observationes in Titum Livium,* composed about 1495–96; the *Satires* of Juvenal — another of his university courses, and one which represented the chosen battleground of his bitter dispute with Angelo Poliziano, the other great exponent of humanist philology; and the satires of Persius. On the latter, following the 1477 commentary mentioned above, Fonzio composed a second treatise, the *Tadeus vel de locis Persianis* (Tadeus, or Passages of Persius), which was dedicated in 1489 to Matthias Corvinus, king of Hungary.

The wide-ranging literary activity of our humanist found further outlets of great interest in the last two decades of the fifteenth century. During the 1480s, for example, Fonzio composed a short but remarkable historical work, the *Annales suorum temporum* (Annals of his own times), in which he set down a succinct account of the principal political, military, and cultural events of the years 1448–83, giving us sometimes valuable information or interesting judgments and points of view. The preparation of the *Saxettus,* a poetical collection dedicated, again in 1489, to King Matthias's son János Corvinus, also goes back to the 1480s, bringing together Latin elegies written in that decade and the '70s. There followed in the period 1489–92 the Latin treatise on poetry, *De poetice,* dedicated to Lorenzo de' Medici. This marked an important stage in Fonzio's literary development. The treatise was innovative in humanist writing, dealing as it did for the first time with poetry in itself and as such, its essence and its history; the treatment is entirely independent of Aristotle's *Poetics,* which Fonzio did not know. But there is much work still to be done on the *De poetice,* in particular on its relationship to the better-known *Nutricia* of Angelo Poliziano. On the vernacular side, it is worth mentioning the little treatise that Fonzio wrote in the 1490s, the *Pelago o Ragionamento sopra alchuni luoghi de' Triumphi del Petrarcha* (The Sea, or An account of several passages in Petrarch's *Triumphs*), which is absolutely original in applying the techniques of philological investigation to the interpretation of problematic passages in the *Trionfi.*

Toward the end of the Quattrocento, Fonzio's support for the message and program of radical moral reform of Girolamo Savonarola (in whose defense he appears to have written an openly apologetic work) did not undermine or weaken his admiration for and profound attachment to the *studia humanitatis* and their educational value, as witnessed by his uninterrupted teaching at the Studio from the middle of the 1490s till 1504. In these years he continued to work on the scholarly analysis of the text of Valerius Flaccus, among other things, and from his university chair often indulged in polemic against the hypocritical religious who criticized the *humanae litterae* and classical studies in general, denying them any legitimacy or purpose. In his last years Fonzio led a relatively tranquil life, divided between the duties attached to his position as priest of the parish of S. Giovanni Battista at Montemurlo (near Prato in the diocese of Pistoia) and the prolonged work of revision and reworking of his Latin and Italian writings. These were to be published in an edition of his collected works, but owing to his death in the autumn of 1513, the work never reached completion.

The *Epistolarum libri* are undoubtedly Bartolomeo Fonzio's most important work. Consisting in the final version of a total of sixty letters arranged chronologically in three books, they embrace a considerable stretch of time, from May or June 1467 to March 1513. They offer not only ample notices of Fonzio's biography and insights into his character, but also much material on the political and cultural history of Florence and Italy between the late Quattrocento and early Cinquecento: they give us in effect a fairly detailed picture of a scholar and his age. With the intention of presenting a fully realized account of his personal and cultural history, Fonzio molded his *opus epistolare* by means of a long, complex, and closely considered choice of material and by a thoroughgoing revision and rewriting of the texts. He did not want, however, to make a systematic collection of all the missives at his disposal, preferring to concentrate his efforts on a limited range of documents that would mark significant moments and events of his biography. The end result was an *epistolario* of slender dimensions but by no means thin in content. It was made up of a harmonious amalgam of carefully selected and balanced texts, designed as pieces of a varied and highly finished mosaic.

At the outset of the collection we find some of Fonzio's dearest friends at once prominent: Pietro Cennini, Pietro Fanni, Francesco Gaddi, the addressees of a large group of letters (1.2–8, 10). In terms of biographical content, what is most striking is the young Fonzio's problems and anxieties as he struggles to find, from the late '60s onward, a more secure position or some sort of patronage that will allow him concentrated and fruitful pursuit of his literary studies. To Cennini, for example, Fonzio confided in ep. 1.2 his chagrin and bewilderment at the lack of any solid backing or secure support. His stay at Ferrara in the last years of Borso d'Este, which extended from about the summer of 1469 until summer 1471, represented a happy parenthesis for him in this regard, and one that was culturally very stimulating; but it came to an end all too soon and was followed by fresh disappointment and frustration. These sentiments clearly emerge from the letters sent in the autumn and winter of 1471–72 to his Hungarian friend Péter Garázda (epp. 1.12–15). With Garázda's help, but to no avail, Fonzio hoped to find a berth in the Hungary of the prelate and patron János Vitéz. At the beginning of the 1470s, though still beset by persistent difficulties and delays, Fonzio nevertheless arrived at an important point in his personal and intellectual development, demonstrating that despite everything he had reached a new maturity and level of educational attainment. Sure signs of this are seen in his two long letters to Battista Guarini in the spring or summer of 1472. Ep. 1.16 gives a long description of the ruins of ancient Rome, modeled on the *De varietate fortunae* of Poggio Bracciolini. It shows Fonzio's strong antiquarian and archaeological interests, which he owed to the influence of the scholarly merchant Francesco Sassetti, with whom in 1472 he began a long association which was significantly to affect the course of his life and the cultural directions he took. Ep. 1.17 is a long letter of consolation for the death of Guarini's wife, Bettina, cut from a delicate and learned literary fabric (one of its principal sources is the Latin version by Alamanno Rinuccini of the pseudo-Plutarchan *Consolatio ad Apollonium*). But it was clearly inspired by real emotion and sympathy for his friend's grief, in wonderfully worked prose, and together with 1.16 is one of the finest of the whole *epistolario*. Another text of great importance is the next, 1.18, addressed to Pietro Cennini. Dated August 26, 1472, the letter is in reality a fictitious composition, never actually sent to his friend and created by Fonzio only about the middle of the 1490s, at a time when he was drawing up the earliest version of the *epistolario*. That does not of course detract from the value of the copious information that the humanist gives on the first twenty-five years of his life, and in particular on the grave material difficulties which from his adolescence onward had obstructed and delayed the course of his studies. Ep. 1.18 is also notable for its presentation of Donato Acciaiuoli as master and guide, with a crucial role in determining Fonzio's cultural education. Fonzio was a mature humanist by the second half of the 1470s, with a substantial armory of historical and rhetorical equipment. Ep. 1.23 is eloquent in this regard, a letter which can be dated to summer or autumn 1476. Here he allows himself to take issue with Marsilio Ficino, then by far the most famous and influential intellectual in contemporary Florence, by criticizing, politely but firmly, some peculiarities of his Latin style.

As the *epistolario* advanced, the focus necessarily came to dwell on the 1480s, a complex period with plenty of important and encouraging new developments, such as his appointment to the Studio of Florence in 1481, mentioned above. But it was also a troubled time for Fonzio, marked by tension and great discomfort. The only Florentine humanist capable of rivaling Angelo Poliziano (up to a point), Fonzio had to suffer a long series of attacks and sly criticisms from the latter, ending inevitably in an open feud with him. The celebrated invective against Poliziano of August 22, 1483 (1.24), documents the violent rupture between the two professors and former friends. It was soon followed by Fonzio's temporary abandonment of Florence, where cultural life was dominated by his enemy. He went to seek better prospects in Rome, and his brief stay there (autumn 1483 to spring or summer 1484) gave rise to several letters (2.1–6) which lament his continued failure to find more congenial employment in the court of Sixtus IV. Addressing himself to his dear companion and patron Bernardo Rucellai in ep. 2.5, Fonzio complains of the impossibility of living amid the corruption of Rome, but he also remembers with still smoldering bitterness the persecution he underwent at the hands of Poliziano when he first took up university teaching. Soon back in Florence, Fonzio returned to teaching there as early as 1484–85, holding his chair until the academic year 1487–88. Various letters of the second half of the '80s are aimed at recording the high esteem in which he was held at home and abroad. Examples are such letters as 2.10, sent in September 1487 to the Senate of Ragusa (Dubrovnik), in which he gracefully declines the offer of a teaching post in the Dalmatian city while professing himself greatly honored by the invitation. A similar line is taken by ep. 2.14, of November 1489, in which Fonzio thanks Roberto Salviati for the gift of a copy of Pico's recently published *Heptaplus*. Fonzio's high-level contacts with another famous name emerge from 2.15, an obsequious missive sent to the chancellor of France, Guillaume de Rochefort, on November 28, 1489; he sends with it a copy of his epigraphic sylloge, which the French politician had shown an interest in acquiring. The years 1488–89 in any case represented a decisive moment in Fonzio's life: in that period, thanks to the good offices of Taddeo Ugoletti, he came into contact with Matthias Corvinus and became one of the principal collaborators in building up the king's library. At that time, in fact, he left Florence once more and took himself off to Hungary, where he lived attached to the royal court for some six months (February or March till August 1489). This appointment was an important recognition of Fonzio's qualities, his learning, and his boundless energy in promoting humane studies. It was only natural for him to recall with pride his involvement in Corvinus's ambitious project, recorded in no fewer than three letters, 2.11–12 to Matthias himself and 2.13 to the king's treasurer, János Móré, his friend and helper in the search for and production of books for the library.

Exemplary events in Fonzio's personal situation are evoked by other letters at the beginning of the sixteenth century, in particular 2.20, of September 22, 1502, with its congratulations to Pier Soderini following his election as Gonfalonier of Justice for life. This is a text that recalls one of the most important episodes in the long political crisis that Florence underwent at the turn of the century, and also one that, together with 2.22, to Francesco Soderini of June 20, 1503 (containing congratulations on his creation as cardinal), forms a sort of diptych designed to display Fonzio's close and confidential relations with the Soderini family, who had assumed a leading role in the political panorama of Florence in the opening years of the sixteenth century. The same bonds are later attested to by the affectionate letter that the elderly Fonzio sent to his friend and pupil Tommaso di Giovan Vittorio Soderini, ep. 3.10, of January 1512.

Among the letters of Book 3, relating to the last part of Fonzio's life, from 1506 onward, we find a number of unhappy events documented, in particular the death of his sister, Brigida, which is recounted with heartfelt grief in ep. 3.1, of August 1, 1506, to his friend and former student Francesco Pandolfini. These letters also reveal developments in his spiritual and cultural life: several of them, for example, emphasize his growing interest in ethical and religious matters and his attachment to a more rigid and orthodox Christian faith. One thinks, for example, of ep. 3.4, a letter given over to a minute examination of excommunication which shows the deep expertise in canon law that Fonzio had acquired, and of 3.5, the well-known discussion of the signs of the Antichrist which he sent to the singular Dominican friar Simone Cinozzi, one of Savonarola's fiercest supporters. Another significant passage occurs in the letter Fonzio sent to Gianfrancesco Zeffi on September 11, 1510 (3.7), where he replies positively to his friend's request for him to produce an edition of his collected writings, though he expresses some moral perplexity as to the publication of literary and scholarly works from a now distant past and, more importantly, ones that jar with his present position as a priest and minister of God. But by far the most eloquent witness to his moral and religious commitment is undoubtedly the apocalyptic ep. 3.9. Sent to Antonio Pucci on December 13, 1511, this beautiful and lengthy letter (the longest of the entire collection) takes us into the heart of the serious conflict then being waged between Julius II and Louis XII, king of France, when the very unity of the Church was being called into question by the schismatic council convened by the king at Pisa. Fonzio launches a vigorous and impassioned protest against it, and while making his personal adherence to the papal cause plain, he takes a reasoned and balanced position overall. He condemns the arrogance of princes and kings but does not hesitate to point out the heavy responsibility of the pope and an ecclesiastical hierarchy corrupted by ruinous worldly ambition. Fonzio forcefully expresses his call for radical renewal of the Church, and likewise for a decisive change in behavior on the part of the secular princes. The moral impetus that he sustains throughout 3.9 reaches its peak in the second part of the letter, which is taken up with a vision of a theatrical confrontation in which the Church and its defenders face the king of France and the schismatic prelates, Satan in person at their head.

The letter to Pucci represents as well in paradigmatic fashion Fonzio's intelligent and attentive observation of the principal events that articulated his age, his marked interest in the unfolding of history as it happened. On closer inspection, this is a trait that emerges at several points in the collection, where other letters besides 3.9 offer reflection on a number of important historical affairs. At times these are hinted at obliquely or touched upon in passing, at others treated, discussed, and judged at length and in some detail, in a critical spirit or even with personal involvement. As background to his own biography, Fonzio several times focused on some of the most important events of the tumultuous period in which he lived: the attempted conspiracy against Piero de' Medici in 1466 and the war with Colleoni that arose from it (ep. 1.1, to Puccio de' Pucci), the military and political disturbances that followed on the Pazzi conspiracy (1.21, to Antonio Calderini), the tensions that filled Italy on the eve of the descent of Charles VIII in 1494 (2.18, to Giovanni Pontano), the election mentioned above of Pier Soderini as perpetual *Gonfaloniere* in 1502 (2.20), the papal election of Giovanni de' Medici in the spring of 1513 (epp. 3.13 and 14, to Pierfrancesco de' Medici and Jacopo Salviati respectively).

Finally, no introduction, however summary, to the *Epistolarum libri III* can omit special mention of one of the defining intellectual bases of the entire work. As indicated earlier, among the themes to which Fonzio was most attached, and one that he meant to inform the entire *epistolario,* was a vibrant portrayal of his unflagging absorption in the life of scholarship, philology, and literature, his profound love of *litterae* and the culture of the ancient world. This ideological current pervades the collection and constantly crops up in a wide variety of forms and expressions. We see it, for example, right from the outset in the young Fonzio's complaints to his friend Pietro Fanni about his failure to find a stable *portus litterarius,* a harbor for letters (1.3); we see it in the desperate pleas to Péter Garázda to secure him a life in Hungary worthy of a scholar (1.12–15); we find it forcefully and emphatically expressed when Fonzio tells Pietro Cennini how the stirring words of Donato Acciaiuoli had deterred him from abandoning his studies (1.18); we find it again in the mature and experienced humanist of the 1480s when he exalts the patronage of Matthias Corvinus, in a piece at once highly rhetorical and sincere (2.11). It is visible in the exhortations he addresses to his pupil Federico Sassetti not to neglect his studies and his education (2.16), and all the more so in the solemn declaration made to Pietro Fanni that virtue, the arts, and the *studia humanitatis* constitute, in a world without true values and sure points of reference, the only solid basis on which human life may rely (2.17).

Book 3 also shows Fonzio's deep attachment to the *humanae litterae* in a number of texts of a pronounced philological or erudite character, such as ep. 3.2 (to Giovanni Nesi, with an analysis of a passage of Leonardo Bruni's *Cicero novus*) or 3.8 (a reworking for Francesco di Matteo Ricci of his old *Epistola de mensuris et ponderibus*, originally sent to Francesco Sassetti in 1472). But it is preeminently in ep. 3.12 that Fonzio's humanist commitment shines forth in its full vigor, in a missive sent to Bernardo Rucellai on March 1, 1513, a few months before his death. Taking its place nearly at the end of the letters, this substantial treatise on *elocutio* and *imitatio* provided an ideal close to the collection. Here Bartolomeo Fonzio summed up for the last time the enduring leitmotif of his existence: the *bonae artes* and the model of civilization, morality, learning, and virtue that they expressed and transmitted. It was a model to which he had enthusiastically devoted his best energies, in keeping with the unwavering faith he had in the foundational values of humanism.

Alessandro Daneloni
(Translation by Martin Davies)

NOTE

1. On Fonzio's life, apart from the many individual notices in my *Commento* on the letters, see R. Zaccaria in *DBI* (s.v. Della Fonte), and Caroti and Zamponi, *Lo scrittoio di Bartolomeo Fonzio*, 12–16.

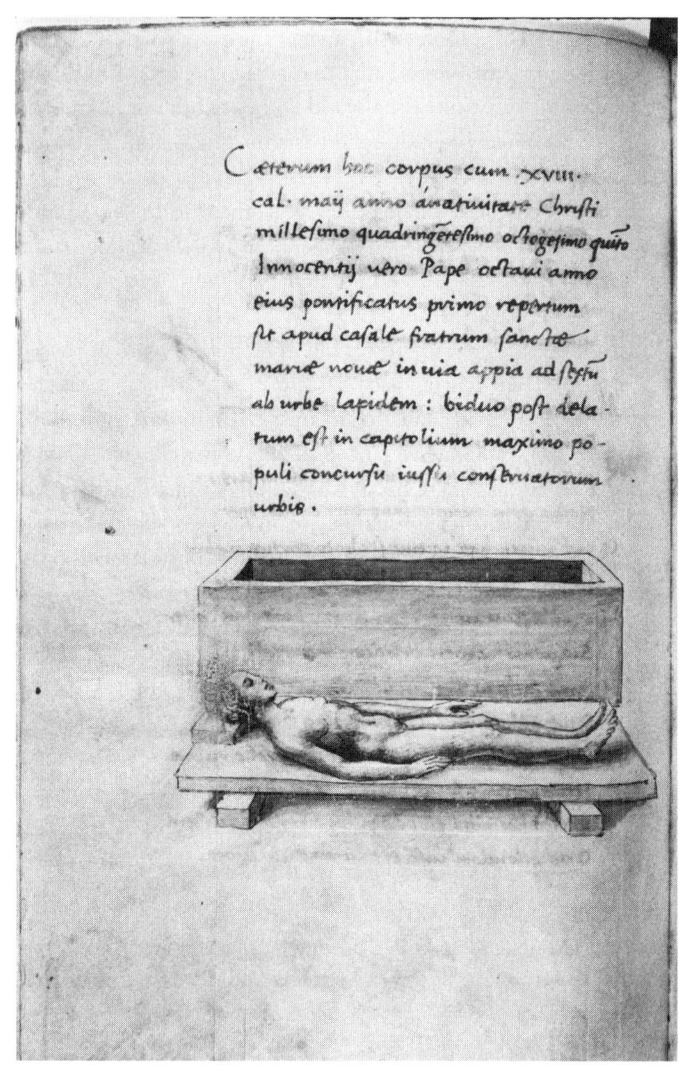

The Roman girl discovered on the Via Appia in 1485 (see ep. 2.7). Fonzio's autograph drawing in Oxford, Bodleian Library, MS Lat. misc. d. 85, fol. 161v. Reproduced by permission.

LETTERS TO FRIENDS

Bartholomaeus Fontius Amerigo Corsino s.

1 Aetatis ne vitio accidit, iam ad senectutem vergentis, an ratione potius animi, cum ipso tempore excrescentis, ut res meas tanquam migraturus componam nescio. Unum scio: mihi quinquagesimum
2 annum agenti non longe hanc abesse discessionem. Quare me ad tantum accingens iter, dum quid cognatis relinquam, quid amicis expedio supellectilemque omnem explico, has inscio me latitantes epistolas, neque adeo multas ut legere extimescas, forte invenio. Quas equidem ad te misi, amicissimum virum et communium studiorum studiosissimum, ut eis, cum vacabit, legendis totius vitae meae cursum, labores studiaque cognoscas. Sunt enim litterae ad amicos praesertim scriptae, quibus nihil esse occultum volumus, iurati ac sancti testes animorum nostrorum et voluntatum.
3 Eas igitur cum pellegeris, nisi, quod maxime vereor, te offenderint, servabis inter alios tuos libros mei monumentum in te amoris; sin certe offenderint, vel tuis ipse conscindes manibus vel ignipotenti Vulcano dabis, ne extent insignes notae iuvenilium mearum ineptiarum. Vale.

Florentia, VIII Cal. Februarii 1495.

[Prefatory Letter]

Bartolomeo Fonzio to Amerigo Corsini, greetings.[1]

Whether it be the fault of my time of life, verging as it is on old 1
age now, or rather the rational act of a mind maturing with the passage of time, that I should be composing my affairs as if about to quit this life, I do not know. But this I do know: in my fiftieth
year, that departure cannot be far distant.[2] And so, as I prepare 2
myself for that great journey, while I am settling what I should leave to my relations and what to my friends and sort out all my possessions, I find by chance these letters hidden away all unbeknownst to me—but not so many that you should be alarmed at the prospect of reading them. I have sent them to you as one of my greatest friends and a passionate student of the scholarly pursuits we share, so that you may read them when time allows and understand the course of my entire life, my struggles and studies. The letters are written to friends for the most part—men from whom I have nothing to hide—and are the sworn and solemn witnesses of my thoughts and feelings. When you've read them, pro- 3
vided that you are not offended by them (my greatest fear), please keep them with your other books as a memorial of my affection for you. But if they *do* offend, by all means tear them up with your bare hands, or consign them to Vulcan's flames, to ensure the destruction of these egregious tokens of my juvenile foolishness. Farewell.

Florence, January 25, 1496.

LIBER PRIMUS

: I :

Bartholomaeus Fontius Puccio s.

1 Summam erga me benivolentiam tuam, multis antea rebus per-
spectam et cognitam, nuper ex Baptista Nellio recognovi, quam
non oratione modo, sed oculis, fronte, vultu, multis praeterea signis quae nequivit exprimere, se plane asserit perspexisse. Quanti
autem me facias vel in se uno expertum esse, quem antea tibi semper incognitum, nostris inspectis litteris, tam comiter et benigne
receperis tamque familiariter sis complexus ac si tecum vixisset
2 diu. Illud vero etiam mihi rettulit, nihil gratius nihilque iocundius
meis ad te litteris posse perferri, quod omnibus de rebus, quae hic
aguntur quaeque actae vel dictae sunt, cumulatissime te erudiunt.
Quod ego ita dici a te arbitror magnitudine tui in me amoris, cum
praesertim non desint tibi qui et celerius queunt et copiosius
cuncta perscribere. Nos enim, quod occupatiores, sumus etiam in
scribendo aliquanto caeteris tardiores. Verum, utcunque sit, nunc
tanta in re tantoque omnium metu quid actum sit quidque agatur
dicaturve volui tibi significare.

3 Patefacta in Petrum Medicem coniuratione, tanti negocii duces
Angelus Acciaiolus in Appuliam, Nicolaus Soderinus in Narbo-
nensem provinciam, Dietisalvius Neronius in Siciliam sunt rele-
gati. Sed Neronius primo Malpagam ad Bartholomaeum Colionem, deinde Venetias profectus est, ubi se illi Soderinus non
multos post dies adiunxit; quorum cohortationibus moti Veneti
4 clam Colionem iusserunt quam maximum parare exercitum. Quod
ubi prospectum est, statim Bernardus Bongirolamus Ferrariam,

BOOK I

: I :

Bartolomeo Fonzio to Puccio, greetings.[3]

Your great warmth of feeling toward me, which I know well and have experienced many times before, I learned of once more from Battista Nelli. He assures me he could plainly see it not just from the way you spoke, but from your eyes and the expression of your face and many other intimations he could not put into words. He readily grasped the high regard you have for me from his own case, for though he was earlier unknown to you, once you had seen my letter, you welcomed him with as much graciousness and friendliness and embraced him as cordially as if he had long been living with you.[4] He also told me that you found nothing more welcome or cheering than my letters for the detailed account they give of everything that is going on here and all that has been said or done. But you said that, I think, out of the great love you bear me, given that you do not want for people who can write all this to you both quicker and more fully. Busy as I am, I tend to be somewhat more tardy in writing than others. Be that as it may, I want now to tell you what is going on, and what's been said and done at this critical moment amid such general fearfulness.[5] 1 2

Once the plot against Piero de' Medici was uncovered, the leaders of the venture were exiled, Angelo Acciaiuoli to Puglia, Niccolò Soderini to Provence, and Dietisalvi Neroni to Sicily. But Neroni went first to Bartolomeo Colleoni at Malpaga and then to Venice, where Soderini joined him a few days later. At their urging the Venetians secretly told Colleoni to get together as large an army as he could muster. When that prospect became known, envoys were at once dispatched to form an alliance, Bernardo Buongirolami to 3 4

Aloisius Guicciardinus cum Thomaso Soderino Mediolanum ac
Venetias, Ioannes Canisianus et Antonius Ridolphus legati Romam et Neapolim missi ad societatem instaurandam, sed cum
rege Ferrando tantum et Galeatio Maria, Insubrium duce, aequis
conditionibus renovata est. Lucenses quoque paulo post in eandem recepti, Senenses vero tergiversati animis esse nobiscum velle
5 non scripto responderunt. Hic curantur omnia diligenter: nam et
decenviri ad belli curam creati sunt et ab his milites scribuntur, a
sociis praesidia accersuntur et omnia ad bellum necessaria summo
studio parantur. Astorem, Faventiae principem, a nobis constat ad
Venetos defecisse, quare vis omnis belli in Flaminiam transferetur.
Eo itaque duodetriginta equitum turmae a rege Ferrando praemis-
sae sunt illisque se Federicus Urbinas adiunget; Roberto quoque
Severino imperatum a nostris est ut eo ire cum suis copiis matu-
6 ret. Bartholomaeum Colionem Padum cum ingenti exercitu per-
transisse magnus est rumor. Quo tanto motu Bononienses perculsi
praeter multorum opinionem in nostras partis concessere: itaque
ad eos Angelus Stupha legatus missus, qui, etsi per se antea satis
firmi fidique nobis extiterant, hac tamen legatione magnopere con-
firmati totis viribus pro nobis contendunt.

7 Intra urbem tamen varii motus animorum sunt: plebi enim rebus novis intentae nihil praeter principes deest, qui non defuturi videntur si in Flaminia succubuerimus. Accedit graviter et iniquis animis multos ferre[1] ad sumptus belli subministrandos honera graviora statuta esse et quinqueviros ad id creatos in res et fortunas omnium potestate permissa.

8 Erit haec aetas, ut multorum fert opinio, plurimarum ac maximarum rerum eventu memoranda: nam et Italia omnis armata est et audimus in Gallia summos Duces cruentissimum bellum parare et Christiani nominis Turchum hostem fidei nostrae interitum

Ferrara, Luigi Guicciardini, along with Tommaso Soderini, to Milan and Venice, Giovanni Canigiani and Antonio Ridolfi to Rome and Naples, but the alliance was renewed on fair terms only with Ferrante and Galeazzo Maria, Duke of Milan. A little later the Lucchesi joined the league, but the Sienese fought shy of it, saying they were with us in spirit but preferred not to sign up. All 5
of this is being given very careful attention: the Ten of War have been appointed and they are raising soldiers, reinforcements are being sought from the allies, and all preparations for war are being made with great energy.[6] It is reckoned that Astorre Manfredi, the lord of Faenza, has deserted us for the Venetians and so the whole brunt of the war will shift to Romagna. Twenty-eight squads of cavalry have accordingly been sent there by King Ferrante, where Federico, the Duke of Urbino, is to join them. Robert Sanseverino too has been told by our authorities to make haste to go there. There is a strong rumor that Bartolomeo Colleoni has crossed the 6
Po with a huge army. Disturbed by this striking turn of events, the Bolognese have unexpectedly (in many people's view) come over to our side, and so Angelo della Stufa has been sent to them as our envoy: even if they were our firm and faithful allies before, this legation strengthens them in their resolve to fight for us with might and main.[7]

Within Florence there are different currents of feeling. The 7
common people intent on revolution want only men to lead them, and there will doubtless be no lack of *them* if we go under in Romagna. Add to that the fact that many are angry and resentful at the taxes that have been imposed in support of the war effort and the power over everyone's property and fortune given to the Board of Five set up for the purpose.

Many people think that our age will be remembered for the 8
great events now unfolding: all Italy is in arms, and we hear that in France high princes are making preparations for a bloody war, and that those enemies of the Christian religion, the Turks, are threat-

minitari. Sed nostrum est, mi Pucci, earum eventa rerum, quae sub Fortunae arbitrio sitae sunt, forti animo expectare. Tu quid agas, quomodo valeas ut sciam cura.

9 Domui tuae pristina illa dignitas magnam in partem est resti-
tuta: nam vix possem exprimere quantum laudis Antonius parens
tuus ex Pisana praetura sit consecutus. Quare et ipse tu, cuius expectatio magna est, cura, elabora, perfice ut is evadas, quem pater,
cognati, affines, amici omnes nosque in primis cupimus et opta-
10 mus. Unum illud emoneo, ne propter iuris civilis studia nostrarum
dicendi artium obliviscare. Nam si ex sola iuris cognitione dignitatem maximam consequuntur ii qui praeter verba legis nihil ex se
non rude atque impolitum promunt, quanto maioribus et honoribus et praemiis honestandus erit is qui ad legum scientiam elegantiam quoque orationis addiderit? Potes autem eodem tempore
utrique facile inservire: non est enim tam ardua iuris cognitio,
quam multi putant, sed potius ampla et diffusa, quam difficilis et
11 obscura. Nostra quidem studia quantum in se iocunditatis atque
utilitatis habeant brevi ostenderem, nisi mecum ad quem scriberem reputarem. Nam cum primam aetatem omnem in his magna
cum laude consumpseris, supervacaneum esse puto tibi longe antea perspecta et cognita enarrare. Te tantum ad ea hortor oroque
ut caepisti pergas meque ames et a me omnia amantissimi hominis
studia officiaque expectes. Vale.

ening the destruction of our faith. But, my dear Pucci, we can only await the outcome of these events with fortitude, and that is in the lap of Fortune. Please let me know what you are doing and how you are.

Your family has in large measure regained its old standing—I 9
can scarcely exaggerate the praise your father Antonio won from his governorship of Pisa.[8] And as you have aroused great expectations, you must for your part strive and work to ensure that you turn out as your father, family, relations, and all your friends (myself above all) desire and hope. One piece of advice: don't forget 10
about our literary pursuits amid your studies in civil law. While it may be true that men can win high status by their legal knowledge alone, even though apart from the phrases of the law everything they say is crude and uncouth, how much greater the prestige and rewards that grace one who can add the power of eloquence to knowledge of the law! You can easily pursue both at the same time. Getting to know the law is not so difficult as many people think; it is a broad subject and a diffuse one rather than difficult and obscure. I would give a brief account of the pleasure and use- 11
fulness of our studies did I not recollect the man I am writing to. But since you have spent the whole of your early life on them and won great praise doing so, I imagine you hardly need to be told things you have long known and understood. Let me just urge and encourage you in that direction so that you may carry on as you have begun, and love me, and look to me for all the devotion and service that a loving friend can give. Farewell.

: 2 :

Bartholomaeus Fontius Petro Cennino s.

1 Vereor ne mora tam diuturna ingens damnum studiis meis attule-
rit, quae profecto si affuisses non remisissem. Quantum enim
superioribus annis potuerit apud me oratio tua sum mihi ipse optimus testis, qui, te fidelissime adhortante et prudentissime admonente, communibus studiis inhaerebam. Nunc vero te absente non
casu aliquo, sed certa potius ratione unde me sustuleras sum revec-
tus. Iactamur enim, ut vides, non imperiti homines saevis undis et
allatrantibus scopulis agitamur. Quae spes autem serenitatis futu-
2 rae, quibus nullum benignum sidus refulgeat? Ergo animus erat,
cum haec scribebam, saevientibus ventis vela convertere, sed illud
me rursus angit, quo me applicem, quid tu probes. Quare consule
mihi, quaeso, per litteras quid agendum putes. Sunt hae profecto
etiam tuae partes, cum nihil habeas separatum a nobis idemque
tibi sit etiam atque etiam cogitandum. Expectabo itaque litteras
tuas atque interim eundem tenebo cursum, non tam ut aliquid
proficiamus, quam ne abiectis animis videamur.

3 Tu quidem recte facis, qui in omnibus epistolis me hortaris ut animo sim erecto; ego vero nedum magno, ut saepe antea, sed etiam nunc animo sum excelso. Verum nos oportet aliquando consulere nobis ipsis: nam etsi summae Diogeni videntur opes habendi cupiditate carere et ad trahendam vitam fontes, herbas, speluncas, pelles sufficere, nobis tamen hoc tempore, hos inter homines, aliter est vivendum. Nosti praeterea naturam stomachi mei quam a sordibus alieni, quam earum rerum, quas tu non

: 2 :

Bartolomeo Fonzio to Pietro Cennini, greetings.[9]

I fear that such a long layoff has greatly damaged my studies, 1
which if you had been here I should never have let drop. How much influence your conversation had on me in earlier years I can myself bear witness: it was with your attentive encouragement and wise counsel that I stuck to the studies we shared together. But now in your absence I am carried back to the spot whence you raised me up, and not by chance but for a particular reason. We are not men lacking in experience, but you see how we are battered by fierce waves and driven onto raging rocks. What hope of peace
can there be for us on whom no kindly star ever shines? I was 2
therefore minded, when I came to write this letter, to turn my sails elsewhere, but still the thought tortures me, where to head for and what you would suggest. Please advise me by letter, then, as to what you think ought to be done. This is really your job too, as nothing you have is not also mine, and you have to consider the selfsame matter time and again. So I shall wait for your letter and in the meantime keep to the same course, not so much because I shall get anywhere with it as in order not to be seen as demoralized.

But you are right to encourage me in all your letters to keep my 3
spirits up. In fact I'm not just in good heart, as often in the past, but in excellent spirits even now. But we have to consider ourselves from time to time: even if for Diogenes the absence of the desire to possess things was the height of wealth, and though he thought that springs, vegetation, caves and skins were enough for life, we have to live a different way in these times and among these men.[10] You know my character as well, how alien it is from stinginess, how passionate for the things you yourself do not despise. And so

contemnis, percupidi. Quare tanquam e specula quadam prospicio quo potissimum advolem, ut tentem et experiar omnia potiusque Fortuna iudicio meo, quam defuisse mihi vel consilium vel animus videatur. Sed haec fortasse pluribus quam fuit necesse. Vale.

: 3 :

Bartholomaeus Fontius Petro Fannio s.

1 Tametsi multo gratius mihi erat verbis potius coram, quam litteris, siqua tibi dicenda erant exponere idque ita facere statueram, tamen, cum te istic diutius quam putaram morari videam, decrevi pauca ad te scribere, quibus animum penitus meum intuens eam mihi a superis mentem datam esse laeteris, quae me, quod in primis quaerendum est, ad virtutem et litteras inflamarit.

2 Ego vero etsi contendi Ferrariam ut Borsium Hestensem viserem, illa tamen etiam causa me commovit, ut quae Bononiae, quae Ferrariae, quae Venetiis litterarum esset conditio quive docti homines plane cernerem. Harum equidem urbium mores et ingenia contemplatus, nihil video in quo nostri homines illis cedant. Uno certe longe praestamus, quod philosophum praeclarissimum atque omnium, qui ubique locorum sunt, facile principem Ioannem Argiropilum habemus, quo doctore ac magistro, nisi casus aliquis retardaverit cursum meum, non me in postremis futurum putem.
3 Sed illud modo fit reliqui, qua ego velificatione in hunc litterarium portum devehar. Expecto igitur te, unum propositi mei non solum laudatorem, sed adiutorem. Itaque reditum tuum accelera: eris enim et consiliorum nostrorum particeps et eorundem socius studiorum. Vale.

as if from a watchtower I'll look out where best to fly to, so that I may try and experience everything, and have it appear that my decisions met with little luck rather than that my wits or courage failed me. But I have perhaps already written too much on this matter. Farewell.

: 3 :

Bartolomeo Fonzio to Pietro Fanni, greetings.[11]

Though I should have greatly preferred to tell you anything I had 1
to say face-to-face rather than by letter, and had decided to do so, still, since I see that you are delayed there longer than I'd anticipated, I have decided to write you a few lines so you may look deep into my soul and rejoice that heaven has given me a character that has fired me to pursue virtue and literature, the things we should seek above all.

Although I went to Ferrara to see Borso d'Este, I was also mo- 2
tivated by the desire to get a clear picture of the situation of literary studies at Bologna, Ferrara, and Venice, and who the scholars were there. But having looked into the manners and talents in those cities, I find nothing in which our men yield to theirs. In one respect we are certainly far ahead of them, having in Johannes Argyropoulos a famous philosopher, by some way the leading philosopher in the world.[12] Under his tutelage and teaching, I think I shall become not the least among them, provided no unlucky event
checks my progress. It only remains to find how to set my sails so 3
as to reach this literary harbor. I'm awaiting you, then—the one supporter of my project, and my one helper too. So hurry up and come back: you will have a share in all my cogitations and be my companion in those same studies. Farewell.

: 4 :

Bartholomaeus Fontius Francisco Gaddio s.

Paenitentiam meam breviter simpliciterque descriptam huic ad te dedi tabellario perferendam, quae, ut puto, non verebitur iudicium tuum, cum abhorreat ab omni barbarie fratrunculorum sitque descripta oratorio quodam, ut in tali re convenit, diserto et eleganti stilo.

Tu vero, si me amas, si nullum officium tuum apud me intermoriturum existimas, da, quaeso, operam diligenter ut libri, de quibus iterum ad te scripsi, mihi quam celerrime transcribantur, quo mihi nihil in praesens facere gratius poteris neque commodius. Vale.

: 5 :

Bartholomaeus Fontius Petro Cennino suo[2]

1 Recordare tuas litteras, quibus mihi recepisti ad omnia te mihi semper paratum fore. Quod ego vere ita esse existimabam propter benivolentiam in te meam, quam si experiendo magis quam loquendo cognosti, in hoc nostrum et tu vicissim negocium nunc incumbas atque ita omnia per te agas, ut me a te mutuo amari re ipsa intelligam.

2 Tu vero, quod proximis ad me litteris subobscure ac breviter attigisti, quicquid evenerit, in meliorem, quaeso, partem accipias. Est enim tuae prudentiae, etiam si secus acciderit quam volueris,

: 4 :

Bartolomeo Fonzio to Francesco Gaddi, greetings.[13]

I have given my [treatise *De*] *paenitentia,* briefly and simply set down, to be taken to you by this courier, and I do not think it need fear your censure, being quite remote from all that monkish barbarousness and written in a certain smooth and elegant rhetorical style, as befits the subject.[14]

But if you love me, if you realize that no service of yours will ever perish from my heart, please give careful attention to having those books copied out for me as quickly as possible—I have already written to you twice about this.[15] At the moment there is nothing you could do that would be more welcome or useful to me. Farewell.

: 5 :

Bartolomeo Fonzio to his friend Pietro Cennini

Remember those letters of yours in which you promised you 1
would always be ready to help me in any matter. And from the goodwill I bore you I actually believed it—had you known that goodwill in practice rather than in words alone, you in turn would now be attending to my problem and doing everything you could, and so I should realize that my love for you is really returned.

As to the matter you touched on briefly and rather obscurely in 2
your last letter, whatever has happened, please take it all in good part.[16] You should have the good sense to bear with things patiently, even if they have turned out contrary to your wishes.

patienter perferre. Ego quidem, re vel desperata vel, quod spero cupioque, adepta, te brevi expecto, ut totius vitae nostrae rationem ineamus. Magna enim spe alor, magnam quoque de te spem habeo, quae futura in dies videtur maior si parueris optimis et fidelissimis consiliis meis, quae divinare iam debes, sed tenebis planius audiendo. Quare iter tuum accelera: nam et haec et plura alia coram agemus, cum veneris. Vale.

: 6 :

Bartholomaeus Fontius Petro Cennino s.

Etsi ea te confido prudenter facturum omnia quae tibi conducere iudicabis, ita me tamen exanimarunt iustissimae querelae tuae, ut non minorem dolorem ceperim ex casu tuo quam si essem in eodem constitutus. Quare te oro in mirum modum ut quid sit subsecutum confestim scribas. Ero enim interim semper de te solicitus, quanquam haec Deus, ut spero, vertet in melius. Quod si erit ut opto, me quasi ab interitu revocabo. Vale.

: 7 :

Bartholomaeus Fontius Francisco Gaddio s.

1 Nulla de causa—sunt enim aliae multae et iustae—tantum cuperem una essemus, quam ut amicitiae nostrae, cuius iampridem

For my part, whether the thing is to be written off or has been successfully concluded, as I hope and desire, I expect you shortly so that we can reckon up where our lives are going overall. I am sustained by great hopes, and I have great hopes of you too, which seem set to get ever brighter if you do but listen to my good and trustworthy advice: that you must for now guess at, but you will have it plain when we speak. So hurry up! We'll talk all this over, and much else besides, when you get here. Farewell.

: 6 :

Bartolomeo Fonzio to Pietro Cennini, greetings.

Even if I'm sure you will attend with good judgment to everything that you reckon to be in your best interests, still your very proper grievances have so prostrated me that I feel no less sorrow for your case than if I were in it myself. I beg you therefore, with all the emphasis at my command, to write what has happened at once. I shall in the meantime be constantly worrying about you, though, as I hope, God will direct all this for the best. And if things fall out as I wish, I shall be brought back from the very brink of death. Farewell.

: 7 :

Bartolomeo Fonzio to Francesco Gaddi, greetings.

Among the many good reasons I have for wanting us to be to- 1
gether, none is better than wanting to reap the pleasant and plenti-

semina sparsimus, iocundos atque uberes nunc fructus meteremus. Sed quaecunque utrique nostrum fortuna erit, quae bona, ut puto, erit, id fiet aliquando. Interim nos armemus validissimis illis armis quae vi nulla contundi possint; quod si ipse facis, est mihi vehementer gratum. Equidem ita me munio, ut iam videar non inglorius esse miles.

2 Musae illae nostrae veteres ita me amplexantur, ita in suam consuetudinem me admittunt, ut, cum amicissimis illis utar, videar mihi sperare debere. Sperarem profecto magis, si studiorum socium te haberem, sed ubi id nequit, explebimus animos nostros crebris litteris cohortando nos invicem et monendo. Me quidem ita delectant epistolae tuae, ita etiam ad te scribens afficior, ut quotiens tua lego, te loquentem audire, te videre, quotiens ad te scribo, tecum esse et colloqui tecum videar.

3 Quod autem tua mihi omnia paratissima polliceris, est id sane minime novum, gratum tamen ac periocundum promissum tuum: ex omnibus enim partibus se se quotidie magis effundit vis et magnitudo amoris tui. De me vero tibi recipio nullam rem unquam futuram tam arduam, quam ego non pro te libenter suscipiam quaeque mihi pro te suscepta non iocundissima sit futura. Vale.

: 8 :

Bartholomaeus Fontius Petro Cennino suo[3]

1 Quod optatis Fortunam tuis acrem quereris adversariam extitisse, pari tecum dolore sum permotus. Verum enimvero fortem virum aequam semper decet servare mentem et invicto animi robore, tanquam fortissimo propugnaculo, uti contra omnem Fortunae temeritatem. Quare, cum intelligam quid tu de rerum tuarum

ful fruits of our friendship, whose seeds we have long since sown. Whatever fortune holds for us both (good things, as I believe), that will happen at some point. In the meantime let us arm ourselves with that strongest of armor which no force can crush. If you do that, I'd be very pleased indeed; I for my part see to my own defense—the figure I cut will not be that of an undistinguished fighter.

Those old Muses of ours have taken me up so strongly and 2
given me such intimate admittance to their company that when I find myself on these friendly terms with them, I really think there's reason to hope. Certainly I should be even more hopeful if I had you as the companion of my studies, but as that cannot be, we shall satisfy our spirits with constant correspondence and mutual encouragement and advice.

As for your assurance that everything you have is completely at 3
my disposal, your promise is by no means a novelty, but very pleasing and welcome all the same: the force and abundance of your love grows ever greater on every side as the days pass. For myself I can promise you there will be no task so difficult that I will not gladly shoulder it for you, and which, having shouldered it for you, I should not find utterly delightful. Farewell.

: 8 :

Bartolomeo Fonzio to his friend Pietro Cennini.

When you complain at Fortune proving a fierce opponent of your 1
desires, I feel your distress as deeply as you do. But the true man ought always to keep an equable mind and maintain an invincible strength of spirit—the strongest bulwark, so to say—against Fortune's fickleness. And since I understand you have maintained an

amissione optime sentias, nihil aliud in praesentiarum ad te scribam, nisi ut, si ante tranquilliora moderate tulisti, nunc turbida sapienter feras.

2 Ego te, quod maxime petis, et Donato commendare non desistam et nihil praeterea, quod ad te tuosque pertineat, praetermittam. Vale.

: 9 :

Bartholomaeus Fontius Donato Acciaiolo s.

Etsi Petrum Cenninum probum et doctum virum propter summum ingenium, suavissimos mores, singularem modestiam satis per se ipsum sine meis litteris tibi commendatum fore confido, te tamen vehementer rogo ut quibus in rebus ei usui esse poteris — poteris autem quamplurimis — facias et amanter et diligenter. Mihi certe nihil efficere gratius unquam poteris, quam si omnem vim tuae in me benivolentiae hunc in unum[4] transfuderis. Quod ut facias te iterum atque iterum oro. Vale.

: 10 :

Bartholomaeus Fontius Petro Fannio s.

1 Quod mihi de optimo statu tuo significasti vehementer placet, quando industria et virtute tua perfectum video ut, quae multi vix tempore longissimo consequuntur, ea tu brevissimo sis adeptus.

excellent attitude in the face of the loss of your property, I have nothing further to write, except that, just as you bore easier times with moderation, so now you must take these upsets as a wise man would.

I shall neither cease to recommend you to Donato [Acciaiuoli], 2
as you particularly ask, nor omit any service where the interests of you and your family are involved.[17] Farewell.

: 9 :

Bartolomeo Fonzio to Donato Acciaiuoli, greetings.

Though I am sure that that good and learned man Pietro Cennini will be sufficiently recommended by his own virtues — his fine intelligence, his civilized manner, his remarkable modesty — without any letters from me, I do nevertheless strongly urge you to help him in a friendly and attentive fashion in any matter (and there are a great many) where you may be of assistance to him. Certainly you could do nothing more welcome to me than if you transfer your whole fund of goodwill toward me to him alone. And I heartily beg you to do so. Farewell.

: 10 :

Bartolomeo Fonzio to Pietro Fanni, greetings.

I received the information on your present excellent situation with 1
great pleasure, as I see that your industry and talent has made it possible for you to achieve very quickly what many scarcely man-

Sunt autem tibi quidem ista praeclara initia tanquam firmissima fundamenta totius vitae iacta, a me ipso, qui te ornatissimum cupiebam, hoc tempore non sperata. Nam etsi cognita industria, probitate, doctrina tua summa de te sperabam, tamen haec nostra doctis viris adversa tempora et inversi Romanae curiae mores faciebant ut vererer interdum quemadmodum tecum ageret ipsa Fortuna. Quare tibi primum, ut debeo, pro adepto Cereti sacerdotio gratulor, deinde mihi ipse etiam gaudeo, qui, dum ea quae in te video in me quoque libenter effingo, bene mecum agi etiam arbitror.

2 Sed nunc, mi Petre, nunc sunt tua officia atque partes (quanquam non haec scribo ut te instituam, neque enim prudentia tua praecepta mea desiderat) omni cura et diligentia vigilare ut assiduitate et virtute tua haec tam clara initia maioribus successibus prosequare. Vale.

: II :

Bartholomaeus Fontius Michaeli Pharcae s.

1 Ex quo tempore te Florentiam studiorum communium causa contulisti, ego nostrorum omnium primus consuetudinem tecum cepi, quam non solum in hunc diem servavi, sed auxi semper diligentissime. Omitto quo interim animo, quo studio, qua liberalitate
2 quibusque officiis prosecutus te fuerim. Cum itaque fides et singularis amor erga te meus extiterit, non queo mecum non admirari cur ita commutatum te viderim ob Petri Cennini discessionem.[5] In quo quidem, fateor, tibi consului ne eius profectionem remorare-

age to do over a long stretch of time.[18] You have made a fine beginning, laying down firm foundations, as it were, for the rest of your life, something that I, who long for your success, was not expecting at this date. Well aware of your industriousness, moral probity, and learning, I was indeed hoping for great things from you, but the times in which we live are unfavorable to the learned and that, added to the perverse ways of the Roman Curia, made me fear from time to time how Fortune would deal with you. So I now first congratulate you, as I should, on getting the living at Cerreto; in the second place I am pleased on my own account, for when I see you achieving those things I should be glad to picture myself achieving, I feel that things are going well for me.

But now, dear Pietro (though I do not write these lines to 2
school you, for your good sense certainly needs no instruction of mine), it is your duty and your destiny to make every effort to see that you follow up this wonderful start with greater successes through your energy and talent. Farewell.

: II :

Bartolomeo Fonzio to Mihály Farkas, greetings.[19]

From the time that you came to Florence to pursue our common 1
studies, I was the first of any of us to get on friendly terms with you, something I have not just kept up to this day but have always taken great pains to strengthen. I pass over the fidelity, devotion, generosity, and acts of kindness I have shown you in the meantime. Since my loyalty and special love for you is thus manifest, I 2
cannot but wonder why I find you so changed on account of Pietro Cennini's departure.[20] In which matter, indeed, I must say I advised you not to hinder his leaving, as I was afraid you were

ris: verebar enim te hominis non indiserti inimicitias absque ulla tua utilitate suscipere. An credebas tuis Antonium Rodulphum, ad Ferrandum regem legatum, verbis ab eo, quod clarissimis viris de illo secum ducendo promiserat, dimoveri? Quod ego cum scirem,
3 tibi ne eum lacesseres recte consului. Sed ne tuae abalienationis causa haec sit, subii equidem libens hanc iacturam tibique quam pecuniam debet de meo misi: malui enim eam perdere quam te amicum, quoniam longe pluris amicorum iacturam facio quam numorum. Non enim mihi ullum aut ex tua aut ex cuiusquam amicitia quaestum propono, sed tantum quaero animum atque mentem longe mihi invidiosis divitiis cariorem.

4 Haec si tibi erunt accepta, ut debent, rem feceris amicitia nostra dignam; si nihil movebunt, ne ego quidem commovebor, cum nulla res tristari me debeat praeter culpam, qua me carere Deum hominesque attestor. Vale.

: 12 :

Bartholomaeus Fontius Petro Garasdae Pannonio s.

1 Tantum est temporum rerumque omnium immutata conditio, ut minime mirandum sit si ego quoque ad tempus patriam mutem. Nam si sapientis est hominis tempestati cedere neque eundem semper cursum tenere, non mihi vitio dari putem si, cum ea, quam proposueram, via ad optatum finem pervenire non possim, alia ire pergam, qua ad exitum tandem perducar. Itaque et horum temporum et mearum rerum omnium ratione prospecta, cum censeam non esse domi amplius desidendum, te, per tuum in me amorem

making an enemy of that not ineloquent man to no conceivable advantage for yourself. Did you really think that Antonio Ridolfi, the ambassador to Ferrante, would be dissuaded by your words from taking him with him when he had promised the city's notables he would do so?[21] When I heard of it, I quite rightly counseled you not to attack him. But in case this is the reason for your 3
alienation, I have willingly borne the loss and sent you the money he owes you out of my own pocket. I have preferred to lose that rather than lose a friend in you, since the loss of friends is much more important to me than loss of cash. I do not think of reaping any gain from your friendship, nor from anyone else's; I seek in a friend only a mind and a temper that to me is far more precious than the riches men envy.

If you find these observations welcome, as you should, you will 4
be doing what our friendship requires; but if they carry no weight with you, I too shall be unmoved, since nothing ought to depress me except the sense of having done wrong, a sense that, as I can call God and men to witness, I am quite free of. Farewell.

: 12 :

Bartolomeo Fonzio to Péter Garázda of Hungary, greetings.[22]

The times and circumstances have been so altered that it is scarcely 1
to be wondered at if I too should change my country to suit the times. If it is the mark of a wise man to yield before the storm and not hold always to the same course, I don't think I can be faulted if, when I find I cannot attain the end I desire by the route I proposed, I take another which will eventually lead to success. And so taking into account present circumstances and the general state of

meumque erga te mutuum, etiam atque etiam rogo ut de nobis quod promisisti conficias. Nullam enim aliam mihi viam ad nostra studia relictam esse perspicio, tota vexata Italia dissensionibus intestinis.[6]

2 Equidem ni mihi persuaderem, cum haec scriberem, te, pro tuo summo in me amore meoque in te pari, tua sponte etiam sine meis litteris esse facturum, plura scriberem meque tibi diligentius commendarem. Tantum oro, si me tui studiosissimum semper nosti, hoc mihi praestes, quod omnium est maximum maximeque necessarium quodque nullius nisi tua unius opera me assequi posse confido. Vale.

: 13 :

Bartholomaeus Fontius Petro Garasdae Pannonio s.

1 Simulac te quartana liberum ex tuis litteris intellexi, incredibili gaudio sum affectus. Sed si me amas, maerore solicitudineque expulsa, aegritudinis tuae potissima causa, ingentes animos erigas. Nam, ut ex multis audio, Pannoniis rebus compositis et tui ad Regem in auctoritate et gratia pristina permanebunt et tu eris brevi inter eos in gradu altissimo constitutus: nihil est enim tam magnum, quod ego te propter egregias virtutes tuas, suavissimos atque optimos mores summamque humanitatem non sperem
2 consecuturum. Donec vero in Pannoniam redeas, incumbe toto animo in hanc curam, ut omnium tuorum expectationem de te exuperes. Hanc, ut spero, etsi ea est ingens, perfacile vinces si ad

my affairs, I've decided I must sit around at home no longer. In virtue of the reciprocal love that you bear me and I you, I beg you again and again to put into action what you promised about my case. With all of Italy racked by internecine quarrels, I can see no other way to our studies left to me.

If I were not persuaded, even as I write these lines, that in the 2
light of your love for me — and mine equally for you — you would do this anyway, unprompted by letters of mine, I should write at greater length and recommend myself more insistently. This only I beg of you: if you have always known me to be utterly devoted to you, do me this service — the greatest and most essential service anyone could do, which I am confident of receiving from the hands of nobody but you. Farewell.

: 13 :

Bartolomeo Fonzio to Péter Garázda of Hungary, greetings.

I was overjoyed to hear from your letter that you have recovered 1
from the quartan fever. But please, now that that unhappiness and worry largely caused by your illness is past, you must lift your thoughts to great things: as I hear from many reports, now that things are settled in Hungary, your friends will retain the prestige and long-standing favor they have had with the king, and you yourself will soon fill the highest office in the land.[23] There is no position so exalted that I may not hope you will achieve it in virtue of your remarkable qualities, the amiability of your excellent character, and your great humanity. Till such time as you return to 2
Hungary, then, you must concentrate all your energies on excelling the expectations that all your friends have of you. And high as they are, you will surpass them with the greatest of ease, as I ex-

nostras te totum artis converteris, unde te Varadinensis praefectura paulum flexit. Igitur eventa rerum Patavii dum expectas cura, elabora, invigila, perfice ut resarcias praeteritam omnem studiorum iacturam. Non succumbas ulli honeri, non iniquis deperditisque temporibus, non saevissimae adversissimaeque Fortunae.

3 Scribo haec amanter ad te, ut debeo, teque rogo ut, licet consilio meo ipse non egeas, hac tamen in re tibi a me consuli patiare. Me quidem semper in omni fortuna fidelissimum amicissimumque habebis; res certe meas omnis, quaecunque sunt, non tibi solum hac tanta tua necessitate promitto, sed ad te ultro libenter defero. Vale.

: 14 :

Bartholomaeus Fontius Petro Garasdae Pannonio s.

Quod quaeris qui meus sit status, is est qui solet et aliquanto deterior, qui, natus ad agendum aliquid dignum viro, ita humiliter vivo ut studiorum ac Musarum suppudeat. Sed, ut alias ad te scripsi, in uno te spem meam omnem reposui. Quare, Pannoniis rebus compositis Polloniisque dimissis ac tuis reconciliatis cum Rege, te Deus optimus maximusque fortunet, ut ad te ego vel ad tuos vel saltem in regionibus tuis non indignam nostris litteris vitam ducam. Vale.

Florentiae, XVI Cal. Ianuarii 1471.

pect, if you do but throw yourself heart and soul into our pursuits, from which your governorship at Várad has somewhat distracted you. So while you await events at Padua, you must work at it night and day to make good all the time you have lost to study in the past. Don't buckle under any burden, don't yield to the treacherous and corrupt times, don't bow before the savage blows of adverse Fortune.

I write all this in a friendly spirit, as is only fitting, and, though 3
you hardly need advice from me, I beg you to suffer yourself to be advised by me in this matter. You will certainly always find in me a most loyal and loving friend, however Fortune looks on you. Everything I have, such as it is, I not merely undertake to give you in this time of your great need, but willingly and spontaneously make over to you. Farewell.

: 14 :

Bartolomeo Fonzio to Péter Garázda of Hungary, greetings.

You ask what my situation is: it is much the same as usual, even a little worse, since though I was made for some great achievement, I live such an insignificant life that I'm somewhat ashamed of my studies and the Muses. But as I told you before, all of my hopes have been placed in you and you alone. And so, now that the affairs of Hungary have been settled, the Poles ejected, and your party reconciled with the king, may God Almighty look with favor on you, so that with you or your people or at least in your part of the world I may lead a life not unbefitting our literary studies. Farewell.

Florence, December 17, 1471.

: 15 :

Bartholomaeus Fontius Petro Garasdae Pannonio s.

Litterae tuae amantissime ad me scriptae cunctas molestias animo depulerunt: non potui enim non dolorem reprimere atque animum, auctoritate tua confirmatum, non constantem habere. Itaque durabo, ut mones, et de te semper optimam spem habebo teque pro tuis in me meritis singulari fide observantiaque amabo. Vale.

Florentiae, Idibus Februarii 1471.

: 16 :

Bartholomaeus Fontius Baptistae Guarino s.

1 Romam ad me tuae litterae sunt allatae, quibus inde rescribere non est visum cum quod certum tabellarium non haberem, tum quod nihil certi referre possem si prius Florentiam non redissem; quo cum veni, nihil mihi fuit antiquius quam ut tuis litteris responderem. Ioanni igitur Bencio quam scripseras pecuniae summam persolvi; Apollonium autem, quem deferre mecum sperabam, idcirco habere non potui, quod Bessario, ad obeundam legationem intentus, non exhibuit; Suetonium per Nicolaum, legatum Herculis, ad te misi,[7] cui quod poema nostrum reddideris, rem gratissimam
2 effecisti. Lyrica tua quidem sunt visa mihi et elegantia et iocunda: quare te rogo, quotiens ocium nactus eris, aliquid simile ad me scribas. Cum enim aut tua lego aut ipse ad te scribo, tuo suavis-

: 15 :

Bartolomeo Fonzio to Péter Garázda of Hungary, greetings.

The friendly letter you sent me has relieved me of all my distress: I could not but put aside my anguish and regain my steadfastness of mind, firmed up now under your influence. So I shall see things out, as you advise. I shall always have the highest expectations of you and will remain your constant, devoted and affectionate friend for all your services to me. Farewell.

Florence, February 13, 1472.

: 16 :

Bartolomeo Fonzio to Battista Guarini, greetings.[24]

Your letter reached me at Rome,[25] but I decided not to write back 1
since I had no messenger I could rely on, and also because I had no definite news to impart until I returned to Florence. But as soon as I got here, I made it my first priority to reply to your letter. So: I paid Giovanni Benci the sum of money that you wrote about; I couldn't get hold of the Apollonius that I was hoping to bring with me since Bessarion didn't produce it, being busy with arranging his embassy; I sent you the Suetonius by Niccolò, Ercole d'Este's ambassador,[26] and I was very grateful that you returned my poem to him. Your own lyrics strike me as elegant and 2
agreeable, so whenever you have the time to spare, do please write something similar for me—when I read your work, or write to you myself, it's as if I were enjoying a pleasant conversation with

simo colloquio perfrui mihi videor. Quo fit ut, cum longitudine tuarum litterarum delecter, ego quoque fiam longior in scribendo.

3 Enimvero te decrevi participem facere totius Urbis antiquitatis,
quam nuper, dum Romae fui, quotidie non sine lachrimis pellus-
trabam, vicissitudinem rerum et Fortunae varietatem considerans,
quae tantam urbem, terrarum quondam orbis imperium atque
arcem, tam foede ac tam immaniter deformasset. Pontem igitur
supra Tyberim, quo in insulam itur, vidi, a L. Fabritio, C. filio,
curatore viarum factum et aedis Concordiae porticus marmoream
quandam partem iuxta Capitolium, quam Senatus Populusque
Romanus incendio consumptam restituit, et Septimii Severi, M.
Aurelii, Titi ac Vespasiani Constantinique marmoreos insignes arcus, Divi quoque Traiani et Divi Antonini duas ingentes cocleas
marmoreas columnas, in quibus eorum gesta miro artificio sunt
4 inscripta. Ad Hostiensem vero portam pyramis est marmorea,
maenia Urbis intersecans, C. Cestii septenviri Epulonum ingens
magnificumque sepulchrum. Est et obeliscus in Vaticano, quem C.
Caligula Divo Augusto et Divo Tiberio sacrum posuit. Sunt et in
Exquiliis duae ingentes marmoreae statuae a Praxitele Phidiaque
perfectae cum duobus infrenis equis. Superest et sacrarium Theo-
dosii, cuius intrinseci parietes marmoreis tabulis caelaturae veteris
exornantur, quod Martino martyri est dicatum. Conspexi omnium
magnificentissimum aqueductum quem Divus Claudius ad Ce-
lium usque montem perduxit et L. Septimius Severus et M. Aurelius Antoninus Pius pluribus in locis corruptum restituerunt.
5 Est et ad Tyberis ripam Divi Adriani, cum nobili supra fluvium
ponte, moles, ingens eius magnificumque sepulchrum nunc Cas-
trum Sancti Angeli vocitatum. Vidi Pantheon, deorum omnium
nobilissimum templum, quod M. Agrippa L. f. consul tertium fe-

you. So it is that since I am delighted to have your long letters, I too write at greater length.

Well then, I've decided to share with you my experience of the 3
antiquities of the entire city—while I was at Rome I wandered all over it, not without emotion, contemplating the way things have turned out and the fickleness of Fortune, which has so foully and brutally degraded a great city that was once the master and stronghold of the whole world.[27] I saw the bridge over the Tiber, then, the one that leads to the island, which was erected by Lucius Fabricius, son of Gaius, when he was Superintendent of the Streets,[28] and a marble portion of the portico of the temple of Concord beside the Capitoline,[29] restored by the Senate and People of Rome after it had been destroyed by fire, and the fine marble arches of Septimius Severus, Marcus Aurelius, Titus and Vespasian, and Constantine,[30] and the vast spirals of the marble columns of the deified Trajan and the deified Antoninus, on which their deeds are
sculpted with wonderful artistry. At the Ostia gate there is a mar- 4
ble pyramid which straddles the city walls, the huge and magnificent tomb of Gaius Cestius, a member of the College of Public Feasts.[31] Then there is the obelisk on the Vatican hill which Caligula erected to the memory of the emperors Augustus and Tiberius.[32] On the Esquiline there are two vast statues fashioned by Praxiteles and Phidias, along with two unharnessed horses.[33] The shrine of Theodosius also survives, its inner walls decorated with marble panels of ancient sculpture, now dedicated to St Martin the Martyr. I examined the grandest of all the aqueducts, the one that the emperor Claudius carried as far as the Caelian hill. It was restored by Septimius Severus and Marcus Aurelius in the
many places where it had suffered damage. At the bank of the 5
Tiber, by a fine bridge over the river, there is the emperor Hadrian's "Pile," a massive and magnificent tomb to him now called the Castel S. Angelo. I saw the Pantheon, a very grand temple to all the gods which Marcus Agrippa, son of Lucius, constructed in his

cit. Extra Urbem vero, ad secundum lapidem via Hostiensi, M. Antonii Antii Lupi marmoreum sepulchrum mire ornatum inspexi cum rerum a se gestarum inscriptione. Ad viam quoque Appiam, secundo ab Urbe miliario, aliud longe maius admirabiliusque perspexi Caeciliae, Q. Cretici filiae, Metellae, Crassi.

6 Haec digna aeternitate quae viderim ex omni restant antiquitate, in quibus litterae sint incisae. Quae subsequuntur, si non titulis, at gravissimorum auctorum testimoniis comprobantur. Nam amphitheatrum illud omnium maximum ex lapide Tiburtino, Colosseum a propinquo olim colosso denominatum, itemque Pacis templum, cuius tres tantum extant ingentes arcus, Vespasiani est opus. Mausoleum etiam Augusti, Flaminiam inter viam et Tyberis ripam quam Augustam hodie quoque dicunt, Octaviani opus ex-
7 cellens fuit. Thermarum autem quaeque Antonianae quaeque Termini nuncupantur, alteras Antoninum Severum, alteras Diocletianum nemo struxisse ambigit. Videntur et marmoreae sex ingentes columnae, tres ad Capitolii, tres ad radices Palatii, quam partem esse pontis a Caligula facti dicunt, quo Palatio Capitolium iunxit. Et in Exquiliis trophea duo marmorea conspiciuntur de Iugurtha deque Cimbris atque Theutonis, primum a C. Mario constituta, deinde a L. Sylla disiecta et a C. Iulio Caesare dictatore
8 reposita. Videtur et Romuli templum post templum Pacis, Capitolium versus, Sanctis Damiano et Cosmo sacrum, et in via Sacra aedes Castoris et Pollucis, quam Sanctam Mariam Novam dicunt, et iuxta Forum Saturni aedes, quod olim Aerarium nuncupatum, modo est sacrum Pontifici Adriano; templum quoque Mercurii, nunc angeli Michaelis, et Apollinis aedes in Vaticano, iuxta basili-

third consulate. And outside the city, at the second milestone on the road to Ostia, there is the elaborate marble tomb of Marcus Antonius Antius Lupus with an inscription recording his activities. On the Via Appia too, two miles from the city, I examined another tomb, much larger and more remarkable, belonging to Caecilia Metella, daughter of Quintus Creticus and wife of Crassus.[34]

These things I have seen deserve eternal commemoration and 6
have been preserved from all antiquity with lettering on them.[35] Those that follow, though they may not have inscriptions, are nevertheless attested by the testimony of ancient authors. That great amphitheater built of travertine, for example, known as the Colosseum from the colossus that once stood nearby, and likewise the temple of Peace, of which only three giant arches remain, are the work of Vespasian. The Mausoleum of Augustus too, between the Via Flaminia and the bank of the Tiber, nowadays also called
Augusta, was a fine work of Octavian. Nobody doubts that the 7
baths called Antonian and those called Termini were built by Antoninus Severus and Diocletian respectively.[36] Six great marble columns may also be seen, three at the foot of the Capitoline and three at the foot of the Palatine, which are said to be part of the bridge made by Caligula to connect the Palatine to the Capitoline. The two marble trophies visible on the Esquiline commemorate victories over Jugurtha and over the Cimbrians and Germans, and were originally set up by Gaius Marius, then destroyed by Sulla,
and replaced by Julius Caesar the dictator. The temple of Romu- 8
lus[37] can also be seen beyond the temple of Peace toward the Capitol, now the church of Sts. Cosmas and Damian, and in the Via Sacra the shrine of Castor and Pollux, now called Santa Maria Nova, and beside the Forum the temple of Saturn, called at one time the Treasury and now consecrated to Pope Hadrian. There is also the temple of Mercury, now S. Michele Arcangelo,

cam Sancti Petri, et Iunonis Lucinae, nunc Sanctus Laurentius in Lucina.

9 Reliqua erant et intra et extra Urbem adhuc quaedam veterum monumenta, quae tibi singula ordine explicassem nisi me, ad te ea libentissime nunc scribentem, adversissimus nuntius enecasset. Nam vir clarissimus Ioannes, Histrigoniae archiepiscopus, a Mathia Corvino rege comprensus est et Ianus, Quinquecclesiensis episcopus, vir doctissimus et poeta clarissimus, in ipsa fuga interiit; Petro quoque Garasdae meo, ne in regias manus pervenerit non mediocriter timeo. O me miserum, qui uno tempore tantos viros tam amicos e tantis fortunis in tantas miserias videam corruisse! Sed quo minus scribam obortis lachrimis et dolore impedior. Vale.

Florentiae, XIII Cal. Maii MCCCCLXXII.

: 17 :

Bartholomaeus Fontius Baptistae Guarino s.

1 Acerbo mihi interitu Bithinae tuae dulcissimae coniugis nuntiato graviter, ut debui, sum commotus: honestissimam enim et pudicissimam feminam, suavissimis moribus et singulari modestia praeditam, immatura morte sublatam vehementer angebar. Vellem autem sub ipsam potius mortis diem quam tam sero eius obitum percepisse, ut in tempore, quemadmodum amici optimi munus erat, aliquod tuo vulneri salutare remedium praestitissem. Veruntamen ne nunc quidem alienum fore putavi aliquid ad te scribere, quod si non radicitus vellere, saltem minuere istum tibi dolorem possit: nihil enim aeque aegritudini animorum ac dulcis amicorum oratio confert.

and that of Apollo on the Vatican beside the basilica of S. Pietro, and that of Juno Lucina, now S. Lorenzo in Lucina.

There remain some other ancient monuments both inside and outside the city which I would have given you a detailed account of if I hadn't been hit by terrible news as I was writing you these pleasant lines—the noble János, Archbishop of Esztergom, has been arrested by King Matthias Corvinus, and Janus, the Bishop of Fünfkirchen, that learned man and distinguished poet, has met his death as he fled.[38] I have no small fear for my friend Péter Garázda too, in case he falls into the king's hands. I feel so wretched to see such men and such good friends fallen from their high estate into such misery! But the welling tears and grief prevent me from writing more. Farewell. 9

Florence, April 19, 1472.

: 17 :

Bartolomeo Fonzio to Battista Guarini, greetings.[39]

I was extremely upset, of course, to hear the bitter news of the passing of your sweet wife Bettina: she was a most upright and chaste lady of pleasant character and singular modesty, and I am greatly distressed at her early death. I wish I had heard of her death at the very time it happened rather than so late in the day, so that I could have given you some salutary remedy for the hurt you have suffered in a timely fashion, as is required of a close friend. But I have reckoned it is not out of place even now to write something which, though it cannot root out your grief completely, may at least lessen it. Nothing can help minds in torment quite so much as the soothing talk of friends. 1

2 Ego vero, ut tu quoque per litteras petis, non te sapientem Stoicorum legibus esse rogo, qui in carissimorum funere nihil omnino nos angi volunt: non enim illis assentio, qui nullis humanis affectibus[8] commoventur. Nam quis est adeo expers humanitatis, qui, si carissimam uxorem amitteret, matrem communium liberorum, quae rem omnem familiarem diligenter conservaret et studiose adaugeret, in quam omnes domesticas curas solicitudinesque reponeret, non vehementius turbaretur? Verum ut carissimorum interitu non tristari immanium potius barbarorum quam piorum hominum est munus, ita quoque dolore nimio cruciari mulierum est
3 potius quam virorum. Bene autem institutus animus neque dolore non commovetur neque plus quam satis est maerore tristitiaque torquetur. Par est enim prudentissimum quenque virum neque se nimium secundis rebus efferre neque adversis concidere, sed bene praeparatum pectus ad utranque fortunam ostendere. Considerare enim debet ut caelum ac pelagus nunc est turbidum nunc serenum, sic nos quoque non posse, pro mortalitatis conditione, semper in uno tenore persistere neminique naturae leges pervertere
4 datum esse. Quae quidem si ab initio nobis perpetuam pacem et securum ocium promisisset, in adversis nostris rebus pro repentino dolore, cuius eo semper acerbior est vis quo magis insperatus acciderit, non iniuria quereremur. Verum quando nobis solicitudines, damna, exilia, bella, clades et innumera mala bonis immixta praedixerit, cum quid adversi contigerit non debemus magnopere commoveri. Harum si rerum humanarum conditionem et duplicem bonorum malorumque urnam, quae Deus in terras iugiter pro arbitrio suo iacit, ipse tecum tacitus reputabis, intelliges adhibendae medelae tuo huic vulneri iam tempus ultimum advenisse.

5 Optima vero medicina doloris ratio est, quae nos admonet cogitare omnibus qui terrae vescuntur munere, sive reges sive inopes fuerint, enavigandum flumen Cocyton esse. Quare cum vitam a

But, as you put it in your letter, I do not ask that you should be 2
the Sage of Stoic theory, which requires us to feel no anguish at all at the passing of dear friends.[40] I do not share the view that we should never be moved by any human emotion. Which of us is so bereft of common humanity that he is not thrown into turmoil by the loss of his dearest consort, the mother of the children they shared, one who took care to preserve the family fortunes and took pains to increase them, in whose hands he placed all his domestic cares and worries? But just as a failure to grieve at the death of loved ones is more a mark of barbarians than men of proper feeling, so suffering an excess of pain is more appropriate to women
than men. A well-tempered soul is certainly not unmoved at pain 3
but neither is it tormented beyond measure by grief and sadness. All the wisest men are rightly neither carried away by success nor downcast by adversity, but display a spirit well prepared for either eventuality. We should realize that just as the sea and the sky are now rough, now calm, so too we must accept that in virtue of the human condition we cannot always maintain the same course, nor
is it open to anyone to overturn the laws of Nature. Had she in- 4
deed held out to us from the outset the promise of eternal peace and carefree leisure, in our hour of adversity we should be right to complain of the sudden blow, which always falls all the more harshly for being unexpected. But since she has held out to us the prospect of anxiety, damage, exile, wars, disasters, and any number of ills mixed in with the good things, we ought not to be greatly disturbed when something goes wrong. If you quietly ponder the nature of the human condition and the double urn of good and ill that God constantly empties over the face of the earth as his whim takes him, you will realize that the right time for healing your wound has now arrived.

The best remedy for grief is reason, which tells us that everyone 5
fed by earth's bounty, be they kings or paupers, must sail over the river Cocytus.[41] And so since we have received from God the gift

Deo mutuam, tanquam aes alienum a faeneratore, sumpserimus,
6 reposcenti quandocunque voluerit laeto animo est reddenda. Neque enim in morte quicquam est mali, cum ea cunctis incommodis
optimum remedium sola praestet humanaeque vitae curas solicitudinesque devitet. Nam etiam si mors animi simul et corporis finis
esset, insensibilitas quaedam tamen ipsam consequitur et requies
cessatioque laborum; at si, quod credimus et speramus, non una
cum corpore animus interit, ab angustiis corporis, quibus mens
variis impletur cogitationibus, liberati quietiorem vitam certe tran-
sigimus. Amore praeterea, spe, metu, cupiditate et diversarum rerum affectibus ita semper exagitamur dum vivimus atque a summi
boni contemplatione abducimur, ut nihil vere possimus sapere donec in corpore permanemus.[9]

7 Itaque si non modo nihil mali in morte est, sed contra plurimum boni, si mors non prece, non pretio, non vi, non arte diffugi-
tur, si cum vita reposcitur aequo animo reddi debet — nam, velis
nolis, reddenda est —, si carissimorum interitum moderate debemus ferre, quid est causae cur tantopere acerbissimo funere dilec-
tissimae coniugis torqueare? An doles quod corporeis vinculis
exoluta ad lucem e tenebris, a labore ad requiem, a terrenis ad
caelestia piissima mulier demigrarit? An vero te potius domesticus
dolor angit, quod necessaria et fida et dulcis coniunx tam insperato
tempore, tam a studiis tuis et liberorum et rei familiaris commodis
8 alieno te solum in medio curarum fluctu reliquerit? Sed an, vir
omnium litteratissime, ignorabas, cum uxorem ex sententia delige-
bas, et eam et liberos, siquos pareret, ac te quoque simul et aegro-
tare et quotidie mori posse, cum nemini sit exploratum vel ad
vesperam[10] se victurum? Quod si haec tibi, ut par erat, ante oculos
proponebas, cur nunc tam vehementi dolore afficeris casibus multo
antea meditatis?

of life—on loan, as it were, from a moneylender—we must cheer-
fully return it whenever he asks for it back. There is nothing evil 6
in death, for it alone provides a sovereign remedy for all our troubles and abolishes all the cares and worries of human life. Even if the soul were to die with the body, it would bring with it only a lack of sensation, rest and an end to our labors; but if, as we hope and believe, the soul does not die with the body, we shall at any rate pass a more peaceful life, free from the bodily limitations that fill our minds with all sorts of worries. In life, besides, we are exercised by love, hope, fear, desire, and the longing for various possessions, and are diverted by them from contemplation of the highest good, with the result that we can attain no true knowledge as long as we remain in the body.

If there is nothing evil in death, then, but on the contrary much 7
good; if death cannot be avoided by prayer or wealth, by force or guile; if we have to surrender life with equanimity when it is asked for—and it does have to be surrendered whether we like it or not; and if we must bear the deaths of our loved ones with restraint, what reason is there for you to torment yourself at the death of your dear wife, bitter as it is? Are you grieving that your faithful partner has slipped her chains and left the darkness for the light, a life of toil for one of rest, earthly things for things in heaven? Or is it rather your domestic afflictions that distress you, that your beloved, trusted, and delightful wife has left you amid a flood of cares so unexpectedly, at a time so unpropitious for your studies
and the well-being of your children and household affairs? But as 8
a man of the highest culture, were you not aware in choosing a wife after your own heart that both she and any children she might bear, and you too, could sicken and die all at once and on any day, since no one knows whether he will live even to nightfall? And if, as you should have done, you did envision these things happening, why now do you suffer such sharp grief at events long held in prospect?

9 Quare age, te collige et res humanas animo revolutans considera
non te solum, non primum, non ultimum his molestiis implica-
tum. Finem maerori luctuique impone, quem si post paulo finiet
ipsa dies, te talem, tam doctum virum, tanta rerum copia et scientia praeditum, tempus ultimum dedecet expectare. Nam cum
prorsus non sani sit hominis in perpetuo luctu persistere, profecto
nos oportet ac decet auxilio rationis longitudinem temporis prae-
venire. Quanquam si lachrimis et maerore possent animae in corpora revocari, concederem sane pro arbitrio te lugere; verum qui
semel occiderit cum non forma, non viribus, non genere, non opibus, non facundia, non pietate restituatur,[11] non debemus, ut ini-
10 tio dixi, plus quam decet tristitie agitari. Neque hoc ea tantum-
modo ratione, quod luctu nostro nihil proficimus, sed etiam quod,
siquis inferis est sensus, illius animam, si te tanto dolore opprimi
senserit, dolituram crediderim, cum te vivens plurimum delectarit.
Praesta hoc igitur illi mortuae, praesta liberis, cognatis, amicis
tuis, qui una tecum tanto tuo dolore maerent; praesta cunctis Latini nominis, qui doctrina et magisterio tuo egent.[12] Quibus omnibus de tua plurimum salute solicitis, nobisque in primis, rem gratissimam feceris et studiis tuis dignissimam si, inanibus querelis
depositis,[13] te ad pristinam vitae consuetudinem revocaris. Vale.

Florentiae, VIII Cal. Augusti MCCCCLXXII.[14]

So come now, collect yourself, and in pondering human affairs 9
consider that you are not the only one—not the first and not the last—to be caught up in troubles like these. Set a limit on your grief and mourning: if in a little while the very passage of time will put an end to it, it is hardly right for you, with all your qualities and learning, your breadth of resources and knowledge, to wait for the last moment. Since it is altogether mad to remain grief-stricken in perpetuity, it is by all means proper and decent for us to forestall the long march of time with the help of reason—though if tears and grieving could recall souls to the body, I should of course allow you to mourn as much as you like. But once someone has died, no beauty or strength, no breeding or wealth, no eloquence or fellow human feeling can bring them back. So we should not, as I said at the outset, be prostrated by grief beyond all measure.
And this not only because we draw no advantage from our grief, 10
but also because, if the dead have any consciousness, her soul must, I think, feel pain at realizing that you yourself are in such pain, when in life she brought you such delight. Do her in death this service, then, and do it for your children, relations and friends, who suffer alongside you in your great grief; do it for all those of the Latin race who need your scholarship and teaching. All of them, myself especially, are greatly worried about your well-being, and you will do us all a great favor—and something worthy of the studies you profess—if you put aside idle complaints and return to your original way of life. Farewell.

Florence, July 25, 1472.

: 18 :

Bartholomaeus Fontius Petro Cennino s.

1 Cum recordor puerilium temporum, quibus cum nostro Fannio periocunde vivebamus in rectis studiis litterarum, et eorum quae postea sunt subsecuta molestias reputo, prae his illa beata fuisse videntur mihi. Nam etsi tunc puer interdum angustiis rerum exagitabar, me tamen ad suavissimas Musas referens ex eis magna solatia capiebam. Illis autem postea necessario decem iam annos relictis, laborum plenam et solicitudinum vitam duxi, ut qui neque foris ornamentum Fortunae ullum neque domi praesidium ullum
2 invenerim. At nunc tandem, cum rerum usu experientiaque edoctus nihil expetendum praeter virtutem censuerim, ad bonas artis revertor cum sponte mea, tum rationibus iis quas paulo post exponam. In quo quidem me pungunt leviter eorum, quos mihi rettulisti, de me sermones, qui cum in me nihil non ferendum inveniant, dicunt tamen non me tamdiu studia relinquere debuisse. Quibus ego si prius ostendero quot mihi per omnem adolescentiam incommoda fuerint ad studia prosequenda, mox tibi sententiam meam aperiam.

3 Me vero a communibus studiis parentum, ut te non praeterit, immaturus interitus invitum avulsit. Tunc enim quintum decimum annum aetatis agens, suscepta necessaria meorum cura, omnem fidem, industriam operamque adhibui eis tuendis. Qua in re tanta assiduitas et diligentia mea septem continuos annos fuit, ut maximo illis adiumento extiterim. Secundo vero aetatis anno supra vigesimum magna ex parte honeribus iam levatus, sorore etiam viro in matrimonium collocata, caepi mecum de me ornando aliquantulum cogitare statuique[15] ad aliquem principem me conferre,

: 18 :

Bartolomeo Fonzio to Pietro Cennini, greetings.[42]

When I think back to the times of our youth which we passed so 1
pleasantly with our friend Fanni in the innocent study of literature, and consider the difficulties that have followed since, I think those times were blessed in comparison to these. Even if as a boy I was troubled by straitened circumstances from time to time, whenever I resorted to the delights of the Muses, I found great consolation in them. I had afterward of necessity to abandon them for ten years and led a life full of labor and care, finding none of
Fortune's distinctions abroad nor any security at home.[43] But I've 2
learned from experience of life that nothing but virtue is worth pursuing, and now at last I return to the humanities, both on my own account and for reasons I shall shortly explain. In that regard, I am indeed somewhat stung by the talk there is of me by those persons you told me about, who though they find in me nothing they cannot abide, still say that I should not have abandoned my studies for such a long time. Once I have shown them how many difficulties have stood in my way throughout my youth, I shall proceed to give you my views.

As you must be aware, the early death of my parents tore me 3
away against my will from our common studies.[44] When I was in my fifteenth year I had to take over the care of my family and I devoted all the trust reposed in me, all my effort and energy, to looking after them. My application and attentiveness in this matter over the course of seven years were such that, as it turned out, I was a great help to them. By my twenty-second year I was already relieved of much of my burden with the marrying off of my sister; I began to consider a little how I might improve my lot and decided to attach myself to some prince, by whose wealth and fa-

4 cuius opibus et gratia vitam honestiorem transigerem. Quare velut
e specula quadam nostrorum Italiae principum vitam et mores
acutum prospiciens, ad Hestensem me Borsium, Ferrariae ducem,
contuli.[16] Is autem, magnitudine animi caeteros longe superans,
me suscepit comiter et benigne. Ego vero eius in me liberalitatem
benivolentiamque expertus, in eo cum spem omnem reposuissem,
non post multo ipsius acerbissimo funere eo corrui magis, quo
5 magis attollere me speravi. Quare contra rebus quam putaveram
succedentibus, cum redire ad vetera studia veluti quietis in portum
excogitarem, Ferraria reversus incidi in quartanam, quasi parum
fecisset ipsa Fortuna si, cum tantum illud mihi decus et praesidium sustulisset, non in corpus quoque meum saeviret. Hac ego
per integrum annum laborans omne litterarum studium, tam longo
intervallo repetitum, non sine magna molestia iterum relinquere
6 sum coactus. Postea vero tam diuturno morbo liberato cum mihi
cum Petro Garasda, viro clarissimo meique amantissimo, tanta
necessitudo intercederet, ut non suam modo sed suorum quoque
omnium gratiam et favorem conciliaret, ecce iterum adversissima
truculentissimaque Fortuna eius et suorum omnium opes fregit.[17]

7 Caeterum, cum ad hunc meum natalem diem, quo sextum et
vigesimum annum ingredior, totius ante actae vitae rationem red-
diderim, cur modo ad intermissa studia toto animo me converte-
rim quam brevissime potero enarrabo. Cum Donato Acciaiolo,
praeclarissimo viro, summa mihi, ut scis, familiaritas intercedit. Is
nuper ad Fovianenses legatus missus ad eorum controversias
finium cum Licinianensibus componendas, me secum duxit. Hac
in legatione, cum saepe dicerem haec tempora doctis esse hominibus multum adversa commutaturumque me libenter, si versura
fieri posset, humanitatis et eloquentiae studia cum quaestuosis,
quanvis minoribus, artibus, ne te pluribus verbis morer, ad me ille

vor I could lead a more distinguished sort of life. When therefore 4
I made a penetrating survey, as if from a watchtower, of the lives and manners of our Italian princes, it was to Borso d'Este, Duke of Ferrara, that I betook myself. Far above the others in his greatness of spirit, Borso welcomed me in a friendly and graceful manner. Having experienced his liberality and generosity toward me, I had placed all my hopes in him, when all too soon I crashed as far down as I had hoped to be raised up in consequence of his untimely death.[45] And so, things turning out so differently from what 5
I had imagined, when I was contemplating going back to my old studies as to a haven of peace, I returned from Ferrara only to fall victim to the quartan fever, as if Fortune had not done enough in robbing me of that high position and support, but had to attack my body too. Suffering from the fever for an entire year, with great heaviness of heart I was once more forced to desist from the literary studies which I had taken up again after such a long interval.
Later, when I was free of this long illness, I formed such a close 6
friendship with Péter Garázda, a man of great distinction and utterly devoted to me, that he secured for me not only his own goodwill and favor but those of all his party. But here again the savagery of adverse Fortune shattered his resources and those of all his men.[46]

But having accounted for the whole of my life up to this my 7
twenty-fifth birthday, I shall explain as briefly as possible why I have now returned wholeheartedly to the studies I dropped. As you know, I am on exceptionally good terms with the illustrious Donato Acciaioli. He was recently sent as the Florentine envoy to Foiano to settle their boundary dispute with the men of Lucignano, taking me with him.[47] I used often to say to him while we were on this mission that the times were adverse to men of learning, and that if change was possible, I would gladly swap the study of eloquence and the humanities for profitable pursuits, even modest ones. To cut a long story short, he turned to me at length and

8 tandem conversus ait: 'officium meum est, pro meo summo in te
amore, tibi consulere et monere ne medio in spatio cursum sistas,
ut, siquid prodesse queam, non videar mea cohortatione defuisse
ac, si minus nunc profuero, saltem posthac intelligas mihi voluntatem egregiam affuisse. Ego vero mecum persaepe reputans quid in
istam te mentem impulerit, nullas nisi duas causas esse video, aut
divitiarum aut vulgarium honorum assequendorum. Sed an decet
pro inani quadam gloriola et pro sordido quaestu eas immensas
opes amittere, quae vivo tibi nunquam adimentur neque earum
laus mortuo quidem? An ignoras quae in Fortunae arbitrio sita
sunt fluxa et instabilia cuncta esse, quae et dum homines quaerunt
et postquam adepti fuerint mille incertis casibus submittuntur?
Quid porro praeclarius est quam non struendis opibus, non falsis
honoribus exquirendis, sed multarum magnarumque rerum cogni-
9 tioni et scientiae inhaerere? Caetera omnia vana et fluxa sunt ha-
bentibusque magis honeri quam honori. Virtus sola aeterna est et
iocunda et utilis possidenti. Sola etenim sapientiae studia, nos ad
honestatem et virtutem instituentia, in adversis rebus consolando,
in prosperis adornando, quid sequendum, quid vitandum sit fideliter admonendo, ad veram laudem et gloriam nos perducunt.
Contra vero aura popularis ac divitiarum cupiditas et quaerendo
habendi spe fatigant animos nostros et quaesita amittendi metu ita
solicitant, ut in eis nullam quietem reperiamus.

10 'Quando autem eorum quae sunt, alia in nostra, alia extra nostram potestatem locata sunt, insani est hominis quae sui iuris non
sunt in potestate sua esse praesumere aut quae propria sunt aliena
existimare. Nostrum est autem appetere, assentiri, eligere, decli-
nare, praeparare, decernere; alienum gloria, robur, pulchritudo,
divitiae caeteraque id genus, quae magis optare quam vendicare

said: "For the great affection I bear you, I am obliged to offer some 8
advice and warn you not to stop when you are but halfway there—if I prove to be of any use to you, I shall reckon my encouragement has not failed, while if I am not of immediate help, at least you will realize later on that I had every good intention. I have often pondered what it is that has driven you to take this attitude, for which as far as I can see there can only be two motives, either to get wealth or attain vulgar honors. But is it right for some empty and paltry moment of glory or for sordid gain to throw away those immense riches which can never be taken from you in life and of which the honor remains even in death? Are you unaware that all things that sit in Fortune's lap are precarious and unstable, subject to a thousand uncertainties, both while men seek them and when they have gained them? And further, what could be more prestigious than to dedicate yourself, not to heaping up riches or seeking empty honors, but to the study and understanding of a multitude of important matters? All the rest is empty and 9
transitory, more of burden than an ornament to those who have them. Virtue alone lasts for ever and gives the possessor both pleasure and utility. Only the study of wisdom, which educates us in integrity and virtue, by consoling us in adversity and dignifying us in prosperity, by giving us faithful advice as to what to seek and what to avoid—only that study can bring us true esteem and glory. But the quest for popular reputation and greed for wealth, on the other hand, wear down our spirits in hopes of attaining them, and once we have them, fill us with such anxiety at the thought of losing them that we find no peace in their possession.

"In any case, since everything that exists is either in our power 10
or beyond it, it is mad for anyone to presume that he controls what is outside his control and to consider as extraneous to him what truly is his. Our proper function is really to seek out, approve, choose, decline, to make plans and take decisions; glory, strength, beauty, wealth, and other things of that sort are indepen-

nobis valemus. Sed earum rerum, quarum te optio penes est, cum eligere utilissimam quanque debeas, utillimum vero procul insania vulgi recte vivere tibi sit. Id autem facere nequeas nisi animum bene colas: iis artibus totum dedere te te debes, quibus illum quam
11 rectissime possis excolere. Sed cum ad bene vivendum sit opus praeceptis et institutis ad felicitatem ducentibus, quae undique ex nostris studiis colliguntur, operae est pretium his incumbas. In quibus etiam prosequendis si lucro animum et honori subiicias, an Leonardum Poggiumque ignoras hac una dicendi scribendique facultate sibi perpetuum nomen et honestas divitias comparasse? An alia, quam hac, duce Schala noster ascendit ad opes, ad honores, ad dignitates? Quare age, expergiscamur aliquando minusque nobis quam possumus, plus tamen quam facimus, assumamus ac iam prope reviviscenti eloquentiae pro virili nostra subveniamus.'

12 His ego adhortationibus tunc mirabiliter sum commotus et iisdem, postquam in urbem redii, mecum saepius repetitis totum ad communia studia me converti. Alii, ut divitias cumulent, Britannos usque adnavigent; alii ante potentiorum fores excubent, ut assequantur aliquam dignitatem. Equidem paupertate contentus, ambitione avaritiaque semota, omne tempus quod a rerum necessariarum cura supererit studiis nostris impertiar. In quo rectissimo atque honestissimo proposito perseverans, contendam efficere quod tabellarii celeres interdum solent, qui si serius mane surgunt, ita mox gradum accelerant, ut citius quam si ante lucem iter ingressi essent ad constitutum locum perveniant.

13 Haec vero ad te potissimum scripsi, suavissime mi Cennine, quoniam cupio te habere in omni meo consilio socium et in omni cogitatione coniunctum. Quae si tibi viro optimo probabuntur,

dent of us, things we may hope for rather than claim as our own. But where you do have a choice over things, you should choose all the most useful of them, the most useful of all being for you to live an upright life far from the madding crowd. And that, indeed, you cannot do unless you carefully nurture your mental life, and so you must devote yourself totally to those arts by which you may best cultivate it. But since for the good life you need the precepts 11
and teachings leading to happiness that are copiously supplied by our studies, it is worth the effort to apply ourselves to them. If you place mental cultivation behind wealth and honors even as you pursue these studies, surely you are not unaware that Leonardo Bruni and Poggio gained eternal fame and honorable riches from their very talent in speaking and writing? Perhaps you think our friend Scala attained his power, his position, and his status by some other route?[48] So come now, let us awake and at length take on the task, in smaller measure than our capacities, certainly, but more than we are doing at present, and to the best of our ability come to the aid of an eloquence now returning to life."

I was greatly impressed at the time by this encouragement, and 12
after I returned to Florence I kept going over it in my mind as I turned to immersing myself in study. Let others sail to distant Britain to pile up riches; let others keep vigil before the doors of the powerful in search of some office. I for my part shall set aside ambition and avarice and be content with poverty, spending all the time I can spare from domestic cares on our studies. In persevering in this proper and honorable course, I shall try to emulate those swift messengers who sometimes rise late in the morning but yet manage by hastening their stride to reach their destination quicker than if they had set out on the journey before dawn.

I have addressed these remarks to you in the first place, my dear 13
Cennini, because I would have you be privy to all my plans and the companion of all my thoughts. And if you as an upright man approve of them, it will mean more to me than the approval of the

gratius erit quam si Senatus et populus omnis probet; Fannio certe nostro vehementer placitura confido, cui honesta et recta omnia semper solent placere. Vale.

Florentia, VII Cal. Septembris MCCCCLXXII.

: 19 :

Bartholomaeus Fontius Petro Fannio s.

1 Cum peccatum animae mortem inferre in *Paenitentia* mea scripserim, sed non eam quae interitus est et finis, cum eius anima sit immunis, quaesivisti hesternis litteris et quid anima ipsa sit et qua ratione immortalem existimem et si eam peccatis honustam putem in Tartareos fluctus demergi ac perpetuo supplicio cruciari, quando quae de inferis scripta sunt ad nostram emendationem, ne cupidi-
2 tatibus moveremur, fabulose dicta non nulli putent. Neque vero haec de me quaerere alienum putasti, quoniam si aut non esset anima immortalis aut inferi ad terrorem, quo pietatem mortales colerent iustitiamque servarent, conficti essent, frustra de paenitentia descripsissem. Ego autem, etsi res tanta maiore ocio longioreque praemeditatione indigeret, per eundem tabellarium tamen, ut aliqua tibi in parte faciam satis, rem totam quanto aptius potero explicabo.

3 Quacunque de re loquimur, duo sunt in primis consideranda, an ea sit et quid sit: frustra enim quid esset, si ea non esset, disquireremus. Esse autem animam inde constat, quod homini motum aut anima aut corpus praestat aut utriusque permixtio. Sed

entire citizenry of Florence. I'm absolutely sure my plans will be welcome to our friend Fanni, one who always approves of all that is right and honorable. Farewell.

Florence, August 26, 1472.

: 19 :

Bartolomeo Fonzio to Pietro Fanni, greetings.

I wrote in my treatise *On Penitence* that sin involves the death of 1
the soul, but not the death which is a dissolution and an end, since the soul is immune from that.[49] And so you asked me in your letter of yesterday what the soul actually is, and on what grounds I believe it to be immortal, and whether I think that a soul weighed down by sins sinks beneath the waves of Tartarus and suffers everlasting torment; for some people think that what is written about hell is invented just to keep us straight, so that we shall not be led astray by our passions. Nor indeed did you think 2
it out of place to put such questions to me, since it would have been pointless for me to write about penitence if the soul were not immortal or if the underworld had been invented to terrify mortals into behaving justly and acting toward one another as duty requires. Though the importance of the matter calls for greater leisure and more prolonged examination, I shall use your same messenger to set out the whole question as best I can so as to satisfy your request in some measure.

Whatever the subject we are speaking about, there are two 3
prime considerations: whether it exists and what it is: any enquiry into what a thing is would be pointless if it didn't exist. The soul's existence is implied by the fact that either the soul or the body (or a mixture of the two) imparts motion to mankind. But since mo-

cum in corpore non sit motus, quia nullum inanimum corpus suo motu cieri potest, si neque etiam animae motus inest, ex duabus rebus motu carentibus nullus motus exorietur. Nunquam enim ex similibus geminatis contrarietas emergit, sicut nec e gemino frigore calor nec e gemino calore nascitur frigus. Verum cum corpus hominis moveatur, neque a se ipso neque etiam a permixtione moveatur (frustra enim ab utroque dicetur moveri, si eorum alterum est immotum), superest ut ab eorum tantum altero, idest ab anima,
4 moveatur. Cum vero esse animam motus hominis causam certum sit, quid tamen ea sit nondum satis inter mortales constat. Probantur a me nostri Christiani tamen, qui eam substantiam esse dicunt carentem corpore seque ipsam moventem ratione a Deoque creatam mortis immunem. Ex quo autem aut quomodo creata sit nec nostra interest quaerere nec humanae coniectatio mentis capit.
5 Immortalem quidem esse, quanquam non me fugit quibus rationibus probent ii qui se Stoicos aut Achademicos profitentur (quoniam scilicet id quod per se movetur semper et est et movetur et sibi ipsi principium motus est; quod vero principium est natum non est, quia nulla principii est origo — nam si aliunde gigneretur principium non esset; quod autem natum non est nec occidit quidem unquam, ergo anima immortalis est), quanquam non hoc me fugit, inquam, longe tamen ab illis aliter sentio, non de immortalitate ac motu, sed de principio eius: non enim, ut illi, immortalem esse censeo quoniam genita nunquam sit, sed quia mortis immunis
6 a Deo creata sit. Duo nanque sunt rerum immortalium genera. Unum vere proprium immortale, quod a se et propter se et non ob alium finem constat, sibi ipsi exordium sine ullo exordio, caeterorum causa et origo, quem Deum aut natum aut interiturum esse non solum impossibile, sed assertu quoque nefarium est. Alterum

tion does not inhere in the body—for no inanimate body can be stirred by its own motion—if there were no motion in the soul either, no motion at all could arise from two entities that both lacked it. For it never happens that from the doubling of two like things their contrary arises, just as heat is never brought about by doubling of cold nor cold by doubling of heat. But since the human body is subject to motion and does not move either by itself or even by a mixture of soul (it would be wrong to say that it is moved by both when one of the two is motionless), the only remaining possibility is that it is moved by one of them alone, that
is, by the soul. And though it is certain that the soul is the cause 4
of human motion, men have not yet reached agreement on what it is. But I favor the view of our Christian writers who say that it is a substance without body, endowed with rational motion and by God's fashioning not subject to mortality. As to when or how it was created, that is not for us to inquire, nor can the conceptions
of the human mind comprehend it. I am aware of the arguments 5
for its immortality made by those who profess themselves Stoics and Academics, namely, that that which moves by itself exists and moves forever and is in itself the beginning of motion; but that which is a beginning is not brought into being, since a beginning has no origin (if it were created from something else it would not be a beginning); and what is not created never dies, and so the soul is immortal.[50] I am not unaware of these arguments, I say, but my views differ greatly from theirs, not in regard to the immortality and motion but concerning its beginning: I do not believe, as they do, that it is immortal because it was never created
but because it was created by God to be immune from death. For 6
there are two types of immortal entities. One is immortal in the true sense that it exists in itself and of itself and not for some other end, it is its own beginning without any antecedent beginning, the cause and origin of other entities: that is, God, whose birth or death is not merely impossible but blasphemous even to

hoc primo longe inferius anima est, quae a Deo principium trahens nullo est unquam tempore defectura.

7 Reliquum est ostendere apud inferos impiorum animas cruciari.
Enimvero si Deus est, ut nullae negant barbarae nationes (nam
quo pacto sine certo moderatore tanta rerum machina tot saecula
tam constanti ordine regeretur?), is etiam sapiens ac iustus est.
8 Cum vero totus bonitas et iustitia undique perfectus virtute sit, an
tu eum aeque putas bonos ac malos homines habiturum? An non
improbi a legibus, a ducibus optimis qui pro legibus sunt coercen-
tur et puniuntur, contra boni laudantur et honorantur? Quae vero
Dei esset sapientia, quae iustitia si scelerum impunitatem non
paenitentibus aeque ac paenitentibus condonaret bonosque a malis, probos ab improbis non secerneret? Qui denique in terris pie-
tati, religioni, fidei locus esset? Quis tot labores, curas, vigilias,
obprobria, damna, caedes pro veritate susciperet? Quare non iure
tantum, sed etiam necessario summus Deus iis qui, voluptatibus et
libidinibus obcaecati, flagitiis omnibus se totos contaminarunt de-
vium quendam a concilioque sanctorum remotum statuit locum,
9 ubi suorum scelerum paenas luant. Qui sicubi locus figendus est,
perquam longissime a Dei beatitudine terrarum in profundo um-
bilico locatus est. Impiorum enim animae terrenis vitiis veluti
compedibus honeratae neque se ex imo attollere neque Deum cer-
nere unquam possunt, qua nulla paena gravior, nulla mors acerbior
reperitur.

10 Caeterum huic iam epistolae modus sit, quae satis tibi si fecerit, pergratum erit, sin minus, plura coram disseremus cum tu redieris. Vale.

Florentia, Idibus Octobribus MCCCCLXXII.

assert. The other, far inferior to the first, is the soul, which in taking its beginning from God is destined never to die.

It remains to be shown that the souls of the impious suffer tor- 7
ment in the underworld. Now if God exists, as not even barbarous peoples deny—how on earth would this great machine of the universe run in such regular order over so many generations without
a definite governor?—he is wise and he is just. But since he is all 8
goodness and justice and in every respect completely virtuous, do you suppose he would treat good and evil men equally? Would not rather the wicked be disciplined and punished by the laws, or by the virtuous rulers who represent them, while the good are praised and honored? What would God's wisdom and justice amount to if he gave the penitent and impenitent alike remission of their sins, if he did not make a distinction between the good and the bad, the wicked and the upright? What place, in short, would there be in our world for piety, religion, faith? Who would take on so many labors, cares, vigils, insults, so much harm and death for the defense of truth? It is therefore not just by right but also by necessity that Almighty God has set those who, blinded by their pleasures and passions, have totally corrupted themselves with all manner of outrages in some remote place far from the congregation of saints, where they may pay the penalty for their
crimes. If we must give a location for this spot, it must be placed 9
as far as possible from God's beatitude in the deep centre of the earth. For the souls of the impious are weighed down with their earthly sins as if with chains, and they can neither raise themselves from the depths nor ever look upon God, than which there is no worse punishment and no harsher death.

But with that, let me make an end to this letter: I shall be very 10
glad if you find it satisfying, but if not, we shall speak further face-to-face when you come back.

Florence, October 15, 1472.

: 20 :

Bartholomaeus Fontius Petro Delphino generali Camaldulensi s.

1 Maurum fratrem se tibi addixisse vehementer gaudeo, non tam quod tu eius Ordinis princeps es, tametsi id quidem permagnum est, quam, hercule, quod vir bonus, quod doctus, quod ab omnibus amandus es. Iampridem enim innotuit morum tuorum sanctitas vitaeque integritas et bonarum artium summum studium summa cum humanitate coniunctum. Quibus rebus ita celeber factus es, ut quicunque virtutem expetunt et ament et praedicent
2 nomen tuum. Ego vero, qui te antea per me ipsum fama compulsus toto animo et cogitatione complexus eram, adiuncta hac necessitudine fratris mei, ardeo desiderio incredibili tecum loquendi. Quod quia propediem futurum spero, propterea brevius ad te scripsi; interim, siqua in re tibi usui esse possim, me ad omnia paratissimum fore polliceor. Vale.

: 21 :

Bartholomaeus Fontius Antonio Calderino s.

1 Desidiae merito abs te arguerer, Calderine, nisi rerum publicarum suspensio hanc mihi tarditatem attulisset. Nam, dum aliquem communibus malis eventum praestolor, diem ex die extrahens nihil adhuc rescripsi litteris tuis Lugduni signatis. Neque vero nunc scribo quod quicquam sit certi et constituti, sed ne me aut hoc

: 20 :

Bartolomeo Fonzio to Pietro Dolfin, General of the Camaldulensians, greetings.[51]

I'm delighted that my brother Mauro has attached himself to you, 1 not so much because you are the leader of the order—though that is itself very important—as because you are a good man, by heaven, and learned too, beloved by all.[52] Your devout character, the integrity of your life, and your passion for the liberal arts, allied to consummate humanity, have long been famous. For these gifts you have become so celebrated that anyone that seeks after virtue loves and exalts your name. For my part, though I had al- 2 ready been driven by report to embrace you with all my heart and soul, now that my brother has formed this close connection, I am gripped by an extraordinary desire to converse with you. This being something I hope will soon take place, I now write this short letter to you. In the meantime, if I can be of any service to you, I am absolutely at your disposal in all matters. Farewell.

: 21 :

Bartolomeo Fonzio to Antonio Calderini, greetings.

You would be right to criticize me for laziness, Calderini, had not 1 my inactivity been caused by the suspension of political life here. While I wait for some development in the bad situation we find ourselves in, I have been putting things off from day to day and still haven't replied to the letter you sent from Lyon.[53] Not that I am writing now because anything has been settled, but only so

pestifero bello putes interiisse aut tui, quod nunquam fieri posset, oblitum esse. Vivo autem et memor equidem tui vivo ac tibi subin-
2 video, quod longe absis ab hac civitatis miseria. Nihil enim, si adesses, vel audires vel cerneres quod non te maximopere angeret: nam nec speratam pacem habemus nec diuturniori bello sufficimus. Laurentius Medices Neapoli adhuc est, Ferrandus quoque illi favet ex animo, sed adversatur maxime Sixtus Pontifex. Veneti Robertum Malatestam imperatorem legerunt maioremque in dies cogunt exercitum. Nos quid agamus incerti sumus: nulla enim aegroto huic corpori absente medico medicina porrigitur.

3 Saxettus occupationibus distractus maximis nihil ad te rescripsit, sed gratae fuerunt illi tuae litterae teque diligit. Vale.

Florentia, III Cal. Februarii MCCCCLXXIX.

: 22 :

Bartholomaeus Fontius Buclero Gallo s.

1 Ex litteris tuis perhumaniter ad me scriptis summam cepi animo voluptatem, quod regiis in rebus te versari esseque in primis aulicis intellexi; quam causam fuisse etiam dicis, ut ad me serius scripseris. Verum etsi excusatio tam honesta minime necessaria apud me est, ob id tamen maxime grata est, quod verebar ne nihil cum scriberes te meus ille tardior *Asinus* offendisset, ita ignavum est animal ac fustis egens.

that you don't imagine that I have died in this ruinous war or have forgotten you—that could never happen. I am indeed alive, and live with you very much in mind, slightly envious that you are so removed from these present calamities of the city. If you were here 2
at Florence, there is nothing you could hear or see that would not bring you utter distress. We have neither the peace we hoped for nor the ability to carry on the war for much longer. Lorenzo de' Medici is still at Naples, Ferrante is sincerely well disposed toward him but Pope Sixtus wholly opposed. The Venetians have chosen Roberto Malatesta as their captain general and are getting an army together that grows by the day. We are uncertain as to what to do: there's no medicine available for our sick body politic while the Medic's away.

Sassetti has been distracted by extremely important business 3
and so hasn't written back to you, but was glad to have your letter and regards you with affection. Farewell.

Florence, January 30, 1480.

: 22 :

Bartolomeo Fonzio to the Frenchman Beauclair, greetings.[54]

I took great pleasure in the very kind letter you sent me, from 1
which I gathered that you are engaged on the king's business as one of his leading courtiers, this being also the reason, you say, that you wrote to me with some delay. But even if this perfectly respectable excuse was for me quite unnecessary, it was nonetheless very welcome since I had begun to worry when I heard nothing from you that my *Ass* had reached you late—it's a lazy animal and needs beating.

2 Sed postquam satis tibi fecit, ut scribis, neque indignus est visus inter maiores misceri equos, non stabuli modo, sed etiam culinae tuae rationem habere decrevi. Quare licet vos, Galli, bonos habeatis popinarum magistros, ad te tamen hunc transmisi cum his litteris, coquorum omnium quot sunt quotque fuerunt aut in posterum erunt sapientissimum. Ex quo sane poteris carnium, piscium, olerum, pomorum bellariorumque omnium pro anni temporibus condituram percipere. In quo uno tantum artis ingeniique deprendes ut non pluris praecepta facias vel Pythagorae vel Platonis. Nam ex eo quicquid hominum generi conferat, quicquid mortales iuvet atque oblectet, quicquid vitandum appetendumve
3 sit edisces. Eum igitur non ut humilem coquum, sed magnum, genialem patronum in urbe, in agro, in ocio, in negocio, in cubiculo, in caenaculo, in ientaculis, in prandiis, in caenis, in commessationibus omnibus, si valitudinem tuam diligis, si rerum naturam scire cupis consulito. Neque vero erit avarior aut gulosior: nam neque aliquid in culina devorabit neque absumet quicquam in cellario aut penu neque etiam in triclinio esse volet, solo odore
4 contentus omniumque abstinentissimus. Unum tantum a te petet, neque sumptuosum nimis, ne pertimescas, ut amicias eum et vestias; quod ego nimiam ob festinationem eius ad te mittendi, simul ut expeditior tam longum iter conficeret, praetermisi. Vesties autem, ut arbitror, eum libenter cum ut eius saluti, tum ut tuae provideas utilitati: nam et ipse nudus in istis frigoribus non perduraret diutius et tu magnam iacturam faceres, si tam sapientem coquum amitteres. Verum iam finis ridendi sit, ne Platiniano in coquo inepti simus, qui *Asinum* Apuleianum tam belle lusimus. Vale.

But since, as you say, he has given you satisfaction and you 2
reckon him fit to be kept with the bigger horses, I have decided to
take account not just of your stable but of your kitchen too. So
though you French have fine master chefs, I send you with this
letter the wisest of all cooks that there have been, are now, or will
ever be. You will certainly pick up from him how to prepare meat
and fish, vegetables, fruit, and all sorts of sweetmeats according to
the season. In this single man you will find so much artistry and
intelligence that you couldn't think more highly of the precepts of
Pythagoras or Plato themselves. From him you will learn all that
contributes to humankind's well-being, everything that helps or
pleases mortal man, whatever is to be shunned or sought after.
Consult him then, not as a humble cook but as a great cheerful 3
patron, in the city or in the country, at leisure or at work, in your
chamber or in the dining room, at breakfast, lunch or dinner, at
each and every meal, if you are fond of your health and want to
know the nature of things. Not indeed that he will prove greedy or
gluttonous, for he will never eat anything in the kitchen or consume anything from the cellar or larder, nor will he even want to
lie down on the dining couch; content with just the fragrance, he
will be more abstemious than anyone. There is just one thing he 4
asks of you — don't worry, it's not too expensive: he wants you to
cover and clothe him, something that in my haste to send him to
you, and also so that he could travel light on that long journey, I
omitted to do. But I imagine you will gladly give him clothes, both
to look after his health and for your own convenience: he won't
last very long without clothes in those frosts of yours, and you
yourself will suffer a great loss if you lose such a sage cook. But let
that be an end on the jesting, in case we become silly over Platina's
cook when we had such an elegant diversion with Apuleius's *Ass.*
Farewell.

: 23 :

Bartholomaeus Fontius Marsilio Ficino s.

1 Non eram nescius Platonem nostrum de omni philosophia non modo caeteris sonantius, sed etiam scripsisse divinius, neque tam eram expers antiquitatis ut orationis et lyrae Cyllenium inventorem dulcisonumque Apollinem ac blandiloquam Venerem ignorarem. Sed insita quaedam animo libertas siquid in te, uno Platonicorum principe, in scribendo desideravit, non tam quid alii nostri facerent, quam quid eleganter te scribere cupientem deceret significavi.

2 Dixi autem et dico prosaicae orationi tam crebro poeticos modos inseri non licere, quoniam in soluto dicendi genere non mediocre vitium est a communi consuetudine et vulgari oratione discedere. Quanquam enim in multis exornandi generibus et in rebus diversis complectendis poetae finitimus est orator, ille tamen maiore licentia verborum numerisque paulo astrictioribus utitur, hic vero laxioribus pedibus aures implens devitat omnem poetici
3 cantus similitudinem. Quod si veteres interdum suis scriptis poetica dicta inseruerunt, longe aliud est an poetarum exemplis testimoniisque utamur, an, quod ego nunquam probavi, solutam orationem in sonos poeticos efferamus. Nam ut illud summorum vatum sapit cognitionem, ita hoc verborum quandam inanem iactationem. Si enim, ut sentire te ostendis, absoluta est musice in qua dissonum nil auditur; si ea sunt carmina quae perfectis numeris et eundem spectantibus exitum concinuntur; si prosaica est oratio quae intra poeticos modos gravi et constanti pedum tenore

: 23 :

Bartolomeo Fonzio to Marsilio Ficino, greetings.[55]

I was not unaware that our friend Plato wrote about all fields of philosophy not only more sonorously but also more penetratingly than the rest, nor was I so ignorant of antiquity as not to know that Mercury was the inventor of eloquence and lyric poetry, along with sweet-sounding Apollo and seductive Venus. But if a certain innate forthrightness in me found anything at fault in your writing as *the* prince of the Platonists, I referred not so much to the practice of our other authors as to what you ought to do if you wanted to write well. 1

Now, I said and still say that one should not insert poetical tropes into a prose composition so frequently, for in prose it is no small fault to depart from regular usage and the common way of putting things. Despite the fact that in many types of ornamentation and in the treatment of a wide range of matters the orator stands very close to the poet, the latter has available to him both a greater license with words and a more restricted selection of metrical forms, while the former in giving his listeners looser rhythms 2
tries to avoid any similarity to the songs of the poets. It's true that 3
the ancients did from time to time introduce poetic vocabulary into their writings, but it is one thing to use examples and quotations from the poets and quite another to turn prose into what sounds like verse. The one imparts the flavor of an acquaintance with high poetry while the other simply gives the impression of empty verbal flourishes. If, as you claim to believe, perfect music is that in which no dissonance is heard, if poems are things sung in regular meters that always aim at the same endings, if prose is speech which proceeds with a stately and steady rhythm but falls

graditur, vitium vel magnum est prosae cum scriptor exeat in poeticam cantilenam.

4 Quod ego non propterea tecum contendo, ut te a tuo stilo scribendi retraham, sed quia utrunque meum est, et quid ipse observem tibi exponere et de te libere tecum decernere, quanquam non sum tuae consuetudinis tam ignarus quin more achademico te mecum obluctatum esse intelligam. Tu vero gratissimum feceris si crebro ad me de studiis tuis et cogitationibus omnibus quam familiariter scripseris. Equidem, cum per multas occupationes meas licebit, tam libenter litteras ad te dabo quam ardenter tua scripta relego teque amo. Vale.

: 24 :

Bartholomaeus Fontius Angelo Politiano s.

1 Non abutetur amplius pudore nostro impudentia tua neque se ulterius patientiam in nostram efferet ista effrenata audacia. Nam quando neque veteris nostrae consuetudinis neque studiorum communium ulla te ratio ad sanitatem mentis potest deflectere, eo te curabo helleboro, quod maxime ad insaniam tuam conferat.

Unde igitur tibi dementia tanta exorta est, ut eruditissimos quosque homines audeas petulantissimis maledictis convellere? Tu nulli defuncto iam vita ignoscis, tu viventibus omnibus detrahis, tu nobis maxime insultas, tu, scire ut unus cuncta videaris, doctos
2 omnis dilaceras. An hos inflatissimos spiritus ulla tibi bonarum artium dedit cognitio, quarum siquam teneres vel mediocriter non tam ab omni humanitate discederes? An te grammaticum profite-

short of turning into verse, then it is a major fault in a prose writer if he falls into poetical singsong.

Not that I am arguing with you in an attempt to deter you 4
from your writing style, but because I think I should both tell you the practice I myself follow and frankly announce my judgment on you to your face, though I am familiar enough with your habits to know that you have engaged me in this debate in your *Academic* style. In any case I'll be very grateful if you send me frequent news of all your studies and reflections in your friendliest manner. For my part, when my many occupations allow, I shall show as much enthusiasm in writing letters as ardor in reading your writings, and in admiring you. Farewell.

: 24 :

Bartolomeo Fonzio to Angelo Poliziano, greetings.[56]

Your impudence will not further abuse my modesty, nor will that 1
reckless insolence of yours any longer launch itself against my patience. Since neither regard for our old friendship nor for our common studies is able to return you to sanity, I shall cure you with hellebore, the best remedy for your madness.[57]

Where has such craziness sprung from that you dare to attack each and every man of learning with your wanton abuse? You spare not one of the dead, all the living you disparage, above all you insult me, you tear all the learned to bits in a bid to appear as
if you alone know everything. Was it some acquaintance with the 2
liberal arts that gave you this puffed-up idea of yourself? — though if you had even a modest mastery of any of them you would not be so devoid of all traces of humanity. Or perhaps you account yourself a grammarian, you who are so far removed from any ex-

ris, ab omni proprietate elegantiaque Latina alienissime? An historicum, cum puerilia furta et ostenta verborum in *Pactiana conspiratione* detexeris? An poetam, cuius te nihil apparet ex conquisitis semifuratisque versibus praeter mentis furorem assecutum? Nam oratorem quidem te dicere non auderes, cum ab omni dicendi consuetudine eloquentiaque abhorreas. Quod si nulla te potuit ad tantam audaciam impulisse bene percepta et cognita disciplina, quid ita, in utris inflati morem, tumidis sermonibus insolescens pestifero tuo spiritu doctos conficis?

3 An adeo tui muneris et Christianae religionis, quae superbiam, ambitionem, dicacitatem, libidinem comprimit, oblitus es ut humana et divina iura permiscens omnia nihil minus quam te hominem esse et Christianum et sacerdotem intelligas? An ignoras magistrum et Dominum et Deum nostrum dixisse «discite a me, quia mitis sum et humilis corde», et ab Apostolo scriptum esse «superbis Deus resistit, humilibus autem dat gratiam»? Quae si aut legisti unquam, ut par est, aut credis, ut debes, quid tam tumentibus animis et inflatis pulmonibus insolescis, non quid dicas sed quam male dicas attendens et confictis mendaciis semper utens?

4 Impudentissimi hominis et parati semper ad lites est in puerorum circulis in probos et doctos viros maledicta congerere. Eruditi nanque ac boni consuevere mandare quae sentiunt litteris et non turpibus contumeliis, sed utilibus scriptis de veritate contendere. Ede, ede, ut risum pavonibus moveas, quae compilasti, denudanda cornicula. Nam cum attrita ista fronte quod tu te ipse conscripseris non tuum esse diffiteri non poteris, tum vero perpetuis voluminibus ignorantiam tuam et depravatum iudicium et inversos a te

actness and elegance in Latin? Or a historian, though you have revealed your childish thefts and inflated verbiage in the *Pazzi Conspiracy*?[58] Or a poet, even though it is plain from your recherché and filched verses that you have attained none of a poet's qualities except mental derangement. Surely you wouldn't dare call yourself an orator when you shun any eloquence and any of the customary practices of rhetoric. But if no proper apprehension and understanding of any field of learning was able to bring you to such a pitch of impudence, why then are you so overbearing, like a blown-up balloon with your windy speech, prostrating the learned with the blasts of your pestilent breath?

Have you so far forgotten your office and the Christian religion (that curb on pride, ambition, ridicule, and wantonness) that by muddling up all human and divine law you have failed to realize that you are nothing but a man, a Christian, and a priest? Are you really unaware that our master, Lord, and God said, "Learn of me, for I am meek and lowly of heart," and the Apostle wrote, "For God resisteth the proud and giveth grace to the humble"?[59] Had you ever read these words, as you should have done, or did you but believe them, as you ought, why are you grown so proud with your swollen spirit and puffed-up lungs; why do you pay so much attention, not to the content of what you are saying, but how ill you say it; why do you constantly make use of invented lies? 3

To heap abuse on the heads of the good and the learned before crowds of boys is the sign of a man of utter shamelessness and one ever ready to quarrel. The erudite and upright generally consign their thoughts to writing and do not conduct debates on the truth by means of disgraceful insults but with useful writings. Go on, publish what you have plagiarized from others to make the peacocks laugh, you crow for the plucking. For when even with your brazen front you find it impossible to deny that what you have written is yours, then in an endless array of volumes I really will unmask your ignorance and depraved judgment and a thousand 4

mille scriptorum locos aperiam, quo tacitus lector scriptis utriusque collatis diiudicet quantum a nostro, qualecunque est, tuum
5 istud distet tenebricosum ingenium. Cum enim ad scriptionem
descenderis et pedem pedi contuleris, cum triario milite cruentum esse tibi certamen senties. Ad hoc ego singulare certamen abs te totiens irritatus nunc te provoco. Ad hanc statariam pugnam tua petulantia impulsus te invito. Ad monumenta virium, siquas habes, totiens lacessitus ostentanda iam te lacesso. Aude in clypeum assurgere, aude manum conserere, aude non latrando sed scribendo aliquod in nos spiculum intorquere.

6 Equidem arbitrabor pugnando tecum non solum contra te, ventosissimum hominem, sed omnes tui similes, ne amplius anseres oloribus obstrepere audeant, dimicare, ut de te docti et boni viri me vindice iustissimum ducant honestissimumque triumphum. Tu modo cognita mente mea tantam petulantiam oris si deposueris, tibi ipsi plurimum consulueris; sin minus graviora his longioraque expectato, ut omnem voluptatem, quam male de me saepe ac multum loquendo cepisti, non bene de te legendo amittas. Vale.

Florentiae, XI Cal. Septembris 1483.

passages in the classics that you have perverted, and from this the
silent reader will be able to compare our respective writings and
judge how far that shady talent of yours is from mine, such as it is.
When you deign to enter the field of writing and fight hand to 5
hand, you will realize you are faced with a bloody struggle with an
experienced soldier. So often provoked by you, I now call you out
to this single combat; stung by your effrontery, I invite you to this
set-piece fight. Challenged by you so many times, I now challenge
you to display a sample of your powers, if any you have. Lift your
shield and make bold to rise up! Dare to join battle, dare to hurl
some lance against me, not by barking but by writing!

For my part, in fighting you I shall regard myself as engaged in 6
a struggle not just with you, vainest of men that you are, but with
everyone like you, so that geese no longer dare to clamor against
swans, so that with me as their champion, educated and upright
men may have a well-deserved and honorable triumph over you.
Now that you know my mind, if you drop your extreme verbal
aggression you will be doing yourself a big favor; if not, you may
expect more and worse, so that all the pleasure you take in your
frequent and lengthy abuse of me will be lost when you read over
things so little to your credit. Farewell.

Florence, August 22, 1483.

LIBER SECUNDUS

: 1 :

Bartholomaeus Fontius Ioanni Rosso s.

1 Tametsi vitae integritas et humanitas et eruditio tua in excolendis iis qui tuo magisterio creduntur nullius commendationem desiderat, tamen, ut aperte intelligas quo amore pietateque complectar Cornelium, sororium nepotem meum quem tibi erudiendum discedens tradidi, tanto iterum studio eum tibi commendo, ut maiore affectu et caritate si filius unicus esset commendare non possim.
2 Quare mihi rem gratissimam et optatissimam feceris si non tanquam discipulum, sed communem potius filium et litteris et moribus instituendum susceperis. Quod equidem pro mutua nostra benivolentia studiisque communibus et amanter et diligenter confido te esse facturum. Nos vero in te neque ingrati erimus neque immemores. Nam quando pro te plus etiam contenderimus quam possimus, nostro tamen desiderio satis nunquam fecerimus. Vale.

Roma, VI Idus Novembris 1483.

: 2 :

Bartholomaeus Fontius Demetrio Chalcondylo s.

1 Quae me antea nova vivendi ratio infirmum atque incertum reddiderat, ea iam et usu ita est confirmata et voluntate constabilita, ut huc me venisse non multum paeniteat. Sum enim in totius

BOOK II

: 1 :

Bartolomeo Fonzio to Giovanni Rosso, greetings.[1]

Though your integrity, humanity, and learning in polishing those 1
entrusted to your teaching have need of no one's praise, still, to let you have a clear idea how close and dear Cornelio is to me, my nephew on my sister's side whom I handed over to you for instruction on my departure, I once again commend him to you — I could not commend him with more affection and esteem if he were my
only son. So you will do me a very welcome and gratifying favor if 2
you treat him not as a pupil but as a son whom we have in common, to be schooled in letters and morals alike. And that is something that I am sure you will do in virtue of our mutual friendship and our shared studies. I for my part shall be neither ungrateful nor unmindful in your regard: even if I exerted myself on your behalf beyond my powers, I should never satisfy my own desires in the matter. Farewell.

Rome, November 8, 1483.

: 2 :

Bartolomeo Fonzio to Demetrius Chalcondyles, greetings.[2]

My new manner of life, which had earlier made me nervous and 1
uncertain, has now been consolidated by my becoming habituated to it and more settled by my wanting it so, to such an extent that I do not repine at coming here too much. I am established in that

Christianitatis theatro amplissimo constitutus, in quo cum patientibus et certantibus magna praemia proponantur enitar pro viribus ferre omnia fortiter et dimicare acriter, ut aliquam laborum et contentionum mearum mercedem consequar. Quod si aut fiet serius quam velimus aut, quod omnino absit, non fiet, laetabor tamen in reliquum vitae tempus me amicorum consiliis obsecutum omnia tentavisse et optatis meis Fortunam, non animum defuisse.
2 Unum iam quidem omnium pulcherrimum sum assecutus, quod in hac urbe, altrice in omni genere litterarum praestantium excellentiumque virorum, ipse quoque ante tempus professor publicus[1] sum adscriptus. Hoc volui nescius ne esses. Vale.

Roma, pridie Cal. Ianuarii 1483.

: 3 :

Bartholomaeus Fontius Ioanni Acciaiolo Petri f. s. d.

1 Dum aliquid, ut par erat, ad te limatius politiusque scribere meditor maiusque temporis spatium commodiusque expecto, gravioribus semper curis oppressus diem die extrahens neque mihi satis neque etiam tibi feci tantopere litteras meas efflagitanti. Quanquam nunc etiam occupatior multo quam soleo, haec scripsi ne nihil scribendo putares, quod nunquam posset accidere, me immemorem tui esse.

2 Te vero etiam atque etiam rogo ut me, qui in his versor allatrantibus scopulis, crebro excites iocundissimis litteris tuis, quas ad me quotiens miseris magnis ac multis curiae huius molestiis me levaris. Demetrio nostro Chalcondylo me plurimum commendato im-

wonderful theatre at the heart of Christendom, where, great prizes being available for those with the patience and persistence, I shall do my best to face everything with fortitude and put up a fierce fight to gain some reward for my labors and struggles. And if that happens later than I could wish, or — God forbid — never, I shall be content for the rest of my life that I followed the counsel of my friends and tried every path, and that it was Fortune that thwarted my desires, not my spirit that failed. But one splendid thing I have 2
already achieved, being appointed before my time to a public professorship in this city that has nurtured such outstanding and wonderful men in every field of letters. I thought you would like to know this. Farewell.

Rome, December 31, 1483.

: 3 :

Bartolomeo Fonzio to Giovanni di Pietro Acciaiuoli, greetings.[3]

While I'm mulling over sending you (as I should) some more care- 1
ful and polished piece of writing, and waiting for a period of greater leisure, and since with my ever-increasing burden of cares I keep putting things off from day to day, I have given no satisfaction either to myself or to you, who demand letters from me with such insistence. Though I am now even busier than usual, I have written these lines so that you should not think that if I have not written, I have forgotten you — that could never happen.

But caught up as I am amid these stormy reefs, I do earnestly 2
ask you to give me the stimulus of your pleasant letters, and that often, for any letter from you lifts the load of the many great troubles here at court from me. Please give my respects to our friend Demetrius Chalcondyles, and tell him of the death of An-

maturumque ei obitum Andreae Brentii, discipuli quondam sui nunc vero etiam collegae familiarisque mei, peste perendie absumpti nuntiato. Vale.

Roma, Idibus Februarii 1483.

: 4 :

Bartholomaeus Fontius Laurentio Medici s.

1 Si post meam discessionem nihil adhuc litterarum ad te dedi, et vitae occupatio et curiae huius pontificiae stupor fuit in causa. Sed hodie mihi ocio ad scribendum concesso et animo iam tempus in reliquum confirmato, si paulo altius exorsus a te petam quod mihi omnium maximum est futurum, dabis longitudini meae veniam.

2 Ego vero cum eam vivendi rationem semper amassem, quae contemplationi rerum coniungeretur,[2] huc tamen ob eas causas, quae te minime latent, me contuli. Quod sane feci libenter sperans mihi fieri aditum ad maiorem sacerdotii dignitatem. At nunc ingeniis horum hominum diligenter inspectis consilium meum damnare cogor. Nam — per immortalem Deum et magistrum et Dominum nostrum Christum! — quae est tanta dicendi vis quae vitia
3 curiae huius narrare possit? Aperuit asylum ab initio urbem cum hanc condidit Romulus, sed illi ex deterrimis in clarissimos industria et labore et legum observantia evasere. Christus autem, qui pro nostra salute, humanitate assumpta, cruci affigi humiliter passus est, cum bonis omnibus et honeste viventibus aeternam beatitudinem et promiserit et tribuerit, hoc templum universae Christianitati aperuit, quod aliquandiu persancte cultum usque adeo

drea Brenta, his former pupil and lately also my colleague and friend, carried off by the plague the day before yesterday.[4] Farewell.

Rome, February 13, 1484.

: 4 :

Bartolomeo Fonzio to Lorenzo de' Medici, greetings.[5]

If I have not yet written you any letters since leaving, the reasons are the busyness of my life and the bewilderment I have felt here at the papal court. But today I've secured some free time for writing, and my mind being now made up as to the way ahead, I hope you will forgive my prolixity if I go back some little way to ask you for something that is of absolutely vital importance for my future. 1

While I had always had a hankering for a style of life that allowed for philosophical contemplation, I nevertheless made my way here for the reasons you well know. And indeed I did it of my free will, in the hope that a higher ecclesiastical position might open up for me. But after closely observing the temper of the men here, I am forced to condemn my decision. By God in heaven and our lord and master Jesus Christ, what powers of oratory would be equal to describing the vices of this court? When Romulus founded the city, he originally opened a refuge for criminals, but from having been the worst of scoundrels, they turned out to be the most notable in virtue of their industry and energy and observance of the law. Christ, on the other hand, who took on human form for our salvation and suffered himself to be nailed to the cross, when he promised and delivered eternal beatitude to all good men and those who led an upright life, opened up this temple to universal Christendom. But after a period in which it was 2

3

postea est pollutum ut omnium scelerum impunitas huc confluentibus concedatur.

4 Nollem tamen, ut libere tecum loquar, non huc venisse atque horum mitratorum capitum consuetudine caruisse. Nam si propterea Ulysses prudens est habitus, quod post sacram eversam Ilion multorum hominum urbes et mores novit, si paucioribus ego mensibus, quam ille annis, longe plura cognovero, non minus hanc arbitror profuturam peregrinationem mihi quam suam illi ad veram sapientiam assequendam. Etenim cum ex tota Christianitate homines huc vel spe vel metu impulsi confluant, non ego Ciconum Lestrigonumve tantum, sed longe plurimarum gentium mores perspexero. Ac si ille Circen, Syrenas, Scyllam Charybdimque non sine magno tandem evasit periculo Ithacamque in illam suam pervenit asperam, ita quoque ipse in his positus portentosis Christianae religionis verticibus, cunctis libidinum illecebris cupiditatumque omnium superatis, in florentissimam istam revertar patriam.

5 Neque vero, si Orpheo, Museo, Melampo, Homero, Soloni, Pythagorae ac Platoni multisque praeterea clarissimis et in omni litterarum genere doctissimis viris magnae laudi est attributum exterarum gentium disciplinas longissimis peregrinationibus didicisse, debebit uni mihi vitio tribui domo procul hos Christianae fidei principes adiisse totque urbium, nationum populorumque mitrata capita in hanc coacta curiam percepisse. Cuius tandem moribus diligenter inspectis omnibusque rationibus et consiliis meis in unum subductis hanc feci summam cogitationum mearum omnium.

6 Equidem si a bonis et sapientibus viris hanc regi Petri apostoli navim cernerem, in ea libentissime navigarem. Nam quid hones-

treated with the utmost veneration, it became so corrupted that freedom from punishment for any and every sin was granted to all who streamed here.

But to be frank with you, I do not regret having come here and 4
I should not want to have missed getting to know these men with miters on their heads. Ulysses is accounted wise for having acquainted himself with the cities and customs of a multitude of men after the fall of sacred Troy;[6] if I then have got to know far more in fewer months than he spent years, I suppose that this trip of mine will be no less profitable than his was for the getting of true wisdom. Since men come here in floods from all over Christendom, driven on by hope or fear, I shall get to examine the characters not just of the Cicones or Laestrygonians but of a far greater number of peoples. And if he managed at great risk finally to escape the clutches of Circe, the Sirens, Scylla and Charybdis and reach his home in rocky Ithaca, so too shall I from my place among these forbidding eminences of the Christian religion return home to my flourishing fatherland[7] after overcoming all the snares of lust and desires of every kind.

And if Orpheus, Musaeus, Melampus, Homer, Solon, Pythago- 5
ras, and Plato,[8] and many other famous men besides who were learned in every department of literature, gathered great praise for having learned the sciences of foreign nations in long sojourns abroad, I shall by no means be singled out for discredit if I have applied myself far from home to the cultivation of the princes of the Christian faith, and got to know the dignitaries of the many cities, nations, and peoples gathered into the Roman court. Having thoroughly acquainted myself with its character and drawn together all my reflections and considerations on the matter, I have at length made this summary of my conclusions.

Well, if I saw that this bark of St. Peter was being steered by 6
men who were good and wise, I should be perfectly happy to sail in her. What could be more honorable, more useful, more laudable

tius, quid utilius, quid laudabilius posset fieri quam tam sancto navigio inhaerendo ad optatum littus magnis cum viris appellere? Sed in ea cum videam agi miscerique omnia, non clavum dirigi, non vela attolli, non remigium disponi, huius autem vitae navigationem inter tot tempestatum procellas periculosam, hanc male rectam et fluctuantem naviculam cum primum facultas data erit egrediar. Nulla enim tanta spes praemiorum aut honorum his me
7 demerget insanientibus fluctibus. Sanctitate quondam vitae, morum integritate, doctrina, religione a maioribus nostris, optimis praestantissimisque hominibus, et constituta et adaucta est Christiana res publica. At nunc ruimus, Laurenti, ruimus: nulla viget amplius Christi fides, nullus amor, nulla pietas, nulla caritas; non virtuti, non probitati, non doctrinae locus est ullus. Nam quid ego latrocinia impunita, quid avaritiam et luxuriam honestatas, quid omnem gulam et libidinem toto ex orbe accersitas commemorem? Afficior, mehercules, tanto stupore haec intuens, ut hinc discedere, si mihi per te licuerit, cito cogitem, ne inficiar huius horrendae luis contagione. Licebit autem per te, ut spero, ea benignitas tua est liberalitasque naturae.

8 Verum enimvero neque apud te litteris impudens ero quicquam petendo neque etiam longior in meo desiderio exprimendo; Petrusphilippus Pandolphinus et Bernardus Oricellarius tecum de me agent. Oro te, quemadmodum semper antea consuesti, ita etiam nunc me ornes. Illa tua erit in posterum vera gloria, quae ob merita summa extabit in cives tuos. Equidem semper ut moribus primum, deinde ingenio a te probarer elaboravi. Spem fidemque meam omnem in te reposui. Huc etiam consulto prius honoratoque te contendi, rerum experientia nunc edoctus reverti duce te atque auspice domum opto. Quare te obsecro ne deteriore condi-
9 tione sit mihi reditus quam discessus. Cum nihil sit in te non

than to reach in such a holy vessel the longed-for land in the company of great men? But since I see everything in it is a confused muddle—the tiller is not held straight, the sails are not set, the oars are not properly arranged—and since I see this life's journey in peril amid so many violent storms, this little boat badly handled and buffeted about in the waves, I shall get out of it as soon as an opportunity offers itself: no hope of rewards or honors, however great, will drown me in these raging floods. Christendom was long 7
ago established and extended by our ancestors, those excellent and remarkable men, with their holy manner of life, soundness of morals, learning and religion. Now we are fallen, Lorenzo, fallen: faith in Christ flourishes no longer, nor love, piety, or charity; virtue, probity, and learning now have no place. Need I mention the robberies that go unpunished, the honor in which greed and extravagance are held, the gluttony and lust of every kind brought here from all over the world? Good heavens, contemplating this state of affairs, I feel such bewilderment that if by your leave it were granted to me, I should plan on leaving here at once rather than risk being infected by the contagion of this dreadful plague. But you, I hope, *will* give me leave, such is your kindliness and generosity of spirit.

But I shall not importune you with a tiresome begging letter, 8
nor shall I expound my desires at length: Pierfilippo Pandolfini and Bernardo Rucellai will put my case to you. I do ask you to show me favor once more, just as you always have in the past. Your true future glory will derive from your great services to your fellow citizens. And I for my part have always striven to win your approval, for my character in the first place, and then my talent. I have placed all my hopes and trust in you. I came here after first consulting you and paying you homage; now I have learned from experience and wish to return home under your guidance and aegis. And so I beg you not to let me return in worse condition than
I left. Though there is nothing about you that is not wholly admi- 9

valde probandum, nihil est tamen amandum magis quam innata quaedam liberalis animi tui bonitas, nihil certe laudandum magis quam ista tua in omnes beneficentia. In eo vero te statu Fortuna posuit, ut multum possis; voluntas autem et ratio ita instituit ut semper velis benefacere plurimis. Nulla sane re clarior fies atque aeternior quam beneficiis dandis, bonis praesertim viris et eruditis. Me quidem semper toto animo ad omnia promptissimum paratissimumque habebis; quicquid studio, industria, diligentia valebo, tibi tuisque liberis semper valebo.

Roma, IIII Non. Martias MCCCCLXXXIIII.

: 5 :

Bartholomaeus Fontius Bernardo Oricellario s.

1 Si te discedens alloqui potuissem, et libenter fecissem et necessario. Nam prudentia tua forsan in sententiam eorum non concessisses, qui amanter quidem sed parum feliciter ut huc venirem persuaserunt. Sed quoniam id neque locorum longissimo intervallo fieri coram neque temporis angustia per litteras a te consilium capi potuit, contigit ut omnino te inscio huc contenderim. Postquam vero e Mediolanensi legatione reversum te intellexi, nihil adhuc scripsi quod, cum essem animo parum firmo, pro certis incerta scribere non volebam, praeoptans accusari abs te tarditatis quam levitatis.

2 At nunc mihi cum discedendum statuerim, omnem tibi mentis atque animi cogitationem aperiendam putavi, ut tua me et auctori-

rable, your most lovable quality is a certain innate and generous goodness of spirit, and certainly there is nothing more praiseworthy than the kindness you show everyone. Fortune has placed you in a position of great power, yet your goodwill and intelligence has led you always to exercise your beneficence on great numbers of people. The one chief thing that will gain you lasting fame with posterity is conferring benefits, on good and learned men especially. For my part, you will always find me ready and willing to perform any service with all my heart. Whatever enthusiasm, industriousness and diligence I may have will always be at your disposal and that of your children.

Rome, March 4, 1484.

: 5 :

Bartolomeo Fonzio to Bernardo Rucellai, greetings.[9]

Had I been able to speak with you before I left, I should gladly have done so, and indeed ought to have done so. In your wisdom you would not perhaps have shared the view of those who, with the best of intentions, certainly, but in the outcome unhappily, persuaded me to come here. But since I could not get your advice in person, owing to the distance between us, or by letter, owing to lack of time, it turned out that I set off for Rome quite without your knowledge. And when I later heard that you had returned from your embassy to Milan,[10] I still did not write, since I was doubtful about what to do and didn't want to give you firm information when there was none, preferring to have you reproach me for sloth rather than fickleness. 1

But now that I have decided to leave, I have thought to lay before you all my thoughts on the matter, so that I may have the 2

tate iuves et gratia. Publicum legendi munus te adiutore cum sus-
cepissem, id mihi laboris plurimum allaturum putavi, ut opinioni
omnium, siqua forte de me esset, responderem; sed neminem aegre id unquam laturum existimavi. Verum in quo meo honestissimo Studio tranquille posse vivere arbitrabar, in eo sum tris an-
3 nos, ut scis, perpetuis molestiis agitatus. Quare dum tempori
aliquantulum cedere et nomini tamen ac quieti consulere meditor,
ecce ultro se, ut tunc putavi, propitia, sed, ut re postea intellexi,
pessima quidem Fortuna obtulit. Zenus enim Baptista cardinalis
invisens Clusentinia nostra Tempe me secum Romam promisso-
rum spe plenum duxit. Ego vero etsi satis in via sagaciter odorabar
qualis mea esset futura venatio et ex una etiam reliquas feras co-
niectabar, nolui tamen primae indagini statim credere, ne a quo-
quam pusilli animi iudicarer si ex ipso itinere, antequam in silvam
4 hanc descenderem, retro cederem. Veni itaque Romam futurorum
prudens ac sciens, tanquam Amphiaraus Thebas, sed non propterea statim reverti volui, ne illaudatus ingloriusque redirem. Qua-
propter magna contentione Idibus Novembribus a Sixto obtinui ut
publice legendi provincia mihi decerneretur. Hesterno quoque Ci-
nerum die, coram eodem Pontifice cardinalibusque omnibus, in
magna patrum frequentia orationem habui non iniocundam. Existimavi autem apud vos, gratissimos cives, meliore conditione me
futurum, si in hoc totius Christianitatis theatro amplissimo osten-
dissem florentissimam nostram urbem non solum opibus, pulchri-
tudine, viribus, sed litteris eloquentiaque excellere.

5 Accepisti qua de causa huc primum venerim, deinde quid
maxime hic quaesierim. Nunc quibus de causis discedendum sta-

support of your prestige and favor. When with your help I took up my public teaching position, I supposed I should be taking on a good deal of work to live up to the general expectations (if such there were) held of me, but I never envisaged anyone would take it amiss. Whereas I imagined I could lead a peaceful life in my well-regarded university, I have, as you know, been dogged by endless troubles there for three years now. And so while I was considering 3
accommodating myself in some measure to the times and taking thought for my reputation and ease, all of a sudden a stroke of good fortune, as I then thought, offered itself, though I later realized that in the event it was the worst of all misfortunes. Cardinal Battista Zeno, on coming to visit our Vale of Tempe in the Casentino, took me off to Rome with him, full of hopes and promises.[11] Though I could already sniff out pretty well on the journey what sort of hunting I was going to have, and had a good idea from one beast what the rest would be like, still I didn't want there and then to trust to my first experience of the hunt, in case people thought me weak-willed if I beat a retreat on the actual journey before I'd even entered the wood. And so I reached Rome, as Amphiaraus 4
reached Thebes,[12] perfectly well aware of what the future held, but unwilling to turn back at once on that account, so as not to return inglorious and unpraised. Against much competition I was therefore awarded a public teaching position by Pope Sixtus on November 13. And just yesterday, Ash Wednesday, I gave a well-received speech before a crowded congregation of clerics, in the presence of the pope and all the cardinals.[13] I thought I should anyway enjoy more favor and gratitude among you and your fellow citizens if I showed on this great stage of all Christendom how this most flourishing city of ours excels not just in wealth, beauty, and power, but in letters and eloquence too.

There you have the reasons for my first coming to Rome, and 5
what I was most set on finding here. Now hear briefly the reasons for my decision to leave. Though I hold nothing more precious

tuerim brevi intellige. Cum nihil apud me sit virtute doctrinaque amabilius, hic vero nullam aut bene vivendi aut recte sciendi rationem haberi videam, nullis adduci praemiis aut honoribus unquam possem, ut ad horum hominum numerum me adiungerem, qui in ovium vestimentis lupi rapaces sunt et sub Christi pastorum nomine ovilia sibi commissa perdunt. Avaritia et luxuries et libido eorum expleri nequit; ignorantia quidem et mentis caecitas tanta est ut litteratos homines pro insanis, bonos autem habeant pro iniquis. Non sacerdotia, non praefecturae, non honores, non dignitates virtuti meritisque praebentur, sed ad gratiam et libidinem
6 conferuntur. Haec ego quotidie oculis cernens et sacra omnia incestari contuens ac ne ad me quoque serpat contagio extimescens, ad vos evolare quamprimum cogito. Quid enim foret aliud horum hominum dignitates appetere quam subiicere me insanis vitiorum gurgitibus, quibus iugiter sursum deorsumque varie tandem agitatus obruerer? Non tamen me paenitet huc venisse. Nam ut semper est animus quarum rerum sit expers maxime cupidus, nunquam, hercule, quievissem nisi huius curiae mores ipsa experientia doctus essem.

7 Caeterum quibus de causis cogitem discedere cum cognoris, superest ut quid maxime velim tibi exponam. Dedi hodie quoque ad Laurentium Medicem litteras quibus scripsi me suppudere quicquam ab eo petere, sed Petrumphilippum Pandolphinum teque simul ei voluntatem esse meam explicaturos. Opto autem ea conditione, quam tibi Giraldus exponet, reverti domum. Novi ego vos magnos viros magnisque negociis impeditos ac propterea eum admonui ut singulos vos, quotiens erit opus, conveniat locumque ac tempus de me agendi communi vestrum voluntate constituat.
8 Pandolphinum tametsi nobis libenter fauturum confidimus, te quoque etiam tamen habere cupimus tuamque auctoritatem et gratiam, qua multum ad Laurentium potes, exposcimus. Quare te quaeso, per meum in te amorem, ut non modo fautorem pro mea

than virtue and learning, I could see that here no account was taken of either right living or true knowledge. No rewards or honors could ever induce me to join with these men here who dress in sheep's clothing and behave like ravening wolves: in the guise of shepherds of Christ they destroy the flocks committed to their care. Their greed and wantonness and lust can never be satisfied. Such is their ignorance and mental blindness that they take men of letters for madmen and good men for scoundrels. Priesthoods, governorships, honors, and dignities are not accorded to virtue
and merit but are instead conferred by favor or at whim. Seeing 6
these things every day, contemplating the defilement of all that is sacred, and fearing that the contagion might spread to me too, I reckon on fleeing to you as soon as may be. To seek the distinctions these men offer would amount to submerging myself in a crazy whirlpool of vice, in which I should be tossed up and down and eventually drown. Not that I regret coming here, for since the heart is always most set on what it has no experience of, I should never have been at rest had I not learned at first hand the ways of the court here.

But now that you know the reasons that I am minded to leave 7
here, it only remains to explain to you what it is that I particularly want. I've also sent a letter today to Lorenzo de' Medici, in which I said that though I was somewhat embarrassed to ask him for a favor, Pierfilippo Pandolfini and you would together put my request to him. I'd like in any case to come back home on the terms that Giraldo will tell you about.[14] I know you are important people and have important matters to deal with, so I have asked him to meet with you separately, as often as need be, and fix a time and
place for dealing with my case that suits you both. Though I'm 8
sure Pandolfini will be happy to support me, I'd still like to have you involved as well, and earnestly desire to have behind me your prestige and favor, which are so effective with Lorenzo. I therefore beg you, in the name of the love I bear you, not just to support my

te dignitate, sed etiam ducem praestes. Quam si per te, ut spero, retinuero, quanquam ad meum singularem in te amorem nihil addi videtur posse, tamen si pro te hanc lucem, qua nihil dulcius est, reliquero, meo erga te incredibili desiderio non satisfecero.

Roma, IIII Nonas Martias 1484.

: 6 :

Bartholomaeus Fontius Ugolino Verino s.

1 Quibus mihi rationibus tarditatem scribendi tuam excusavisti, me quoque eaedem tibi purgabunt atque eo fortassis aequius, quo molestioribus curis cogitationibusque praepedior. Vivo enim in hoc inflatissimo Euripo totius Christianitatis ac sursum deorsumque ita quotidie agitor ut nedum scribendi, sed ne quidem quid scribam cogitandi liberum spatium concedatur. Itaque mecum interdum imbecillitatem humanam reputans non conniveo his insanis fulgoribus, quos fere omnes admirantur et cupiunt. Una enim est virtus quae et facere nos et servare beatos potest, quam si scientia multarum magnarumque rerum exornemus, tum vero etiam aeterni et clari sumus.

2 Non pandam igitur, ut mones, aspiranti Fortunae sinus, ne demergar illius procellosis verticibus; tu vero, quod facis, te ipsum ne increpes neve tuam cunctationem redarguas, sed laeteris quod vivis in patria et gaudeas quod industriae tuae invideatur. Non enim surgentis fama *Carliados* ullum tibi honorem abstulit, sed veram laudem attribuit. An tu, poeta clarissime, dignitatem esse putas id assequi quod est commune cum multis imperitis improbisque hominibus? Quod vero proprium est tuique caelestis ingenii non

claim for office but to take the lead in securing it. And if, as I hope, I keep it thanks to you, though it seems could nothing could increase the love I bear you, yet if I were to lay down my life for you, than which nothing is more precious, I would still not match the extraordinary feelings I have for you.

Rome, March 4, 1484.

: 6 :

Bartolomeo Fonzio to Ugolino Verino, greetings.[15]

1 The same reasons you offer to excuse your delay in writing must excuse me too, and perhaps more reasonably in that I am weighed down by a greater burden of worry and trouble. I live amid the seething tide[16] of all Christendom and every day I am tossed hither and yon, so that I have not a moment to myself for thinking what to write, let alone writing it. And so when from time to time I ponder the weakness of humankind, I cannot turn a blind eye to those mindless glories that practically everyone admires and hungers after. Virtue alone it is that can make us happy and keep us so, and if we can ornament it with wide-ranging and significant knowledge, then indeed we attain immortality and fame.

2 So I shall not spread my sails before Fortune's fair wind, as you advise, in case I sink in her stormy whirlpools. For your part, you should cease to criticize yourself or blame your hesitancy. You should instead rejoice to be living in your homeland and take pleasure in the envy that your industry provokes: the fame of the burgeoning *Carlias* has brought you no dishonor; rather it has won you genuine praise. Do you, a celebrated poet, think it a distinction to attain what many ignorant and bad men have likewise attained? But what really comes from you and your immortal genius,

gloriam existimas singularem? An putas fore ullam tam ingratam
ac tam rudem posteritatem quae non te honoratissimum semper
3 habeat? Vellem affuisse tuis Pannoniis epigrammatis non, ut cu-
piebas, adiutor, sed potius inspector atque laudator. Nam quae ad
me Sixto tradenda misisti, ei sunt fideliter reddita, quanquam nihil est quod hinc speres: nam qui non meritis poema dictat consu-
mit studio dies inani. Tu tamen perge aliquid quotidie scribere
dignum te, dignum immortalitate. Is enim divinus et rectus et sa-
nus furor laudabitur semper ab omnibus, quo te suavissime ur-
gente atque impellente non harenas istic fodis, sed sacros Musarum latices hauris eosque amenissimos campos colis, unde fructus
4 uberrimi colligantur. Neque vero te paucorum ingratitudo com-
moveat, ut alienas et barbaras sedes incolas: nulla enim regia sunt
praemia amicis et liberis et patriae conferenda. Quod ego antea
cum multa lectione percepissem, nunc ita experior in me ipso,
nulla ut re tam angar, quam quod absim a vobis patria procul.

5 Caeterum elegiam tuam concitatius ad me scriptam et libenter pellegi et diligenter, qua nihil tersius elegantiusve hac aetate hominum est perscriptum. Eam, ut iubes, ostendam nemini, non quia nocituram tibi, si edatur, existimem, sed ut obsequar voluntati tuae. Vale.

Roma, VI Id. Martii 1484.

do you not think *that* the special glory? Do you think any posterity will arise so ungrateful and uncouth that it will fail to hold you ever in the highest esteem? I should like to have been associated 3
with your Hungarian epigrams, not (as you wanted) as a helper but as an onlooker and admirer. The ones you sent me to give to Sixtus IV have been duly passed on, though there is nothing to be hoped for from that quarter: anyone who writes poetry for those who don't deserve it is spending his days in pointless labor. But you must carry on every day writing something worthy of yourself, and worthy of immortality. For that divine (and noble and *sane*) frenzy will always find universal praise: under its sweetest suasion and solicitation, you won't be digging sterile sand but drinking the sacred liquor of the Muses and cultivating those charming fields from which fruit is gathered in abundance. And do not let the 4
ungratefulness of the few drive you to live in foreign and barbarous lands: no rewards a king may give can compare to your friends, your children, your homeland. This is something I had discovered after much reading, but am now experiencing for myself: nothing troubles me so much as the fact that I am absent from you and far from home.

As for the ardent elegy you wrote for me, I have read it through 5
with pleasure and attentiveness: this age has written nothing with such polish and elegance. As you ask, I'll show it to no one, not that I think it would damage you if it were published, but simply to abide by your wishes. Farewell.

Rome, March 10, 1484.

: 7 :

Bartholomaeus Fontius Francisco Saxetto s.

1 Petiisti a me, Saxette carissime, cadaver ut illud femineum, in Appia via nuper inventum, cuiusmodi esset tibi significarem. Qua sane in re non solum probo, sed etiam laudo vehementer studium tuum in tantis occupationibus antiquitatis noscendae percupidum. Sed vellem aequare posse scribendo cadaveris huius formam et venustatem, quae incredibilis videretur fideque ad posteros careret nisi totam Urbem testem haberet.

2 Nam, ut rem totam ordine tibi aperiam, operarii quidam, fundamenta sepulchrorum ad inquirenda marmora ad sextum ab Urbe lapidem in via Appia eruentes, munitum undique lateritium arcum humi decem depressum pedes cum evertissent, marmoream capsam adinvenere. Qua aperta cadaver in faciem cubans, odoro oblitum cortice, repertum est, digitorum duorum ad crassitudinem; capsa quoque omnis interior eisdem erat odoribus tanquam tecto-
3 rio quodam circumlita. Eo suave fragranti amoto cortice, facies, ut a capite ordiar, erat subpallida ac si eodem puella die sepulta esset. Capilli et longi et nigri cuti tenaciter adhaerentes, in nodum torti comamque in geminam puellari more distincti, reticulo erant serico intertexto auro obvoluti. Aures exiguae, frons brevis, supercilia nigra, decentes oculi albidique intus apparebant. Nasus quidem integer atque adeo mollis ut digito pressus flecteretur et cederet. Labra erant in rubro pallentia, dentes nivei et exigui, lingua tota a palato coccinea. Genas, mentum, collum, iugulum spirantis credas.
4 Brachia integra, humeris pendentia, quacunque duceres sequebantur. Manus in longitudinem patentes digitique teretes et oblongi

: 7 :

Bartolomeo Fonzio to Francesco Sassetti, greetings.[17]

You've asked me, dear Sassetti, to give you some details about that female corpse recently found on the Appian Way.[18] In this connection I admire and heartily praise your great eagerness to learn about antiquity amid your many occupations. I only wish I could do justice in words to the beauty and attractiveness of the cadaver, which would seem amazing to posterity and quite incredible were it not that it was witnessed by the entire city. 1

To explain the whole matter in order: some workmen were dig- 2
ging out the foundations of tombs in search of marble on the Via Appia six miles out of Rome. They had destroyed an arch faced with brick on all sides some ten feet down when they came across a marble box. Opening it up, they found a corpse lying on its face, covered by a layer of fragrant bark two inches thick; all of the inside of the casket was likewise smeared with the same fragrant
mixture like some sort of plaster. When this sweet-smelling bark 3
was removed, the girl's face (to begin at the top) was rather pale and as if she had been buried that very day. Her hair, long and dark and firmly fixed to the scalp, was gathered in a knot and divided into twin tresses in girlish manner, all covered by a hairnet of silk interwoven with gold. Then there appeared small ears, a short forehead, dark eyebrows, the eyes beneath shapely and bright. The nose was still intact, and so soft that if it was pressed by a finger it would flex and yield. The lips were a pale red, the teeth snow-white and small, the tongue from the roof of the mouth all scarlet. The cheeks, chin, neck, and throat—you'd think
they belonged to a living person. The arms hung down from the 4
shoulders entire, and would follow wherever you led them. The hands were stretched out, the fingers rounded and tapering with

cum translucidis unguibus atque adeo haerentes et firmi, ut velli ab internodiis nequirent. Pectus autem et stomachus venterque se in latitudinem coaequabant et odoro amoto cortice candicabant. Cervix quidem et renes sedesque statum suum et gratiam obtinebant. Coxarum quoque ac feminum crurumque ac pedum decus viventis faciem praeferebat.

5 Ad summam et formosissima simul et generosissima haec puella florente adhuc Roma urbe apparet. Sed cum insigne monumentum, quod supra terram extabat, multis ante nos saeculis eversum fuerit, nullo titulo apparente et nomen et genus et aetas latet huius tam insignis et admirandi cadaveris. Quod XVIII Cal. Maii, anno a nativitate Christi quinto et octogesimo supra mille quadringentos, Innocentii vero octavi anno pontificatus primo, repertum biduo post delatum est in Capitolium, maximo populi concursu, iussu Conservatorum Urbis. Vale.

Roma, XV Cal. Maii 1485.

: 8 :

Bartholomaeus Fontius Petrophilippo Pandolphino s.

1 Cum nulla sit ea melior institutio, qua ad rationem vitae et sapientiam erudimur, nihil a me putavi praestari posse Francisco filio tuo
utilius, quam si ea praecepta tradidissem, quae cum ad eius tum
vero ad caeterorum incolumitatem pertineant. Est enim operae
pretium a teneris eum annis imbibere salutaria laudabiliaque ad-
monita quibus et ipse in posterum beatus vivat et haec insignis
patria maxime floreat. Nam qualiscunque fuerit educatio puerilis,
2 talis aetas reliqua subsequetur. Te vero minime praeterit non modo
hanc nostram, sed quascunque alias civitates semper tales fuisse
quales earum gubernatores extiterint. Ex quo tibi vehementer ela-

translucent nails, and so firmly fixed that they could not be torn from the joints. Her breast, stomach, and belly were equally broad, and appeared white when the fragrant bark was taken away. The nape of her neck, her back and buttocks retained their position and shape and graceful appearance. The beauty of her hips, thighs, shins, and feet likewise gave the impression of a living person.

In short, this girl who had lived when Rome was in its prime 5
seemed as shapely as she was noble. But since the fine monument which stood on the surface had been destroyed many centuries before our time, without any visible inscription the name, family and age of this remarkable and wonderful corpse remain unknown. Two days after it was found, by order of the Conservators it was taken to the Capitol amid vast throngs of people on April 14 in the year of our Lord 1485, the first of the reign of Pope Innocent VIII. Farewell.

Rome, April 17, 1485.

: 8 :

Bartolomeo Fonzio to Pierfilippo Pandolfini, greetings.[19]

Since there is no sort of education better than one that instructs 1
us in practical wisdom and how to live, I thought I could give your son Francesco nothing more useful than to hand on those precepts which conduce to his well-being, as to that of everyone else. It is worth his while to imbibe from earliest years those salutary and laudable lessons that will enable him to lead a good life in future and his famous homeland to flourish as much as may be: whatever education one has had in boyhood sets the style for the rest of
one's life. I'm sure you are aware that not just our own city but all 2
others too have always had the same character as their governors.

borandum est ut non ipse tu modo, quod perfecisti, sed etiam tui liberi, quod maxime curas, ita consuescant et vivant ut populo de se specimen aequitatis et modestiae praebeant. Nam cum vulgus primorum sequatur vitam, hi vel probi malos corrigere vel improbi bonos civitatis mores possunt corrumpere.

3 Ego quidem, ut filio tuo valde consulerem, ei dicavi Phocylidem, aequissimum et continentissimum hominem, ut eius admonitionibus perfecte vivere consuescat; quem si colet et diliget, vir iustus fiet et temperans et clarissimus civis sapientissimusque evadet. Vale.

Florentia, pr. Id. Augusti 1485.

: 9 :

Bartholomaeus Fontius Petro Delphino generali Camaldulensi s.

1 Summa tua in me humanitas et mea erga te observantia adhortantur id a te per litteras petere, quod rebus est meis percommodum et tuis quoque non alienum. Popilianae ecclesiae ad undecimum a Florentia lapidem rectore aliquo indigemus cum ad sacrorum curam, tum etiam vectigalium. Qui id valeat aut diligentius agere aut fidelius domno Mauro non habemus. In tua ista benignissima manu locatum est et plurimum prodesse nobis et dignitati tuae, cuius cupidissimi sumus, non obesse: sacerdotio enim huic honeste legitimeque incumbet; Clusentinio agro erit vicinior; poteris

From which it follows that you must not only make every effort to accustom yourself to living a life that offers the populace a model of fairness and modesty, as you have done, but that your children, your greatest concern, do too. For since the common people follow the manner of life of their leaders, the latter, if they are good, may reform the bad morals of the citizenry, or corrupt its good morals if they are bad.

I for my part, to be of service to your son as best I may, have 3
dedicated Phocylides to him, a man of the utmost fairness and self-control, so that by following his advice he may come to live the perfect life.[20] If he cultivates and learns to love him, he will become a just and moderate man, and turn out to be a distinguished and wise citizen. Farewell.

Florence, August 12, 1485.

: 9 :

Bartolomeo Fonzio to Pietro Dolfin, General of the Camaldulensians, greetings.[21]

Your great kindness toward me and my reverence of your person 1
encourage me to ask something of you by letter that is greatly in my interest, and not adverse to yours. At the church of Popigliano, eleven miles out of Florence, we have need of a rector to take charge both of divine worship and of the parish income. We have no one who could do this more carefully or faithfully than Don Mauro.[22] It is in your generous hands to help us greatly in this way, nor will it be detrimental to your dignity, of which we are the keenest supporters. He will perform the office of this priestship with honesty and dutifulness; he will be closer to the Casentino region, and you will be able to avail yourself of his labor and

opera et industria eius cum voles uti, ipse siquidem promptus paratusque est per omnem vitam et consiliis nostris obsequi et parere mandatis tuis (nam sic recepit mihi ac multis amicis communibus). Eius autem eum constantiae puto fore ut nunquam propositi huius paeniteat.

2 Quare te oramus, per Dominum nostrum Christum, qui nunquam paenitentes neglexit, nunquam petentes reiecit, nunquam pulsantibus non aperuit, ut supplicantibus nobis eum concedas. Quod si, ut speramus atque optamus, praestiteris, et maximo commodo nos affeceris et tibi nos universos in aeternum devinxeris. Vale.

Florentia, pridie Nonas Septembris 1485.

: 10 :

Bartholomaeus Fontius Senatui Ragusiensi s.

1 A vestris honestissimis civibus qui Florentiae negociantur vestro sum nomine vestrisque litteris adhortatus accedere ad iuventutem Ragusiensem erudiendam humanitatisque artibus informandam. Qua sane re potuit animo meo contingere nihil suavius: a tali enim Senatu in istam urbem aequitate, prudentia, opibus, libertate in primis insignem ultro vocari cui non debeat esse quam optatissimum? Verum quanquam pergrata est mihi vestra de me voluntas atque iudicium, oblatam tamen a vobis conditionem suscipere non permittit cognatorum pietas de me pendentium et amicorum ratio a tam longa discessione me dehortantium.

2 Vobis autem, praeclarissimi patres, quod me tali magisterio dignum iudicaveritis, immortalis gratias ago et habebo dum vixero vosque oro ut in me, vestrae rei publicae amantissimum, qua cae-

industriousness whenever you like, since he is ready and willing to follow our advice and obey your bidding all his life (as he undertakes to me and many of the friends we have in common). I think he will prove sufficiently steadfast never to regret this move.

We therefore beseech you in the name of our Lord Jesus Christ, who never ignored the penitent, never rejected supplicants, never failed to open the door to those who knocked, that you give us Mauro at our request. And if, as we hope and desire, you do grant it, you will settle a great benefit on us as well as securing the eternal devotion of all of us. Farewell. 2

Florence, September 4, 1485.

: 10 :

Bartolomeo Fonzio to the Senate of Ragusa, greetings.[23]

I am invited by your honorable citizens who do business in Florence, in your name and with a letter from you, to come to Ragusa to teach your youth and instruct them in the humanities. Nothing could have given me greater pleasure: to be summoned without solicitation by such a government to that city of yours, so specially distinguished for its justness, wisdom, wealth, and liberty—who would not find it utterly desirable? But however flattering I find your opinion of me and your intentions toward me, the duty I owe the relations that depend on me, and the consideration of friends who dissuade me from removing myself so far away forbid me to take up the offer you have made. 1

But I give you infinite thanks, noble senators, for having judged me worthy of such a teaching position, and shall as long as I live. As a sincere friend of your republic, I beg that you continue to 2

pistis benivolentia prosequentes, me licet absentem non minus omnium vestrum fore, quam si vobiscum viverem, existimetis.

Florentia, VI Cal. Octobris 1487.

: II :

Bartholomaeus Fontius Mathiae Corvino regi Pannonio[3] *s.*

1 Erat, Mathia Corvine rex invictissime, nostra constans in urbe fama quemadmodum felicitate ac virtute validas bello nationes domueras et quacunque victricia signa converteras perinde ut alter Mars ingentes hostium strages semper edideras. Sed nondum, quae potiora sunt armis, cognoveramus ut fortitudini animi et scientiae militari studium quoque vehemens adiunxeris omnium artium optimarum. Verum ex quo Tadeus Ugholettus[4] hanc in urbem concessit ad tuam bibliothecam perficiendam, tum vero mirificus ardor Musarum et divina mens tua ista cunctis innotuit.

2 Quotiens enim Florentina civitas eum de tua benignitate in homines studiosos deque rectissimarum artium reparandarum immortali voluntate loquentem audivit, totiens est erga Maiestatem tuam incredibili amore inflamata et magnitudinem animi admirata, qui, in tantis maximarum rerum agendarum molibus, et antiquorum scriptorum monumenta non sinas interire vetustate et novorum ingenia excites magnis propositis praemiis et honoribus. Quod si superiores fecissent reges, non tam multi scriptores nobiles deperissent neque tamdiu in tantis tenebris humanissima studia iacuissent.

regard me with the benevolence you have so far shown and that though absent, you think of me as being as much among you as if I were living with you.

Florence, September 26, 1487.

: II :

Bartolomeo Fonzio to Matthias Corvinus, King of Hungary, greetings.

Matthias Corvinus, invincible king: there has been in our city 1
constant report of how by your fortune and valor you had vanquished nations mighty in war and how, wherever you turned your conquering standards, you had always, like a second Mars, wrought vast slaughter on the enemy. But we had not yet learned of something better than arms: that to bravery of spirit and grasp of warfare you had joined ardent study of all the finest arts. But as soon as Taddeo Ugoletti came to this city to arrange for the completion of your library, your amazing passion for the Muses and that godlike mind of yours became known to all.[24]

Whenever the citizens of Florence heard him speaking of your 2
encouragement of scholars and of your undying wish to restore the noblest arts, they were inflamed with extraordinary love of Your Majesty and admiration of your magnanimity, in that amid such burdens of the highest office, you not only decline to allow the monuments of the ancient writers to wither and die, but also stir the intellects of the writers of today with the prospect of great rewards and honors. And if earlier kings had done the same, fewer of the great writers would have perished, nor would humane studies have lain hidden in deepest dark for so long.

3 Tu unus, serenissime rex, his turbidis temporibus affulxisti Maiestatisque tuae splendorem ad illustrandas artis honestissimas convertisti. Qua quidem ex re et in praesens afficeris per omnem orbem sempiternis honoribus et ad omnem posteritatem aeterniorem laudem consequeris quam aut Athenis Pisistratus aut Alexandriae Ptolemaeus aut Eumenes Pergami aut olim Romae Caesar, nuper vero Nicolaus quintus Pontifex bibliothecis insignibus pu-
4 blicandis. Illi enim praestantissimi principes iis civitatibus imperaverunt, quae liberalissimis disciplinis maxime tunc florerent, iisque viguere temporibus quibus de nominis claritate inter se urbium moderatores ingenti aemulatione contenderent. Tu vero et primus et solus istud amplissimum regnum, quod rerum a te sapienter feliciterque gestarum magnitudine decorasti, nunc quoque litteris et scientiis excolis et amabilius reddis mansuetissimis Musis, quae pridem ex tota Graecia eiectae, modo etiam a nostris principibus destitutae, a Gallis vero Germanisque neglectae ad te confugiunt teque unicum suum decus et certum praesidium venerantur. Unde tua quidem perpetua et singularis gloria fuerit sustulisse cunctis studiosis hominibus in regia tua signum, quo ex omnibus gentibus, urbibus, nationibus, populis ad te Regem liberalissimum viri litterati conveniant.

5 Ego certe[5] tanta nominis tui fama compulsus tantaque tua benignitate in studiosos commotus incredibiliter ardeo pro mea virili conferre aliquid rectissimo tuo laudatissimoque consilio bibliothecae et Studii publicandi. Itaque nunc, quod potui pro angustia temporis, hoc tenue *De locis Persianis* opusculum ad te misi, quod non longo post tempore maiora nostra volumina subsequentur ac tua celsitudine digniora. Vale.

Florentia, III Cal. Februarii 1488.[6]

You alone, most serene king, have shone forth in these turbulent times and have turned the splendor of Your Majesty to adding luster to the noble arts. This, certainly, is something for which you even now garner eternal praise throughout the world, and for which in the eyes of posterity you will attain more enduring fame than Pisistratus did at Athens, Ptolemy at Alexandria, Eumenes at Pergamum, Caesar in the Rome of those days or Pope Nicholas V more recently, in founding their famous public libraries. Those outstanding princes ruled cities that were then the most flourishing in the liberal arts, and they lived in times when rulers of cities were hugely competitive in vying among themselves for renown. You, on the other hand, first and alone now ennoble your extensive kingdom, already adorned by the greatness of your wise and prosperous undertakings, with the arts and sciences too, and make it more welcome to the gentle Muses — the Muses long since cast out of Greece, now abandoned by our own princes too, neglected by the French and Germans, who now seek refuge in you and revere you as their sole glory and most certain defense. Hence it will be your undying and peculiar glory to have raised the standard at your court for all learned men, whither men of letters from every race, city, nation and people will gather themselves to you as their most liberal king. 3 4

Driven by the great fame of your person and moved by your great kindness toward men of learning, I for my part burn with incredible desire to contribute something, such as I may, to your splendid and laudable plan of opening to the public a library and a university. And so for want of time I now send what I can, this slight work *On Passages of Persius,* on which will follow before too long some of my more substantial writings, and ones worthier of your highness.[25] Farewell. 5

Florence, January 30, 1489.

: 12 :

Bartholomaeus Fontius Mathiae Corvino regi s.

1 Ni veritus essem ne meum officium ostentando memet ipsum putarer extollere, scripsissem pluribus quae per omnia loca istinc revertens de Maiestate tua veris et sempiternis laudibus enarrarim quantoque studio et ardore apud omnis magnitudinem animi, aequitatem, prudentiam, liberalitatem extulerim cunctis libenter audientibus et collaudantibus. Unum tamen praetereundum non putavi, Florentinos meos in primis esse totis animis erga serenitatem tuam conversos tibique summam optare felicitatem neque officiis neque studiis erga te ullis Italiae potentatibus cedere.

2 Studiosi quidem et boni viri et artium rectissimarum percupidi bibliothecae istius fama ad tuum nomen celebrandum una mecum scriptis perpetuis convertuntur. Quae adeo quosdam excitavit insignes viros, ut apud nos etiam Laurentius Medices nobilem Graecam ac Latinam paret bibliothecam. Ego tamen affirmare locis omnibus non desisto Maiestatem tuam, quemadmodum vel pace vel bello rerum fortiter ac sapienter gestarum magnitudine caeteros antecellat, ita etiam in hac bibliotheca superaturam. Quo autem ea possit celerius perfici atque facilius, misi ad Ioannem Morenum scriptorum omnium indicem cum gentilium tum sacrorum eique quid mihi videatur agendum a Maiestate tua significavi, cui me vehementissime commendo.

Florentiae, XVI Cal. Octobris 1489.

: 12 :

Bartolomeo Fonzio to King Matthias Corvinus, greetings.

If I were not afraid of being thought to be celebrating myself in showing my devotion to you, I should have written at greater length of what I said with sincere and perpetual praise on the subject of Your Majesty at all points on my journey back from you, and of the energy and ardor with which I extolled before everyone your magnanimity, fairness, wisdom, and liberality, all listening eagerly and joining in the praise. But one thing I thought I could not pass over, the fact that my fellow Florentines are specially devoted to your highness with all their hearts and wish you every success, nor do they yield to any power in Italy in their respect and deference toward you. 1

Scholars, indeed, upright men, and those with a passion for the noblest arts, through the renown of your library join with me in turning to celebrate your name in deathless writings. It has so enthused some notable men that here in Florence Lorenzo de' Medici is also getting ready a fine Greek and Latin library. But I never cease to state on all occasions that, just as Your Majesty surpasses all others for grandeur of achievements accomplished with courage and wisdom in peace and war, so with this library you shall likewise prevail. And to accomplish this the more quickly and easily, I have sent János Móré[26] a list of all writers sacred and profane, and have indicated to him what I think should be done by Your Majesty, to whom I most heartily commend myself. 2

Florence, September 16, 1489.

: 13 :

Bartholomaeus Fontius Ioanni Moreno s.

1 Postquam istinc discessi, nihil adhuc ad te scripsi quod ex itinere quem Budam mittere non habebam et corpore nondum valido ingenioque eram ad scribendum languidior. Ex quo autem veni Florentiam, ea statim sum executus quae, pridie quam discederem, a Mathia Corvino rege te praesente mihi mandata sunt. Verum quoniam eo animo est Rex ut quemadmodum caeteris in rebus omnibus ita quoque in hac bibliotheca alios principes antecellat, misi ad te cum his litteris librum cum veterum tum novorum auctorum omnium, et gentilium et Christianorum, in omni genere doctrinarum, a me non sine multo labore et diligentia collectorum, ut videre possitis ea quo sit ordine vobis instituenda. Vos autem recte feceritis si librorum, qui Viennae describuntur, indicem ad nos miseritis, ne hic iterum transcribantur.

2 De Italicis rebus nihil est novi: nam ubique in pace et ocio vivitur neque, ut nunc se habent res, aliquod bellum cernitur. Exinanitis enim urbibus diuturnis stipendiis neque a Venetis neque ab aliis ullis Italiae potentatibus quicquam movetur. De Mathia vero Corvino nostro expectatio magna est et quam pacem cum Imperatore sanciverit et quid praeterea gesturus sit. Sunt qui pro Dalmatia recuperanda depugnaturum, sunt qui gloriosius contra Turchos iturum putent; non desunt etiam qui fore ociosum existiment non prospera valitudine atque annis ad tranquillitatem vergentibus.

3 Quod ad me attinet, tua in me humanitas et egregia liberalitas quanquam cogunt quotidie meditari quibus officiis tibi facere satis possim, nondum tamen facultas concessa est amoris tibi mei sig-

: 13 :

Bartolomeo Fonzio to János Móré, greetings.[27]

Since leaving your country, I have so far written you nothing because on the journey I had no one I could send to Buda and I was too feeble to write while my mind and body had not yet recovered. As soon as I reached Florence, however, I at once carried out the instructions given me by King Matthias in your presence the day before I left. But since the king is minded to surpass other princes in this matter of the library, just as he does in everything else, I've sent you with this letter a book listing all authors, ancient and modern, pagan and Christian, in every field of learning, which I have compiled with considerable labor and care, so that you can see how the library should be arranged. You for your part will oblige me if you can send me the list of the books that are being copied at Vienna, so that they are not transcribed a second time here. 1

There is no news to pass on regarding the situation in Italy: life goes on in peace and quiet everywhere, and as things stand, there's no hint of war. The cities have been cleaned out by years of payments to mercenaries, and there's no move on the part of the Venetians or any other of the Italian powers. There is considerable interest in what our Matthias Corvinus will do, what sort of peace he will strike with the emperor, and what he'll do then. Some think he will fight to recover Dalmatia, others that he will make a more glorious expedition against the Turks; some even think he will remain at leisure, since his health is not good and his years suggest a tranquil life. 2

As for me, though your kindness and extraordinary generosity toward me compel me to wonder every day what services I could perform to pay you back, I have not yet been given the chance to 3

nificandi. Sed, mihi credas, remunerabor te brevi aliquo insigni diuturnoque munere. Nunc enim ingenium tibi non possum praestare meum, dum conor pro viribus Mathiam regem et illustrare insignius et exornare magnificentius; cui me etiam atque etiam commendabis Balaschumque praefectum curiae et Morepetrum et caeteros convictores nostros consalutabis. Vale.

Florentiae, XVI Cal. Octobris 1489.

: 14 :

Bartholomaeus Fontius Roberto Salviato s.

1 Siquid unquam summa cum voluptate, Roberte, legi, Picum tuum proxima nocte legi duabus de causis: et quod a te viro amicissimo missus erat et quod auctorem operis per se amabam, quem adhuc non legisse turpe mihi putabam fore. In quo ambigo[7] magis ne mirer plurimarum maximarumque rerum complexionem, an in tanta varietate tam incredibilem ordinem, an in tam laboriosis descriptionibus elegantiam tantam orationis. Nam quid in *Heptaplo* commemorem, quae maxime operum auctores commendant, nullam esse loquacitatem, nullum tumorem et sine ulla livoris suspi-
2 tione modestiam in omnibus singularem? Utinam vero huic tuo suavissimo muneri consimile donum mittere potuissem, quo cerneres animum in te meum significantius. At, quod potui, Budae orationem a me habitam ad te misi,[8] quam tu ipse cum legeris Pico quoque nostro legendam dabis; quem omnium aetatis nostrae, quorum scripta adhuc viderim, in eo doctrinarum genere praestantissimum iudico. Vale.

VIII Cal. Decembris MCCCCLXXXIX.[9]

demonstrate my love for you. But, believe me, I shall repay you before long with some splendid and enduring gift. For the moment I cannot devote my talent to you while I am trying as best I can to render King Matthias even more illustrious and deck him out with even greater splendor. Please commend me heartily to him, and pass on my greetings to Balázs, the judge at court, to Móré Péter and the rest of the friends we share. Farewell.

Florence, September 16, 1489.

: 14 :

Bartolomeo Fonzio to Roberto Salviati, greetings.[28]

If ever I have read anything with the utmost pleasure, Roberto, it 1
was your Pico last night, and for two reasons: first, because it was sent by you, my great friend, and second, because I loved the author of the work on his own account, someone I'm ashamed not to have read before. In reading him, I don't know whether I admire more his grasp of so many deep matters, the extraordinary clarity of argument amid all this complexity, or the great elegance of the writing on such difficult subjects. I need scarcely mention the points that specially commend authors to us, the absence of verbosity in the *Heptaplus,* the absence of pomposity, the singular
modesty toward everyone, no shade of envy. I wish I could have 2
sent you a present to match your delightful gift so you might see my feelings for you more clearly. But I send you what I can, the speech I made at Buda, which please give to our friend Pico to read when you have finished it—him I judge to be in this sort of learning the finest of all our contemporaries whose writings I have yet seen. Farewell.

November 24, 1489.

: 15 :

Bartholomaeus Fontius Guglielmo Roccifortae Galliarum cancellario s.

1 Cosmus Saxettus cum propter amicitiam quae mihi summa cum Francisco parente fuit, tum propter suavissimos eius mores et praecipuam quandam humanitatem est animo meo perquam carissimus. Is per litteras mihi significavit antiquitatis noscendae te cupidum valde optare quae olim veterum monumenta collegerim. Quare cum me totum ad te amandum iampridem fama tui nominis excitaris, hanc meae erga te optimae voluntatis declarandae idoneam nactus occasionem, eum ad te librum transmisi ut huic
2 tuo honestissimo desiderio inservirem. Nam cum tantum studiosos et doctos ames, quantum quotidie a multis intelligo, incredibiliter cupio tibi, Galliarum primario et litteratorum patrono, gratificari; cui rem cum pergratam effecero, non ipse tibi officium praestitisse, sed a te accepisse mihi videbor. Vale.

Florentiae, IIII Cal. Decembris 1489.

: 16 :

Bartholomaeus Fontius Federigo Saxetto s.

1 Ex quo non vulgari amore facti amici sumus, sed liberalis disciplinae communione, qua in una plus est fidei quam in ullo alio necessitudinis vinculo, ea te absentem hortari cogor, quae totius vitae tuae conferant dignitati. Cum nihil virtute sit amabilius aut prae-

: 15 :

Bartolomeo Fonzio to Guillaume de Rochefort, Chancellor of France, greetings.[29]

Cosimo Sassetti is very dear to me, thanks not only to the close 1
relations I enjoy with his father Francesco but also to his pleasant character and a very obliging disposition. He has told me by letter that you are a keen student of antiquity and are very eager to have the ancient monuments which I once assembled. Since the renown of your name has long stirred in me utter devotion to your person, I therefore seize this opportune moment to show my great goodwill toward you and have sent you the book so as to oblige your
noble yearning. Since you love students and scholars so much, as I 2
hear every day from many quarters, I have an overwhelming desire to gratify you, the leading light of France and patron of men of letters; and in giving you this pleasure, I shall not think I have done you a service so much as received one from you. Farewell.

Florence, November 28, 1489.

: 16 :

Bartolomeo Fonzio to Federico Sassetti, greetings.[30]

Since we have become friends—and with no ordinary friendship 1
but one based on a shared interest in the humanities, in which alone one may place more trust than in any other bond of intimacy—I feel constrained, even though you are absent, to offer you advice that may conduce to your dignity your whole life through. Since there is nothing more lovable or excellent than virtue, and

clarius, ea vero rectissimis artibus nostris perficiatur, nunc dum res et aetas patitur haec nostra humanissima studia toto animo complectare, quae nisi quis cito, dum potest, perceperit, nunquam omnino consequi poterit. Qui vero in his a puero multum profecerit facile ac brevi cunctos disciplinarum gradus ascenderit.

2 Tu quidem cum et ingenio valeas et institutione nostra plura intelligas, si quae a nobis accepisti et quae iam per te potes saepe ac multum recolueris, brevi cursu optatam metam contigeris. Ante omnia pudorem et verecundiam cole, quae cum omnem aetatem tum maxime pueritiam adolescentiamque exornat. Te vero non nisi probis modestisque viris et earundem artium laudisque studiosis adiungas: cum his enim si frequens fueris, opinionem cunctis afferes te eorum futurum persimilem, quos tibi ad imitandum delegeris. Vale.

Ghiacceti, XII Cal. Augusti 1490.

: 17 :

Bartholomaeus Fontius Petro Fannio s.

1 Putares ne me unquam fore tam inconstantem ut certo in proposito non persisterem? Querebar in urbe tecum multis rerum angustiis agitari ad levandasque curas animi in agro vivere satius arbitrabar. Huc postquam veni, rursus doleo carere urbe, amicis, necessariis omnibus. Itaque infirmus ac levis ubique torqueor, incertus quid consilii capiam aut quid agam. Huius autem distractionis animi est causa quod, nullis adhuc iactis in vitam reliquam fundamentis nullisque validis praesidiis constitutis, nunc ad

that is accomplished through the exercise of those noble arts of ours, now, while your circumstances and age permit, embrace with all your heart our humane studies: if one does not seize them while one can, they will never be acquired. But someone who has made good progress in them from boyhood will easily and swiftly mount the steps of learning at every level.

In your case, since through my instruction you have a good in- 2
tellect and a good understanding of things, if you constantly recall to mind what you have learned from me and what you have attained through your own efforts, you will reach the desired end in short order. More than anything else you should cultivate decency and modesty, which ornament any time of life, but boyhood and youth most of all. Keep company with none but upright and sober men and with lovers of these same arts and of glory: if you frequent them, you will convince everyone that you will turn out just like the men you have chosen to imitate. Farewell.

Ghiacceto, July 21, 1490.

: 17 :

Bartolomeo Fonzio to Pietro Fanni, greetings.

Did you really think I would ever be so inconstant as not to per- 1
sist in a course of action once I had made up my mind? I complained to you of the myriad annoyances in the city and thought that living in the country would better raise my spirits. But after coming here, I'm sorry to find I miss the city again, my friends, all my relations. And so, weak and capricious, I'm tormented everywhere, uncertain what to do or what plan to adopt. The reason for this mental distraction is that I've laid down no foundations for the rest of my life, I've acquired no solid security, and so at one

maiora trahor, nunc vitio forsan aetatis retrahor aestuantis in undae morem. Quandoque enim cum cogito me et natura non ineptum et rerum non minimarum scientia instructum, suppudet istic me tanquam in tenebris et hic velut in solitudine vivere. Quare anxius segnitiem meam reprendo reges magnosque duces adire meditans.

2 Interdum vero cum rerum humanarum imbecillitatem considero atque oculos mentis in caelum erigo, inani rerum mortalium spe reiecta, praesentis vitae statui acquiesco; quod cum saepe alias, tum hodierno die maxime contigit. Nam cum Pelagi triduum fuissem apud Paulum nostrum nullis in aliis sermonibus quam de rebus communibus, Ghiaccetum reversus, de via fessus et aestu solis defatigatus in cubiculo cum quiescerem, horum temporum conditionem et civitatis nostrae corruptos mores et vitae huius varieta-
3 tem considerans mecum talia sum locutus: 'o me miserum, qui cum hac mortali vita nihil imbecillius esse cernam, in qua tot fluctibus circumdamur, ut ne momento quidem horae non agitemur, me velim saevientibus undis immergere! Quid enim est aliud humanas appetere dignitates, opes ac divitias quaerere quam subiicere me immensis vitiorum gurgitibus, quibus iugiter vexatus sursum deorsumque fluctuans tandem obruar? Errant quidem mortales, errant haec turbida maria dum adnavigant vel ambitioni deservientes vel colla iugo avaritiae subiicientes, quasi vero nobis vivere datum sit ut terrenis cupiditatibus serviamus, non ut caelestia bona contemplemur, ut huius vitae navigationis bene confecto
4 cursu in portum sempiternae aulae veniamus. Quid ergo demens excogito in rebus inanibus et caducis tempus absumere? Honores ne quaero? At cum verus honos praemium sit virtutis, quis honos,

moment I'm drawn to higher things, at another I'm dragged back as if into a raging sea, the fault, perhaps, of my time of life. When I consider that I am not naturally foolish and have a fair knowledge of the world, I'm rather ashamed to live so much in the shade when I'm in your parts and to live here in such a solitary fashion. And that is why I peevishly curse my laziness as I plan to approach kings and great princes.

But when from time to time I consider the frailty of human 2
affairs and raise my mind's eye to heaven, I put aside the vain hopes in mortal things and am reconciled to my present state of life; as it often has before, so it happened to me in particular today. I had spent three days at Pelago with our friend Paolo engaged in conversation only about matters of common concern to us. Returning to Ghiacceto tired from the journey and exhausted by the heat of the sun, as I was resting in my bedroom, I fell to contemplating the present state of things, the rotten character of our city, and the ups and downs of this life, saying to myself something like
this: "How wretched I am! Though I see that nothing is more 3
fragile than this mortal life, in which we are surrounded by such great waves that we are battered without a moment's intermission, I yet propose to throw myself into the raging swell! To search for human honors, to seek wealth and power, would amount to nothing less than subjecting myself to a vast whirlpool of vice, by which I should be continually vexed and tossed up and down and eventually overwhelmed. Mortal men are certainly in error: they err when they sail these turbulent seas, becoming enslaved to ambition or bending their necks beneath the yoke of avarice, as if indeed we are given the gift of life only to serve worldly desires and not to contemplate heavenly goods, so that having creditably covered the course of our voyage through this life, we may reach the
port of the halls of heaven. Why then am I mad enough to con- 4
template wasting my time on empty and transitory things? Am I looking for honors? But since true honor is the prize awarded to

quae dignitas, quae gloria maior erit quam quae bonis artibus acquiretur? Divitias ne appeto? At quot[10] labores et solicitudines praebent, dum aut qui non habet ut inveniat nunquam quiescit aut postquam habuerit semper metuit ne amittat!

5 'Ad haec nullum vitium est cuius non avaritia sit parens: pervertit enim animum, rationem aufert, consilium impedit ac veri iudicium tollit. Cur igitur stabilia pro infirmis, certa pro dubiis, tranquilla pro turbulentis, perpetua pro caducis relinquo, ac non potius ea mihi certa praesidia vitae paro, quibus nullae rerum mutationes, nullae Fortunae turbulentissimae tempestates nocere possint? Auferet haec quaesitas opes cum libuerit et honores, virtutem vero scientiamque non adimet.'

6 His et multis aliis eiuscemodi, quae longum esset enumerare, inter cubandum tacite repetitis, refecto corpore et exhilarato animo assurrexi haecque statim ad te scripsi, quem cupio habere ut socium studiorum ita etiam cogitationum mearum omnium. Vale.

Ghiacceti, XI Cal. Augusti 1490.

: 18 :

Bartholomaeus Fontius Ioanni Pontano s.

1 In communi maerore omnium, tam importuno tempore, expectatione magnarum rerum, cunctis Gallis Italisque suspensis, gratuler ne tibi magis an doleam, Pontane, nescio. Nam ut Ferrandum amissum regem, quem cunctae Italiae urbes revererentur, degravat

virtue, what honor, what status, what glory can be greater than that which may be acquired by the liberal arts? Is it riches I am after? But how many trials and worries they give us, as one without riches never rests in his quest to acquire them, while he who has acquired them is ever fearful of losing them!

"Add to that the fact that there is no vice without avarice for a parent: it corrupts the spirit, deprives one of reason, obstructs good counsel and takes away one's discernment of the truth. Why, then, do I quit stable things for things that are feeble, certainty for uncertainty, peace for trouble, the eternal for the transitory? Why do I not rather furnish myself with those secure aids to living which no change of circumstance, none of Fortune's wild tempests can harm? Fortune may make off with the wealth one has sought whenever she likes, but virtue and learning she cannot take away." 5

Having quietly gone over these considerations as I was resting, and much more of the sort which it would take too long to rehearse here, with my body refreshed and my spirits recovered, I got up and at once wrote them down for you, wanting to have you as the companion of all my thoughts just as you are the companion of my studies. Farewell. 6

Ghiacceto, July 22, 1490.

: 18 :

Bartolomeo Fonzio to Giovanni Pontano, greetings.[31]

Amid universal grief and at a time of such difficulty, with every Frenchman and Italian anxious at the prospect of momentous events, I don't know whether to congratulate you, Pontanus, or offer you condolence. For just as the loss of King Ferrante, whom all the cities of Italy revered, depresses the spirits, so they are 1

animum, ita etiam levat Alphonsus paterno regno hereditario iure parto. Te vero decet quam maxime a cogitatione amissi ad spem modo assumpti regis mentem reflectere ac tantum alumnum tuum tuisque praeceptionibus optimis institutum ad aequitatem ac fidem in pace, in bello autem, quod acerrimum a Gallis instat, ad animi robur fortitudinemque incendere.

2 In eo quidem te gradu et industria et eruditio et, quae cuncta humana vertit, Fortuna posuit, ut, cum omnia unus ad eum possis, quodcunque vel recte vel perperam illi cesserit tibi sint omnes homines adscripturi. Quare quas Italas potes urbes ei adiunge, Hispanos ac Germanos concilia, ante omnia quacunque conditione cum Gallis paciscere. Sin minus, invicto animi robore dimicantes, virtuti si vestrae Fortuna inviderit non incruentam victoriam hostibus linquite. Vale.

Florentiae, Idibus Martiis 1493.[11]

: 19 :

Bartholomaeus Fontius Raphaeli Brandolino s.

1 Si ei benivolentiae, quam mihi tecum fama prius conciliavit deinde tua humanissime ad me scripta epistola confirmavit, ut non defuit studium et voluntas, ita etiam temporis oportunitas affuisset, honesto desiderio tuo satisfecissem. Quaesivi enim et quaero summa cura et diligentia qualem petiisti adolescentem idoneum legendo et scribendo et ministrando et mandatis omnibus exequendis. Sed mira talium adolescentium est hic paucitas ac, siqui sunt, neque precibus neque adhortationibus neque pollicitationibus ullis divelli possunt ab amantissimis patronis eorumque liberis, quos et dili-

raised by Alfonso's succeeding to his father's realm by hereditary right.[32] But you more than anyone should turn your mind from reflection on the dead king to the hopes placed in the newly enthroned one, and inspire your great pupil, raised under your excellent instruction, to justice and loyalty in time of peace, and in time of war (which now presses violently upon us at the hands of the French) to strength and fortitude of spirit.

Your industry and learning — and Fortune that holds sway over 2
all human life — have placed you in such a position that, since you alone have power with him, whatever turns out well or badly for him, all men will lay at your door. So you must ally him with any Italian states that you can, win over the Spanish and the Germans, and above all come to an agreement with the French on any condition whatever. If not, though you fight with invincible strength of spirit, if Fortune grudges you your prowess, you will leave the enemy a far from bloodless victory. Farewell.

Florence, March 15, 1494.

: 19 :

Bartolomeo Fonzio to Raffaele Brandolini, greetings.[33]

If I had had a favorable opportunity (for I was very ready and will- 1
ing) of exercising my goodwill toward you, first arising from your repute and then confirmed by your courteous letter to me, I should have satisfied your honorable request. I have looked and do still look with all energy and persistence for a youth such as you seek, one fitted for reading, writing, serving, and carrying out all your orders. But there's a remarkable shortage of such young men here, and those that there are cannot be parted from their affectionate patrons, or the patrons' sons that they love and instruct, by

2 gunt et erudiunt. Instabo tamen grammaticorum ludis, rimabor civium domos, scribam ad propinqua oppida. Tu quoque in ista Romana curia, in quam confluunt ex omni Christianitate vegetissima quaeque ingenia, elabora ut, si nos hinc tibi quem cupis mittere non poterimus, istic invenias quem exoptas. Vale.

: 20 :

Bartholomaeus Fontius Petro Soderino
iustitiae vexillifero perpetuo designato s.

1 Legatis ad Attalum regem missis, ad Matrem Idaeam Pessinunte Romam advehendam, oraculum Delphicum consulentibus responsum est compotes voti Romanos fore, sed in Urbem cum advexissent, qui optimus Romae esset hospitio deam susciperet; qua de re P. Scipionem G. f. optimum in civitate centum conscripti patres
2 iudicavere. Te absentem vero bis mille senatores liberis suffragiis tertium repetitis semperque numerosius redditis—quod faustum felixque tibi ac tuis et patriae sit—non modo optimum, sed magnis rebus gerendis aptissimum moderandaeque civitati fide, consilio, aequitate, prudentia praestantissimum iudicantes perpetuum iustitiae vexilliferum creaverunt, omni Florentino populo approbante. Quod totius civitatis de te iudicium quisque sibi mallet quam opulentissima regna validissimaque imperia.

3 Itaque cum egregia corporis dignitate gentilitioque splendore et patris tui clarissimi viri grata memoria et fratrum ac nepotum

any sort of entreaty, encouragement or promise. I'll press on, however, with the grammar schools, I'll investigate the households of citizens, I'll write to all the nearby towns. Being in the Roman court to which the liveliest minds of all Christendom gravitate, you for your part must work at finding there the one you're after, if we prove unable to send you one from here. Farewell. 2

: 20 :

Bartolomeo Fonzio to Pietro Soderini, designated Gonfalonier of Justice for life, greetings.[34]

When the ambassadors sent to King Attalus to transport the 1
Great Mother of Ida from Pessinus to Rome consulted the Delphic oracle, they got the response that the Romans would attain their desire, but that when they had taken her to the city, the best man in Rome should give the goddess lodging; and on that account a hundred senators decided that Publius Scipio, son of
Gaius, was the best in the city.[35] Yet in your absence, by electing 2
you Gonfalonier of Justice for life, with the approval of the whole people of Florence, two thousand members of the Great Council, in a free election thrice repeated and with an ever growing number of votes (may it be a happy omen for you and yours and your homeland!), judged you not only the best person but the man best fitted for handling great affairs of state, and the strongest for governing the city with integrity, judgment, fairness, and wisdom. Anyone would prefer to have such a judgment as was made of you by the entire citizenry to the wealthiest kingdoms and mightiest empires.

And so now that you have reached the highest office of govern- 3
ment by the stateliness of your person, the splendor of your fam-

tuorum popularitate atque modestia et scientia et virtute et magnitudine animi ascenderis gradum altissimum civitatis, decet et aequum et pium est te publicae utilitati consulere Florentinique populi erga te benivolentiam singularem conservare facilitate, mansuetudine, fide, beneficentia et urbium conservatrice iustitia, pro qua graves et fortes cives malunt mortem oppetere quam honestatem iustitiamque deserere. Ego vero tanta tua potestate et immortali gloria incredibiliter laetor tibique ac rei publicae gratulor, quam scelerum impunitate oppressam duce te suas pristinas opes brevi recuperaturam confido. Vale.

Flor., X Cal. Octobris 1502.

: 21 :

Bartholomaeus Fontius Francisco Soderino cardinali s.

1 Minimus equidem tuorum omnium, reverendissime pater, sed observantia et fide erga te maximus non tam cardinali tibi nuper creato, quam bonis et studiosis viris et Ecclesiae Dei gratulor, siquidem nos habebimus rectarum artium et communium studiorum praesidium, in quo nostra honesta desideria conquiescant. Sed ipse tu vexabere gravioribus curis et infinitis laboribus. Nam si episcopus antea expectationi multorum non sine crebris vigiliis et solicitudinibus respondisti, nunc positus eminentiore in specula meditare tecum et cogita, universo Christiano orbi si facere satis

ily, the fond memory of your famous father, the popularity of your brothers and nephews, your modesty, learning, virtue, and largeness of spirit, it behooves you, as is right and proper, to take thought for the public advantage and maintain that remarkable benevolence of the Florentine people toward you by your affability, clemency, integrity, and beneficence, and by the justice that preserves cities. For that, true and brave citizens would prefer to seek death rather than abandon honor and justice. I for my part am extraordinarily happy at the great power and undying glory you have attained, and I congratulate you and the republic, which I am confident will soon regain under your leadership its earlier prosperity after being prostrated by crimes that went unpunished. Farewell.

Florence, September 22, 1502.

: 21 :

Bartolomeo Fonzio to Cardinal Francesco Soderini, greetings.[36]

Least of all your people as I am, reverend father, though greatest 1
in respect of loyalty and attentiveness toward you, I do not so much congratulate you on your recent creation as cardinal as I congratulate upright and learned men and God's Church, since we shall now have protection for the liberal arts and our common studies, in which all our honorable desires may find repose. But you yourself will be burdened with heavier cares and infinite labors. If, before, as a bishop you met the expectations of a multitude of people at the cost of constant vigils and endless anxiety, consider and ponder how much sharper will be the troubles that consume you now that you are placed at a higher eminence, if you wish to give satisfaction to the whole Christian world, as surely

voles, quod certe ut par est et decet voles, quanto asperioribus
2 conficiere molestiis. Te Italae multae urbes, multae exterae nationes, multi excelsi principes, multi suspitiunt reges. Nostra quidem res publica non minus in te confidit quam in suum perpetuum iustitiae vexilliferum, fratrem tuum. Sacrosancta Romana Ecclesia hanc speratam exoptatamque dignitatem tuam existimat sibi magnopere profuturam teque posthac divino munere sublimius fastigium ascendente se tandem aliquando victuram sperat antiquis legibus et apostolicis moribus. Itaque vides quanto studio, labore, industria, cura, diligentia, contentione maiore quam unquam antea nitendum sit ut virtute ac meritis adeptam invidiaeque subiectam amplitudinem serves.

3 Experiere, mihi crede, nihil in vita praesenti durius, nihil in futura periculosius quam cardinalatum pontificatumque gerere, Deoque simul hominibusque placere. Veruntamen tibi cum sit adnavigandum tempestuosum hoc pelagus et agitatae Ecclesiae sapienter et fortiter consulendum, etiam atque etiam te adhortor non aurata corymba, non sericeos rudentes, non purpurea vela, non remos argenteos, non Attalicas vestes, sed ingentes illas animi tui virtutes et singulares ingenii dotes spectandas admirandasque cunctis in Ecclesiae navi explices, ne te magis cardinea sublimitas illustrasse, quam tu illam decorasse sanctissimis moribus et sapientissimis
4 consiliis videare. Ac quoniam quanto quis magis opibus et honoribus fulget, tanto magis ministris et familiaribus indiget, quorum improbitate minus interdum felices, magni et excellentes apparent principes, et hoc quoque prospectent omnes: te tui habere persimiles studiorum tuorum consiliorumque socios et gerendarum rerum participes. Hoc erit iocundum bonis, gloriosum tibi, pergratum Deo, quem orare non desino te diu praestet nobis et patriae et Ecclesiae suae sanctae incolumem. Vale.

Flor., die XX Iunii 1503.

you rightly and properly do. You have the admiration of many Italian cities, many foreign nations, many high princes, many kings. 2
Our republic has no less faith in you than in its perpetual Gonfalonier of Justice, your brother. The Holy Roman Church believes this much-longed-for appointment of yours will be greatly to its advantage and hopes that if by divine providence you ascend to an even higher role, it will at last conduct its life under its ancient laws and apostolic character. You see, then, how much application, effort, care, and thoroughness—and greater exertion than ever before—will be needed to ensure that you preserve this high position, one you have won through merit and virtue but which is yet exposed to envy.

Believe me, you will find that nothing is harder in this present 3
life, nothing in a future life more dangerous, than to act as cardinal or pope and be pleasing to God and man at the same time. But since you must sail this stormy sea and take wise and bold thought for the Church in turmoil, I emphatically urge you not to spread out in the ship of the Church gilded sterns, no hawsers of silk, no purple sails, no silver oars, no vestments woven with gold, but rather expose those great spiritual virtues and remarkable mental gifts of yours for all to look on and admire, so that the majesty of the cardinalate does not seem so much to add luster to you as that you rather adorn it with your holy character and sagacious counsels. And since the more one glitters with riches and honors, the 4
more one needs servants and ministers whose depravity sometimes makes great and distinguished princes appear less successful, let everyone see this too, that you have as companions of your studies and counsels, and sharers in your activities, men just as you are. This will be satisfying to men of good character, it will bring you renown, and will prove highly pleasing to God, to whom I never cease to pray that He may keep you safe for us, the homeland, and His Holy Church. Farewell.

Florence, June 20, 1503.

LIBER TERTIUS

: I :

Bartholomaeus Fontius Francisco Pandolphino s.

1 Brigidae sororis discessione cum vitae meae portio maxima demigrarit, non potui non dolere, amantissime Francisce, et vehementius forsan angi quam decuit studiosum et gravem senem. Dolui tamen et doleo non ulla animi mollitudine, sed recordatione eius in me officiorum et molestia secutorum incommodorum. Dilexit enim illa me semper affectu sororio et de me valde solicita, magis quam ego ipse, mihi metuebat, aegrotanti ministrabat, bene valenti providebat, comiter amicos excipiebat; ipse domesticis curis solu-
2 tus quieto animo litteris et sacerdotio incumbebam. Quibus omnibus nunc privatus commodis, multis praeterea amicis et Mauro fratre intra paucos annos orbatus, cum neque publice profitendo foris habeam quo avertam dolorem meum neque domi inveniam quod unicum solamen relictum erat, in hoc novissimo funere omnes acerbitates superiorum funerum recruduerunt.

Veruntamen Paulo apostolo admonente neque contristor de fratre neque de amicis dormientibus. De sorore vero, cum semper pudice moderateque vixerit et me fratrem et Cornelium filium moriens viderit et sacramenta Ecclesiae cuncta susceperit ac septimum et quinquagesimum annum agens in ulnis meis decesserit,
3 nulla est aequa causa cur contrister. Homo tamen cum sim non alienus a sensibus, sororis unicae incredibiliter semper a me dilectae desiderio moveor, exemplo etiam magnorum sapientissimorumque hominum. Nam et Abraam Sara coniuge defuncta indulxit lachrimis; et Ioseph faciem deosculans extincti patris amare flevit;

BOOK III

: I :

Bartolomeo Fonzio to Francesco Pandolfini, greetings.[1]

Since the greatest part of my life departed with the passing of my 1
sister Brigida, I could not but mourn, dearest Francesco, and perhaps felt more intensely tormented than was fitting for a scholarly and serious old man. Yet I grieved, and still do, not from any weakness of spirit, but from remembering her solicitude toward me and from the vexation of the difficulties that have followed on her death. She always loved me with a sister's affection, was always highly attentive in my regard—more than I was myself—she feared for me, tended me when I was sick, looked after me in health, welcomed my friends affably. Free of domestic cares, I devoted myself to letters and to my priestly office undisturbed. Now 2
stripped of all these advantages, deprived, too, of many friends and my brother Mauro in the space of a few years, since my public teaching brings no relief from the pain abroad, nor do I find at home the only consolation that was left to me, in this latest death all the bitterness of the earlier ones has welled up again.

But as Paul the Apostle counsels, I am saddened neither by my brother nor by my friends as they sleep.[2] And in truth there is no good reason to grieve over my sister: she always lived a chaste and modest life; on her deathbed she was able to see me, her brother, and her son Cornelio; received all the sacraments of the Church, and in her fifty-seventh year died in my arms. Yet as I am no 3
stranger to sentiment, I miss my only sister, for whom I always felt extraordinary love, following in this in the footsteps of men of grandeur and wisdom. Even Abraham indulged in tears when his wife Sara died, and Joseph wept bitterly as he kissed his dead fa-

et David in Saulis ac Ionatae Abnerisque ac Absalonis funere lachrimis et luctui non pepercit; quin etiam Dominus ac Deus noster Iesus Christus ut humanitatis mortalitatisque nos moneret ad
4 Lazari monumentum infremuit spiritu. Ego tamen non immemor
rationis et mentis memorque nostrae mortalitatis non tam illius
defunctae vicem lugeo quam meam indoleo, qui meorum et sanguine et amore coniunctissimorum funeribus supervixerim, relic-
tus multis ferendis humanis incommodis. Instant morbi et mortes
carissimorum, instant exilia et egestates, instant amarae solicitudines finemque mali unius sequitur accessio semper alterius.

5 Quare mihi quidem bene videtur actum cum Petrophilippo parente tuo, viro praeclarissimo meique amantissimo, cumque Paulo Ghiacceto amico optimo caeterisque amicis dormientibus, quoniam adepti finem praesentium aerumnarum sunt procul ab omni metu futurarum calamitatum. Sorori quoque meae bene consultum existimo quod me non viderit morientem, non illachrimarit ad tumulum, non se luctu et squalore confecerit. Quae tamen cum esset aetate minor iustius illi me deflere quam mihi illam contigisset. Ego vero solus et senex non amplius eam aspicio, nulla verba referentem audio, casta oscula offerentem non deosculor. Nil mihi sine te, soror, amplius erit iocundum, nil me tristem solabitur, nil me levabit afflictum.

6 Haec gravant, Francisce, animum, haec continue opprimunt, haec defunctae augent desiderium. Quas certe amaritudines, si adesses, magna ex parte delinires iocundissima consuetudine et collocutionibus suavissimis. Sed nimis longo intervallo abes et locorum et temporum, siquidem legatio ista gallica videtur mihi futura longior quam sperabam. Nanque publicam rem apud Regem

ther's face; and David spared no tears or grief at the deaths of Saul and Jonathan, Abner and Absalom; why, even our Lord God Jesus Christ groaned in his spirit at the tomb of Lazarus, to remind us of his humanity and mortality.[3] For my part, however, I am not 4
unmindful of reason and rationality, and very mindful of our mortality, and so I do not so much mourn the lot of my dead sister as lament my own, survivor of the deaths of those closest to me by blood and friendship, and left behind to endure the many ills to which mortals are subject. Diseases threaten me, and the deaths of those dearest to me, exile and poverty threaten me, sharp anxieties threaten, and another evil always arises hard on the heels of the last one.

On that account they seem to me to have acquitted themselves 5
well — your father Pierfilippo, that distinguished man so devoted to me, Paolo da Ghiacceto, best of friends, and all the other sleeping friends — since they have reached the end of their troubles and are free from fear of any future calamity.[4] Things have gone well with my sister, too, I think, in that she has not seen me on my deathbed nor wept at my tomb, she has not been eaten up by grief and mourning; though since she was younger than me, it would have been more reasonable had she had to mourn me rather than I her. But now I'm alone and old and shall see her no more, never hear her speaking again, never kiss her as she returns chaste kisses. I shall have no pleasure in anything any more without you, sister; nothing will raise me from my dejection.

Such are the concerns, Francesco, that weigh on my spirit and 6
continually oppress me; they make me miss my dead sister all the more. These sorrows you would no doubt soothe, if you were here, with your pleasant company and agreeable conversation. But you are too far away in time and space, since I think that that embassy of yours to France will take longer than I had anticipated: you are dealing so wisely with the king over the Republic's affairs, and from time to time make such sound forecasts of the way things

tam prudenter agis, tam diligenter interdum futura significas, ut
7 multi dicant legari tibi successorem non oportere. Quae de te constans opinio quanquam grata mihi est, me tamen laedit quod et careo dulcissima consuetudine tua et vereor ne res etiam laedat privatas tuas. Nam de te pendentes uxor et nubilis soror praesentiam tuam desiderant domusque iam nimis diu te absente non retinet pristinam dignitatem suam. Ioannes autem frater, qui haec omnia diligenter curaret, abesse, ut scis, ab urbe Roma non potest: quare tu pro tua prudentia quod optimum putabis efficies. Ego Montemurlensibus tuis rebus multo magis quam meis providebo et cum mente paululum conquievero te faciam de illis et de toto statu meo diligentissime certiorem. Vale.

Ex Gignoro, Calendis Augusti MDVI.

: 2 :

Bartholomaeus Fontius Ioanni Nesio s.

1 In *M. Tullii vita* a Leonardo Aretino edita haec te ad verbum legisse scribis:

> denique abeuntem consulatu habere concionem et apud populum loqui de rebus suis, ut mos erat, Metellus prohibuit; tantum ut iuraret sibi permissum. Ille autem magna voce iuravit non solitum iusiurandum, sed aliud pulcherrimum, quod populus postea magna voce ‹ipsum vere›[1] iurasse iuravit,

atque haec Leonardus ex ea sumpsisse tibi videtur epistola quam ad Q. Metellum Celerem in quinto volumine scripsit Cicero, ubi ait:

will turn out, that many people are saying there is no need to send another legate to replace you. This settled opinion of you, though 7
welcome to me, also upsets me: not only do I lack your delightful company but I fear the affair is damaging to your own interests. For your dependents, your wife and marriageable sister, need you there and the house in your over-long absence has lost some of its former prestige. Your brother Giovanni, who would take care of all this properly, cannot, as you know, be away from Rome.[5] So you should do what in your wisdom you think best. I'll look after your business at Montemurlo (much more carefully than I'll attend to my own affairs there), and when I've recovered a little in my mind, I'll tell you about it and all about how I am in detail.[6] Farewell.

From Il Gignoro, August 1, 1506.

: 2 :

Bartolomeo Fonzio to Giovanni Nesi, greetings.[7]

You write that you find the following in Leonardo Bruni's *Life of* 1
Cicero:[8]

> When he was finally leaving his consulate, Metellus forbade him from giving a speech and talking of his achievements before the people, as was customary. He was allowed only to give his oath. But in a loud voice Cicero not only swore the usual oath but another very fine one, which the people then in a loud voice swore that he had truly sworn,

and you think this was taken by Bruni from the letter that Cicero wrote to Quintus Metellus Celer in Book 5 of the letters, where he says:

> nam cum ille mihi nihil nisi ut iurarem permitteret, magna voce iuravi verissimum pulcherrimumque iusiurandum, quod populus item magna voce me vere iurasse iuravit.

2 His tamen verbis cum quid iuraverit Tullius non expresserit et Leonardus etiam non adverterit, de me quaeris an apud quempiam veterum unquam legerim quod illud fuerit iusiurandum. Equidem apud Asconium Pedianum, super oratione Tullii *In Pisonem,* ita scriptum legisse memini:

> ego cum in concione abiens magistratu a tr. pl. dicere prohiberer ea quae constitueram, cum is mihi tantummodo iurare permitteret, sine ulla dubitatione iuravi rem publicam atque hanc urbem mea unius opera esse salvam.

Vale.

: 3 :

[. . .]

Ut Romani veteres Saturnalibus, ita nos Domini nostri Iesu Christi natalibus amicis munera missitamus. Unde ego nullas habens tabulas neque signa, hoc tenue munusculum ad te misi; sed quanquam tenue nec antiquis vatibus conferendum, non tamen ullis imaginibus posthabendum. In illis enim nihil apparet praeter effigiem corporis, quae nullam vel vivis vel mortuis laudem parit; in hoc vero, si qualem cupimus fuerit, in dies clarior apparebis. Vale.

> For when he allowed me only to give the oath, in a loud voice I gave that very true and excellent oath, which the people likewise with a loud voice swore that I had sworn truly.

However, since Cicero does not reveal in this passage what it 2
was that he swore, and Bruni equally does not mention it, you ask me if I have ever read in some ancient writer what the oath was. I remember reading this passage in the commentary of Asconius on Cicero's *Oration against Piso*:

> I was stopped by the Tribune of the people from saying what I had intended to say in the public assembly held when I was leaving my consulate, being allowed only to make an oath, so without hesitation I swore that the Republic and this city were saved by my efforts alone.[9]

Farewell.

: 3 :

[To an unknown correspondent][10]

Just like the old Romans at the Saturnalia, we have the habit of giving our friends presents on the birthday of our Lord Jesus Christ. Having no pictures or sculptures, I therefore send you this tiny little gift. But slight as it is, and not to be compared to the ancient poets, you should not think it inferior to any portrait. In them there is nothing to be seen but an image of a body, which brings no credit to either living or dead; but in this one, if it is as I hope, you'll appear more distinguished day by day. Farewell.

: 4 :

Bartholomaeus Fontius Spicae s.

1 Non recte a quopiam quae sit excommunicatio potest percipi, qui quae sit communicatio non cognoverit. Ea vero est vitae ac victus communis participatio, quae quidem bifariam sumitur: una saecularis pertinens ad communicationem temporalis huius praesentis vitae, de qua consulti iuris secundum leges et instituta saecularium principum civitatumque tractant, ad aequitatem iustitiamque servandam; alia ecclesiastica secundum sacros canones spectans ad animam in vitam aeternam perducendam. Atque haec ecclesiastica communicatio, de qua sententiam meam quaeris, bifariam quoque accipitur: nam vel ad Deum vel ad proximum pertinet.

2 Ad Deum communicatio facientis gratum gratiae status est, cui adversatur excommunicatio omnis quae ex mortali peccato gignitur. Atque haec excommunicatio minor dicitur, latens quidem et quae paenitenti et confitenti a solo confessore dimittitur, de qua dictum est a Domino illi leproso a se mundato 'vade, ostende te sacerdoti et offer munus, quod ostendit Moses, in testimonium illis.'

3 Ad proximum vero communicatio patens et publica est eorundem sacramentorum Ecclesiae allocutionumque ac vitae victusque communio, cui ecclesiastica excommunicatio et irregularitas adversatur. Quae consideratur dupliciter: nam quaedam est omnino sine mortali peccato, veluti bigamia et lepra et servitus et mutilatio et sententia lata de morte hominis ex officio et caetera id genus, ab exercitio divinarum administrationum et ab ordinum susceptione repellentia; quaedam vero est ex peccato vel existente vel praesumpto, veluti excommunicatio latae sententiae ab homine vel a

: 4 :

Bartolomeo Fonzio to Spica, greetings.[11]

No one can grasp what excommunication is without understanding what "communion" is. It is participation in a shared life and manner of living, which can be taken two ways. One is secular and pertains to sharing this present temporal life, on which the legists discourse according to the laws and institutions of secular princes and cities with a view to securing fairness and justice; the other is ecclesiastical, based on sacred canons and aimed at leading the soul to eternal life. And this ecclesiastical communion, on which you seek my views, is likewise to be taken in two senses, as it pertains to God and as it pertains to one's neighbor. 1

Communion with God is the state of grace of one who does a thing pleasing to Him, as opposed to all forms of excommunication, which arise from mortal sin. And this is said to be a "lesser excommunication" when it is hidden and can be remitted by a confessor alone in one who is penitent and makes confession, on which matter our Lord spoke to that leper he had cleansed: "Go thy way, show thyself to the priest, and offer the gift that Moses commanded, for a testimony unto them."[12] 2

Being in communion with one's neighbor is that open and public sharing of the same sacraments and doctrines of the Church, and of one's life and manner of living, as opposed to ecclesiastical excommunication and irregularity. And that is to be taken in two ways: one is, to be sure, altogether without mortal sin, such as bigamy, leprosy, enslavement, mutilation, a fixed penalty for imposing a death sentence in the course of one's duties, and others of the sort; such cases preclude one from the exercise of divine service or taking orders. The other derives from a sin either existing or presumed, such as excommunication *latae sententiae*[13] imposed 3

iure propter mortale peccatum, cum contumacia vera vel praesumpta.

4 Quae a iure fertur generalis est in transgressores omnis, ut in homicidas, in sacrilegos, in incendiarios et id genus caetera; atque haec utilis et necessaria et apostolica est. Quae vero modo hunc, modo illum nominatim alligatis fertur a iudice vel ab homine spetialis est, in qua et causa et voluntas inferentis et patientis consideranda est, cuius quisque sibi conscius est. Deus certe et Apostoli ferri eam in debitorem non potentem solvere aegre ferunt ac tanto aegrius quanto debitum minus est. "Non ob aes alienum, sed ob contumaciam!' scio, hic iudices exclamabunt. Sed videant ne forsan ipsi excommunicentur a Domino, quia fuerint causa contumaciae.

: 5 :

Bartholomaeus Fontius fratri Simoni Cinozo Ordinis Praedicatorum

1 Cum non probares, frater carissime, quod Petrus apostolus in *Itinerario* quod Claementi adscribitur de veris signis venturi loquitur Antichristi auctoremque operis iudicatum apocriphum elevares, quoniam contradiceret Paulo ad Thessalonicenses scribenti de signis Antichristi mendacibus, ubi primum reverti domum in Augustini *De civitate Dei* libro vigesimo et capite decimo nono haec ad verbum scripta legi:

> praesentia quippe eius erit, sicut dictum est, secundum operationem Sathanae in omni virtute et signis et prodigiis mendacii et in omni seductione iniquitatis his qui pereunt.

by man or the law for a mortal sin with real or presumed contumacy.

The one sanctioned by law is general and aimed at all transgressors, such as murderers, the sacrilegious, arsonists, etc.; and this is useful and necessary and of apostolic authority. Excommunication imposed by a judge or other man, however, with allegations against this or that named person is particular, and here the motives and intentions of the offender and victim must be taken into account, of which everyone is in himself aware. God and the Apostles would surely not approve of the excommunication of a debtor who cannot pay, and all the more so the smaller the debt is. I know the judges will exclaim at this point, "It is not because of the debt but because of his contumacy!" But they should take care that they are not themselves excommunicated by the Lord because they were the *cause* of the contumacy. 4

: 5 :

Bartolomeo Fonzio to Fra Simone Cinozzi, O.P., greetings.[14]

Dear brother, learning that you place no credit in what the Apostle Peter says about the true signs of the advent of the Antichrist in the *Itinerarium* ascribed to Clement,[15] and that you disparage the author of this supposedly apocryphal work because he contradicts what Paul says about the false signs of the Antichrist in his letter to the Thessalonians, as soon as I got home I read the following words in Augustine's *City of God*, Book 20, Chapter 19: 1

> His coming, so it is said, will assuredly be after the working of Satan with all power and signs and lying wonders, and with all deceivableness of unrighteousness of them that per-

> Tunc enim solvetur Sathanas et per illum Antichristus in omni sua virtute mirabiliter quidem, sed mendaciter operabitur. Quod solet ambigi utrum propterea dicta sint signa et prodigia mendacii, quoniam mortales sensus per phantasmata decepturus est, ut quod non facit facere videatur, an quia illa ipsa, etiam si erunt vera prodigia, ad mendacium pertrahent credituros non ea potuisse nisi divinitus fieri, virtute diaboli crescente maxime quando tantam, quantam nunquam habuit, acceperit potestatem. Non enim, quando de caelo ignis cecidit et tantam familiam cum tantis gregibus pecorum sancti Iob uno impetu absumpsit et turbo irruens et domum deiiciens filios eius occidit, phantasmata fuerunt; quae tamen fuerunt opera Sathanae, cui Deus dederat hanc potestatem.

2 Haec Augustinus, cui astipulatur Ioannes Gerson, theologus excellentissimus, in libro *De verarum visionum a falsis distinctione* ita scribens:

> nec reclamaret propter Antichristi miracula, quae non nulli vera fore contendunt ad probationem electorum et reproborum subversionem, licet tamen Antichristus minister miraculi mendacissimus erit et in vita sceleratissimus; sed Deus ipsi suisque miraculis ne crederetur per suas aliorumque praenuntiationes innumeras reclamavit atque contradixit; propter quod inexcusabilis erit sibi credens.

3 Idem eisdem in *Visionibus* non multo post ait:

> nihil bonis moribus aut sincerae fidei contrarium angeli sancti et prophetae veri praedicunt aut praecipiunt. Non sic

ish.[16] For then Satan will be loosed and through him the Antichrist will work "with all power" in a wonderful though deceitful fashion. The question is often asked whether these are called "signs and lying wonders" because Satan will deceive mortal senses by illusions—by seeming to do what he does not really do; or because, though they are truly wonders, they will draw men into falsehood nonetheless, in that, being ignorant of the devil's strength—and especially his strength when he has received such power as he never before possessed—they will believe that such things could only have been achieved by the power of God. For when fire fell down from heaven and at one stroke consumed all the large household and numerous flocks of holy Job and a great wind rushed down and smote the house and slew his children, those things were not illusions; and yet they were the work of Satan, to whom God had given the power to do such things.[17]

So Augustine, with the support of that excellent theologian 2
Jean Gerson in his book *On Telling Apart True Visions and False Ones,* in the following words:

Nor would he object to the miracles of the Anti-Christ is said in relation to the miracles of the Antichrist, which some maintain will be true miracles to confirm the elect and destroy the damned, even though the Antichrist will be the most deceitful agent of miracles and leading an abominable way of life. But by innumerable predictions of his own and others, God has objected and spoken against any credit being given him and his miracles, and anyone believing in him will not be justified.

Gerson again says a little later in the same *Visions:* 3

Holy angels and true prophets preach and propound nothing that is contrary to good morals and genuine faith. Not so

> daemones vel Antichristus, quorum signa dicuntur signa mendacii quia ad mendacium credendum inducunt.

4 His duobus gravissimis praestantissimisque theologis accedit Nicolaus Lira, super eisdem verbis Pauli sic scribens:

> nam aliqua fient per illusionem sensuum a daemone, quae videbuntur esse et non erunt, et aliquae erunt res verae, sicut daemon super oves Iob fecit ignem verum descendere. Dicuntur tamen signa mendacia quia fient ad assertionem mendacii.

5 Accedit his quartus Georgius Benignus, insignis aetate nostra theologus, libri octavi *De natura angelica* capite decimo septimo haec referens:

> possunt itaque daemones multa omnibus hominibus admiranda facere, applicando causas activas passivis. Quae quidem non erunt phantasmata, sed re ipsa talia. Omnia tamen dicuntur signa mendacia ex eo, quia fiunt ab eis animo decipiendi.

6 Ex his facile datur intelligi Petrum apud pseudo Claementem non dissentire a Paulo, cuius *Itinerarium,* licet apocriphum in *Decretis,* distinctione quindecima et sextadecima, iudicatum, equidem non erubui testem adducere quando etiam Gerson verarum falsarumque visionum testem protulerit. Tu vero iam potes et certe debes tantis auctoribus credere signa prodigiaque mendacia Antichristi, non quia non vera multa futura sint, sed quia credituros ad mendacium pertrahent, ab apostolo Paulo appellari.

7 Negasti etiam, amantissime frater, moveri caelos ab angelis Dantemque poetam contempsisti, quanquam non ea primum opi-

> demons and the Antichrist, whose signs are said to be signs of deceit because they induce belief in lies.[18]

To these two very weighty and authoritative theologians may be added Nicholas of Lyra, writing as follows on the same passage in Paul: 4

> For some things will happen in virtue of sensory illusion induced by a demon, things which will seem to be so but are not, while others will be true, such as when the demon caused real fire to fall on Job's sheep. They are nevertheless called signs of deceit because they will happen on the basis of a lie.[19]

A fourth authority alongside these is Giorgio Benigno, the famous theologian of our own day.[20] In the eighth book, Chapter 17, of his work on *The Nature of Angels,* he has this to say: 5

> Demons can perform many things astonishing to all mankind, by applying active causes to passive ones. These will assuredly not be illusions but actual realities. They are nevertheless all called signs of deceit because they are done with a view to deceiving.

From these passages it is easy to see that Peter in Pseudo-Clement is not at odds with Paul. Though his *Itinerarium* is judged to be apocryphal in the *Decretum* (Dist. 15 and 16),[21] I do not blush to produce it as witness since even Gerson cites it as evidence for true and false visions. You can and now certainly should believe with such great authorities that these signs and prodigies are called lies of the Antichrist by the Apostle Paul, not because many of them will not prove to be true, but because they will induce those who believe in them to lie. 6

You have also denied, dearest brother, that the heavens are moved by the angels and you hold Dante in contempt on this ac- 7

nio Dantis fuit, sed peripateticorum principis Aristotelis, a quo nostri quoque theologi non dissentiunt. Inter quos idem Ioannes Gerson in *Trilogio astrologiae,* propositione tertia decima, scribit 'angelos vel intelligentias non animare sed regere caelum cum sideribus et planetis ad Dei gloriosi voluntatem.' Georgius quoque Benignus *De angelica natura* primo ac quarto voluminibus de caelorum motoribus scribit angelis. Te vero etiam atque etiam rogo ut Dantem legas, quem docti viri et admirantur et diligunt; quo diligenter inspecto non vereor de tanto vate maximoque theologo te sententiam mutaturum.

: 6 :

Bartholomaeus Fontius Bernardo Oricellario s.

1 Non modo ad portum Neapolitanum commissum praelium, sed historiam totam Gallicam tuis in hortis biduo legi attentius cum Dante Populescho, utriusque nostrum amantissimo. In qua nescio magis ne laudem genus dicendi grave crebris exornationibus perpolitum an dilucidum ordinem in locis et castris et certaminibus referendis, an singulare iudicium in consiliis principum et bellorum causis cum imperatorum ac militum vel vitiis vel virtutibus enarrandis. Quae abs te omnia tam dilucide, tam apposite, tam fideliter sunt relata ut, cum summo artificio singula quaeque decenter scripseris, in omnibus tamen artis suspitionem vitaveris egregius et excellens scribendi artifex, omnium nostri temporis ingenio et eloquio eminentissimus.

count,[22] even though the idea was not originally Dante's but Aristotle's, the prince of the Peripatetics, and our theologians do not disagree with him. Among them is the same Gerson in his *Trilogium astrologiae*, proposition 13, where he writes "angels or intelligences do not *animate* the heavens but *regulate* them with their stars and planets in line with the will of God in His glory."[23] Giorgio Benigno, too, in the first and fourth of his books on *The Nature of Angels* writes of angels as "the motor of the heavens." I earnestly urge you to read Dante, a writer that scholars admire and love. After a careful reading of him, I'm sure you will change your opinion of that fine poet and great theologian.

: 6 :

Bartolomeo Fonzio to Bernardo Rucellai, greetings.[24]

In the space of two days in your garden I read with great attention not only the battle at the port of Naples[25] but the whole history of the French Wars, in the company of our great friend Dante Popoleschi.[26] I don't know whether to praise more the solemn and highly polished style, or the pellucid arrangement of its account of places and encampments and combats, or the extraordinary penetration it shows in explaining the deliberations of the leading figures and the causes of the wars, along with the strengths and defects of the commanders and soldiers. All of it has been related by you with such clarity, relevance and accuracy that, though you have given a graceful account of each and every event with the utmost skill, in all this, as a superbly able writer, you yet escape any suspicion of artifice, showing yourself the most prominent man of our time for talent and eloquence. 1

2 Quare te etiam atque etiam hortor ad exitum perducas tantam historiam, tibi quidem aeternum nomen, legentibus magnam utilitatem, patriae summum decus allaturam. Quae in Gallorum regis tanta felicitate atque victoria tantoque totius Italiae metu desiderat iocundissimum conspectum tuum sapientissimumque consilium, quo ne prives cives tuos, liberos, cognatos, affines, amicos omnis nosque in primis te vehementissime oro. Caeterum ne locorum gallicorum quae petis oblitus videar, ea penes me non sunt et quae Saxetti erant iampridem ad Pannonios migravere; sed passim circumferuntur in impressis Caesaris *Commentariis*. Vale.

Florentiae, Cal. Iuniis 1509.

: 7 :

Bartholomaeus Fontius Ioanfrancisco Zeffio s.

1 Tanti fuere litterae tuae amantissime ad me scriptae, ut hyeme adventante statuerim, qualiacunque sunt, quae scripsi edere et obsequi tibi magis quam mihi ipsi. Distuli autem hactenus non limae causa, quem vel ad stomachum usque laborem nunquam effugi, sed aequi, honesti pudoris. Quid enim minus decet nunc sacerdotem quam insudasse tamdiu poetis interpretandis gentilibus et modo Latiis modo Tuscis decantasse carminibus?

2 Nam Politiano Ficinoque exceptis, quos belle adducis, longe alia fuit ratio Schalae, Landini, Pici, Nesii et Criniti, qui dare in lucem quae poterant etiam debebant nulla religione impediente. Nos vero ministri Dei possumus quidem, sed nescio quae saecula-

So I do emphatically urge you to carry your great history to the end, something that will procure you undying fame, great benefit for your readers, and the highest glory for your homeland. During that great success and victory of the king of France and amid such anxiety throughout Italy, your homeland missed your welcome presence and your sage counsel, of which I earnestly beg you not to deprive your fellow citizens, your children, your family and relations, and all your friends, us above all.[27] As for the notices of places in France that you ask me about, in case you think I have forgotten, I no longer have them with me, and those that belonged to Sassetti have long since left for Hungary; but they are widely published in editions of Caesar's *Commentaries*. 2

Florence, June 1, 1509.

: 7 :

Bartolomeo Fonzio to Gianfrancesco Zeffi, greetings.[28]

Your very kind letter was so persuasive that I have decided as winter approaches to publish what I've written, such as it is, and to oblige you rather than myself. I have put it off so far not for want of the final polishing, work that I have never avoided, even to the point of nausea, but from a natural and proper reserve. For what could be less becoming to a priest than to have labored over the interpretation of the pagan poets at such length and to have produced verse by turns in Latin and the vernacular? 1

If we except Poliziano and Ficino, whose example you do well to mention, the situation as regards Scala, Landino, Pico, Nesi, and Crinito was quite different: they actually had an obligation to publish what they could, since no scruple of religion barred their way. We as ministers of God certainly can, but I don't know 2

res adhuc lusimus an salva conscientia debeamus. Itaque vereor ne tu mihi ad Deum fias particeps culpae huius, quem oro tibi persuadenti et mihi ignoscat non renitenti.

3 Extorsisti a me profecto quod multis mei amantissimis semper antea denegavi. In quo tamen etiam illis puto gratificari et Danti Populescho pro me tibi, ut scribis, recipienti et Petrofrancisco, Laurentii filio, candore ingenii et morum optimorum suavitate splendorem inclytae suae gentilitatis Mediceae referenti, quem equidem gaudeo nostris et studiosorum virorum congressibus delectari, quoniam si, ut Melanthius Homericus loquitur in Ulyssem, *αἰεὶ θεὸς τὸν ὅμοιον ἐς τὸν ὅμοιον ἄγει*, ea inter bonos similitudo est inditium manifestum excellentis ingenii et acquirendae conservandaeque virtutis. Qua nihil peregrinantibus nobis, dum vivimus vel potius hic dum morimur, est suavius, nihil melius, nihil amabilius, nihil ad vim inferendam caelesti regno, quod vim libentissime patitur, expeditius.

4 Hoc ei Christianum dictum non displicere si videris, hortaberis, quoque meo nomine, ut ascendat bene vivendi recteque intelligendi laboriosum quidem sed gloriosum curriculum. In quo si nostra aurigatione, impulsu, clamore, verbere ad metam currentis equos excitari placuerit, tunc ei libenter nostrum studium, curam, industriam, diligentiam omni loco et tempore polliceberis. Nos subinde quod maximum operae pretium visum fuerit ei cumulate praestabimus multo libentius. Vale.

Ex Genioro, III Idus Septembris 1510.

whether in all conscience we *should* publish what we amused ourselves with as laymen. So I'm afraid you'll become complicit in my guilt in the eyes of God, whom I pray to forgive you for pressing me on this — and me for not refusing.

You have wrung from me something that I have often denied to many of my closest friends. In doing so, however, I think I shall oblige them, and Dante Popoleschi too (who as you write vouchsafes for me), and Pierfrancesco, the son of Lorenzo,[29] a youth who in the brilliance of his intellect and pleasantness of his fine character reflects the splendor of his famous Medici family; I am glad he takes pleasure in our meetings and those of other scholars, since if, as Melanthius says to Odysseus in Homer, "God always leads like to like,"[30] the likeness between good men is a clear indication of a fine mind and of a virtue that is to be acquired and kept hold of. Than this nothing is more agreeable to us on our journey through life — or rather as long as we are *dying* here below — nothing better, nothing pleasanter, nothing handier for thrusting our way into the kingdom of heaven, which indeed very happily endures such thrusts. 3

If you see that this Christian sentiment is not displeasing to him, encourage him, in my name too, to ascend that difficult but glorious path of good living and right thinking. If on this course he is pleased to have the horses straining for the line, driven on by my guidance and urging and shouting and whipping, then you may readily assure him of my eagerness, application, solicitude, and attentiveness at any time or place. Whatever he thinks most worth doing, I shall at once provide him with in abundance all the more willingly. Farewell. 4

From Il Gignoro, September 11, 1510.

: 8 :

Bartholomaeus Fontius Francisco Riccio Mathaei filio s.

1 Quaesisti ex me tuis humanissimis litteris ut quaedam vocabula mensurarum, quibus Romani veteres utebantur, ad te praescriberem. Quae brevi a me collecta, plura etiam quam petieras, ad te misi ut mea scribendi tarditas ubertate muneris compensetur.

2 Mensura proprie ea est quae a membris hominis sumpta est, quanquam eius appellatione continetur quicquid pondere, capacitate, longitudine, latitudine animoque finitur. Verum ea quam requiris plurium et inter se aequalium intervallorum mensura determinatur. Mensurarum autem appellationes sunt digitus, uncia, palma, sexta, pes, cubitum, passus, decempeda, clima, actus, iugerum, stadium, miliare, centuria.

3 Digitus est minima mensurarum, infra quem, siquid dimetiamur, partibus respondemus, ut dimidiam, tertiam quartamve digiti partem. Digitorum porro observatio duplex est: quadratus enim dicitur et rotundus. Sed cum simpliciter appellamus rotundum accipimus, qui quidem est sextadecima pedis pars, tribus quartis decimis suis quadrato minor: nam si quadratum in quattuordecim
4 partes dividas, tribus ex illis partibus rotundum superat. Uncia vero digitum unum et eius tertiam partem habet, siquidem unciis duodecim pes integer definitur. Palmam duplicem esse reperio, extensam scilicet et compressam. Extensa est quantum expansa manus a pollice ad minimum se extendit, quae sane est duodecim digitorum; compressa est quantum digiti quattuor simul iuncti excepto pollice se expandunt. Verum palmam simpliciter nominantes de compressa intelligimus. Sexta digitos duodecim continet: eandem enim mensuram quam extensa palma complectitur.
5 Pes vero est sexdecim digitorum. Ex pede autem et semis cubitum fit. Ex pedibus quinque fit passus, quanquam spatium quoque il-

: 8 :

Bartolomeo Fonzio to Francesco di Matteo Ricci, greetings.[31]

Your very kind letter asked me to explain for you some of the words for measures that the ancient Romans used. I soon gathered together even more than you'd asked about, and now send them, so that the richness of the gift may make up for my slowness in replying. 1

"Measure" properly speaking is that which is derived from human limbs,[32] though the term includes whatever is defined by weight, capacity, length, breadth, or spirit.[33] What you asked me about is in fact determined by the size of many intervals of equal measure. The terms for such measures are finger, inch, palm, sixth, foot, cubit, yard, ten-foot, *clima, actus,* acre, furlong, mile, century. 2

A finger is the smallest measure, and if we must measure something smaller, we use fractions of it, as half, third or quarter of a finger. A finger in turn has a double aspect: it may be called square or round. But when we speak simply of a finger, we mean the round finger, that is, a sixteenth part of a foot, and smaller than a square finger by three fourteenths (if you divide a square finger into fourteen parts, it is longer than a round finger by three of those fourteenth parts). An inch is a finger and a third, since a whole foot is made up of twelve inches. I find that a "palm" has two senses, that is, open and closed. When open it is the distance of the extended hand from thumb to little finger, which amounts to twelve fingers. Closed it is the breadth of four fingers joined together, without the thumb. But when we talk simply of "a palm" we mean the closed one. A "sixth" contains twelve fingers, i.e., the same distance as the open palm. A "foot" is sixteen fingers. A foot and a half makes a cubit. A yard (*passus*) is made up of five feet, 3 4 5

lud, quod inter ambulandum est inter pedes, passus denominatur, dictus quia gressibus mutuis pedes patescunt. Decempeda ex pedibus decem constat, unde etiam nomen sumpsit; quo vocabulo in Clodium pro Milone utitur Cicero sic scribens: 'qui cum architectis et decempedis villas multorum hortosque peragrabat.' Sex vero decempedae clima reddunt, quod quoquo versus pedum est sexa-
6 ginta. Actus dicitur quod in eo boves agerentur cum araretur uno impetu iusto, qui erat centum viginti pedum. Tris autem actus esse invenio: minimum, quadratum et duplicatum. Minimus quattuor pedes patescit, quod spatium in agris erat inter vicinos; quadratus undique centum viginti pedibus praefinitur; quadratus duplicatus iugerum praestat, dictum quod ex duobus quadratis actibus sit coniunctum vel, ut maiori Plinio placet, quod id spatium uno iugo boum in die arari posset. Protenditur itaque iugerum in longum pedes ducentos et quadraginta, in latum vero centum viginti. Stadium passibus quinque ac viginti supra centum describitur. Milia-
7 rium stadia octo, hoc est passus mille, complectitur. Centuriam primi Romani veteres ex centum iugeribus effecerunt, iuniores ex ducentis quoque iugeribus servato centuriae nomine expleverunt. Neque vero praeterire te arbitror in re militari centuriam centum militum numerum continere et centurionem appellari qui illis praeest subcenturiatosque dici milites non primae, sed secundae centuriae, ubi ad insidiandum maxime locabantur: ex quo 'in subcenturiis' quasi ‹in›[2] insidiis quempiam positum dictitabant. Centuriatim quoque adverbium, quod abundantiam copiamque designat, a centuriis, quae in comitiis ferebant suffragia, derivatur, unde et centuriata sunt dicta comitia.

8 Caeterum mensuris omnibus quanto brevius fieri potuit explicatis, brevi quoque ponderum vocabula enarrabo, nequid honesto studio tuo desit. Ponderum omnium minimum siliqua est, quod granum ex ea est siliqua quam fabam Graecam plerique nuncu-

though the distance between the feet when walking is also called a *passus* (pace), so called because the feet are stretched out in alternate strides.[34] A "ten-foot" is made of ten feet, whence its name. Cicero uses the word in his attack on Clodius in the *Oration for Milo,* thus: "who with architects and ten-foot measuring poles would stroll around many people's villas and gardens."[35] Six ten-feet then make a *clima,* which is [a square of] sixty feet on each side.[36] An *actus* ("driving") is so called because it is the distance 6
oxen were driven when a field was plowed at a single stretch, equivalent to 120 feet. I find there are three sorts of *actus:* the basic, squared, and doubled. The basic *actus* is four feet wide, which was the space in the fields between neighboring properties; the squared *actus* is defined as 120 feet in both directions; a double squared *actus* makes an "acre" (*iugerum*), so called because it is made of two squared *actus* yoked together, or, as the elder Pliny would have it, because that was the area that a yoked pair of oxen could plow in a day. An acre accordingly measured 240 feet in length, 120 in breadth.[37] A "furlong" measures 125 yards. A "mile" is eight furlongs, that is, a thousand yards. For the ancient Romans a "cen- 7
tury" originally comprised 100 acres; later, they kept the same name but made it 200. I think you're aware that in the military context a century is a unit of 100 soldiers; also that the man in charge of them is called a centurion and that "subcenturiated" is a term applied to soldiers of the second, not first, century, where they were stationed with a particular view to carrying out ambushes; whence the phrase *in subcenturiis* to mean someone placed in ambush. There's also the adverb "by centuries," denoting abundance and plenty and derived from the centuries which voted in the assemblies, from which they are also called "centuried assemblies."

But now that I have explained as briefly as I could the whole 8
vocabulary of linear measurement, I shall briefly expound the terms for weights too, so that your laudable study of the matter

pant. Sex autem siliquae scrupulum faciunt, a scrupo brevi perexi-
guoque lapillo denominatum, qui et obolus appellatur, quem hodie
denarium pensum dicimus; est vero quarta et vigesima unciae
pars. Supra obolum drachmam ponimus, quae ‹ex›[3] scrupulis tribus constat. Sextula autem ex quattuor fit scrupulis, sic dicta quod
sit unciae sexta pars. Hanc unicam vetustiores quandoque denarium appellavere (denarius enim tunc argenteus numus erat ponderis siliquarum quattuor et viginti, quanquam denarius proprie
decem assium pondo constet); atque haec erat apud antiquos minima aeris signati pars. Supra sextulam semunciam legimus, dimi-
9 dium unciae continentem. Uncia ab uno denominatur, quod ex
duodecim ea unica est pars assis. Unciae duae sextans, quasi sexta
pars assis. Quadrans quarta pars, hoc est tres unciae, quod etiam
triuncium dicitur. Triens tertia pars assis, unciae quattuor. Quincunx unciae quinque. Semissis dimidium assis, unciae sex. Septunx septem unciae. Bes unciae octo, quasi des, dempto triente ex
asse. Dodrans dempto quadrante, novem unciae, quod et nonuncium dicimus. Dextans decem unciae, dictus quoniam assi
deest sextans. Deunx undecim unciae, quasi una uncia ex asse
10 dempta. Inde as ex duodecim unciis constans, mna a Graecis,
mina a nostris interpositione litterae appellatur. Hanc etiam li-
bram dicimus, cuius diminutivum libella, a qua et deliberare, quia
animo tanquam libra res perpenditur, tractum est. Libellae dimidium est sembella, quae semis est assis. Supra assem dupondium
est, librae duae, a duobus ponderibus: pondus enim et pondo assis
pondere dicebatur, unde assipondium unum pondus est appella-
tum. Ultra dupondium est sestertius, librae duae et semis, dictus
quasi semistertius, hoc est post duos sequens tertio loco semis:
quia enim fiebat ex duobus assibus et tertio semisse veteres nuncu-

may be complete. The smallest unit of weight is the *siliqua,* which
is a grain of the carob-tree fruit, called by most people the Greek
bean. Six *siliquae* make a scruple (so called from *scrupus,* a tiny and
minute stone), also known as an obol, which today we call a penny
weight; it is actually the twenty-fourth part of an ounce. Beyond
the obol we have the drachma, consisting of three scruples. Then
the *sextula,* made up of four scruples, so called because it is a sixth
of an ounce. The ancients sometimes called a single *sextula* a denarius (a denarius was then a silver coin weighing twenty-four *siliqua,* though properly speaking it consisted of ten asses by weight);
and this *sextula* was in antiquity the smallest unit of the bronze
coinage. Above the *sextula* we read of the *semuncia,* weighing half
an ounce. Ounce (*uncia*) itself derives from "one" (*unum*), because 9
it is a single part of the twelve that make up an *as.* Two ounces
make a *sextans,* as it were a sixth part of an *as,* and a *quadrans* is a
quarter of an *as,* three ounces, also called a *triuncium.* A *triens* is a
third of an *as* or four ounces, a *quincunx* five ounces, a *semissis* half
an *as* or six ounces, a *septunx* seven ounces. *Bes* (also *des*) is eight
ounces, made by taking a *triens* from an *as.* A *dodrans* is an *as* minus a *quadrans,* i.e., nine ounces, which we also call a *nonuncium.* A
dextans is ten ounces, so called for being an *as* minus a sextans,
deunx is eleven ounces, an *as* minus an ounce. Then we have the *as* 10
consisting of twelve ounces, in Greek called a *mna,* by us in Latin
mina with an inserted letter. We also call this a pound (*libra*), with
diminutive *libella,* from which we also get *deliberare,* when a thing is
weighed in the mind as on a scale. Half a *libella* is a *sembella,* which
is half an *as.* Above the *as* is the *dupondius,* or double pound, from
duo and *pondus:* a *pondus* or *pondo* was so called from the weight of
an *as,* whence one pound is called an *assipondium.* Beyond the *dupondius* is the sesterce, two and a half pounds, as if from *semistertius,* i.e., a "half in third place" following two units; because it
was made up of two asses and half of a third, the ancients called it

11 pavere sestertium. Supra quem tressis a tribus assibus dicitur, quo vocabulo noster usus est Persius: 'hic Dama est non tressis agaso.' Octussis quoque ac nonussis decussisque reperitur: octo, novem decemque asses. Denarium vero ut decussem a decem assibus veteres interdum denominarunt. A duobus deinde decussibus fit bicessis, idest viginti asses, a tribus tricessis, triginta asses. Persius etiam centusse utitur: 'et centum Graecos curto centusse licetur.' Supra centussem maius aeris vocabulum non invenio: nam ducentos, trecentos quadringentosve cum dicimus, non magis asses quam denarios aut alios numos significamus.

12 Infra centussem autem talentum est, cuius variae speties cum pondere, tum materia extitere: nam secundum diversas gentes diversi quoque ponderis invenitur. Verum, quod celebrius est, Atticum maius et minus talentum extat: minus assibus sexaginta, maius tribus et octoginta assibus ac triente describitur, licet aliqui octoginta assium tantum fuisse scribant. Plinius maior talentum Atticum ex Varronis sententia sexdecim sestertiis taxari scribit. Sed haec satis de pondere. Materiam vero talenti variam extitisse gravissimi attestantur auctores. Nam nedum aurum, argentum, aes hoc pondere aestimari comperimus, sed quaecunque alia ponderantur. Curtius enim candidi ferri talenta centum et Herodotus aluminis mille talenta scribit.

13 Haec habui quae breviter de mensuris ac ponderibus ad te scriberem. Siqua in re alia tibi usui esse possum, omne meum studium tibi paratissimum semper erit. Vale.

a *sestertium*.[38] Beyond that, the *tressis* is named for its three *asses*, a word used by our friend Persius: "This Dama is a lackey not worth three *asses*."[39] *Octussis*, *nonussis*, and *decussis* are also found, meaning eight, nine and ten *asses*. The ancients also occasionally called a denarius a *decussis*, from the ten *asses* it was made of. From two *decusses* is then formed a *bicessis*, or twenty *asses*, and from three a *tricessis*, thirty *asses*. Persius also uses *centussis* in "and he offers a clipped hundred-*as* coin for a hundred Greeks."[40] Above the *centussis* I find no word for higher denominations in bronze, for when we speak of two hundreds, three hundreds, or four hundreds, we do not mean *asses* but the silver denarius or some other coinage. 11

Lower than *centussis*, on the other hand, is the talent, of which there are various forms, both in weight and material. It appears that it had different weights among different nations, but the best known is the Attic talent, large and small. The small was equivalent to sixty *asses*, the large to eighty-three *asses* plus a *triens*, though some writers say it was only equivalent to eighty. Pliny the Elder says on Varro's authority that the Attic talent was valued at sixteen sesterces.[41] But that's enough on the weight. As to the material of the talent, authoritative authors bear witness to its variousness. We find that not only gold, silver, and bronze are reckoned in talents, but any other materials that are weighed. Curtius, for example, writes of a hundred talents of white iron, Herodotus of a thousand talents of alum.[42] 12

There you have, in brief, what I have to tell on weights and measures. If I can be of use to you in any other matter, my every exertion will be at your service. Farewell. 13

: 9 :

Bartholomaeus Fontius Antonio Puccio suo s.

1 Quotiens oculos mentis verto super hoc damnato scismate, in quo veluti magno in pelago agitatur vicarii Christi navis et ei desponsa catholica apostolicaque Ecclesia, totiens ingenti metu deterreor, quod nautas[4] aliquot remigesque prospicio, magistri imperio non parentes, conari eam illidere saevos in scopulos tempestatis. At cum me converto ad caput primarium sacrosanctae Romanae Ecclesiae, Dominum nostrum Iesum Christum habentem sacerdotium pontificatumque sempiternum, totus equidem recreor pie ac fideliter credens secundarium quoque caput ad consummationem saeculi duraturum, cui ascensurus ad Patrem Filius Dei unigenitus
2 omnem potestatem ligandi atque solvendi attribuit. Hunc tamen clavum Christianae navis et unitatem Ecclesiae moderantem aequalemque Deo in terris potestatem habentem, pro dolor!, hoc insano calamitosoque saeculo deseruere non nulli, viribus atque armis saecularium principum freti, navigio eum detrudere cogitantes ac propterea ad futurum concilium appellantes. Unde iam qui a vero catholicoque Pontifice defecerunt quique se illis temere adiunxerunt censurae ecclesiasticae gladio, iure divino atque humano districti sunt et ipsi apostatae, ab unitate Ecclesiae segregati, qualiacunque tela in eum coniiciunt 'concilium! concilium!' clamitantes.

3 Equidem sanctorum de more patrum celebrari concilium a vero Pontifice, totius Ecclesiae uno et solo capite, magna praelatorum et cleri frequentia, licere et expedire et maxime decere non solum confiteor, sed opto etiam vehementissime ad consultandum de statu, de vita, de moribus ecclesiasticorum et saecularium princi-

: 9 :

Bartolomeo Fonzio to his friend Antonio Pucci, greetings.[43]

Whenever I cast my mind's eye over this damnable schism, in 1
which the ship of the Vicar of Christ and his Spouse, the Catholic and Apostolic Church, are battered as if on the high sea, I shrink back in terror, for I see some of the sailors and oarsmen, no longer obedient to their master's direction, trying to smash it onto dreadful rocks in the storm. But when I turn my gaze to the supreme head of the Holy Roman Church, our Lord Jesus Christ, with his eternal priesthood and pontificate, I find myself absolutely comforted, in the pious and trusting belief that the second head too, to whom the only-begotten Son of God gave full power of binding and loosing as he was about to ascend to the Father, will endure to
the end of the world. And yet, alas!, some in this crazy and ca- 2
lamitous time have abandoned him who holds the tiller of the ship of Christianity and governs the unity of the Church, the one that has powers on earth equal to God. They rely on the might and arms of secular princes with a view to casting him out of the vessel, and to that end appeal to a future Council of the Church. For which those who have now defected from the true and catholic pope, and those who have rashly gone to join them, have been struck by the sword of ecclesiastical censure, by human and divine law, and the apostates themselves, separated from the unity of the Church, have launched any weapons they could against him, shouting "a Council! a Council!"[44]

Yet I for my part not only confess that to have a Council cele- 3
brated after the custom of the holy fathers by a true pope as the one and only head of the whole Church, with a great concourse of prelates and clergy, is lawful, desirable and entirely proper, but I also earnestly wish for it, so as to deliberate on the condition, way

pum et ad regendos moderandosque iuste populos et ad corruptos perversosque mores corrigendos, ut optata cunctis mortalibus pace omnis Christianitas perfruatur. Nam si non verba sed opera monente Domino inspexerimus, multa apud clericos, non pauciora apud laicos cernemus grave olentia ulcera et ad interitum tabida
4 corpora, nisi medela adhibeatur, ducentia. Medicina autem, nisi prius fuerit morbi causa intellecta, ad sanitatem non exhibetur apposite. Causam vero cognoscere aegritudinis et pro loci, aeris, temporis qualitate, pro corporis habitu, complexione, victus consuetudine mederi paucorum est prudentium medicorum. In his qui sunt eminentissimi asserunt destillantem a capite pituitam reliquum corpus inficere variosque morbos et mortem gignere. Gentes et nationes et populi unum sunt corpus totius humani generis; capita gentium sunt ecclesiastici saecularesque principes. Hi morbis gravissimis, ambitione, libidine, avaritia, ira, odio, invidia
5 laborantes exemplo suo genus humanum inficiunt. Siquidem, ut a nobis incipiam, si minores dignitate sacerdotes capita nostra episcopos haberemus non quae sua sunt, sed quae Dei et Ecclesiae cogitantes suasque dioceses annis singulis visitantes et cunctas parochias corrigentes, non obrueremur tot ac tantis ignorantiae tenebris et vitiorum gurgitibus. Si episcopi superiores cardinales inspicerent modestius viventes et quae clericali statui conveniunt observantes, ipsi quoque continentius viverent. Si cardinales intuerentur summum Pontificem non quae ad pompam et luxum et vanitatem, sed quae ad aeternam salutem pertinent meditantem,
6 non tam praecipites in vitia laberentur. Imperatores autem ac reges et caeteri saeculi principes si suis contenti finibus alienos non occuparent, si subditos iniquis honeribus non urgerent, si a divina, si a naturali, si a communi hominum lege non deviarent, si iuste

of life and morals of the princes of Church and state, and to govern and regulate the populace in a fair manner and correct corrupt and perverse morals, so that the whole of Christendom may enjoy in full the peace all men long for. For if under God's admonishment we weigh not words but deeds, we see among the clergy many stinking sores, and no fewer among the laity, and putrefying
bodies that will lead to death if no remedy is applied. But medi- 4
cine is not seen to be effective in curing disease unless its cause is first understood. Knowing the cause of the illness, and healing it in the light of the nature of the place, the air, the time, the physical condition, complexion, and way of life—all this is a gift of a few expert doctors. Those most eminent in these matters assert that it is the phlegm dripping down from the head that infects the rest of the body and causes the various diseases and death. Tribes and nations and peoples are the single body of all mankind. The heads of these peoples are the ecclesiastical and secular princes. If they suffer from the terrible diseases of ambition, lust, greed, anger, hatred, envy, they infect by their example the whole human
race. If (to begin with our own case) we priests of lesser rank had 5
as our heads bishops who thought not of their own interests but of those of God and the Church, and visited their dioceses every year and reformed their parishes, we should not be overwhelmed by such dense clouds of ignorance and whirlpools of vice. If the bishops could see their superiors, the cardinals, living more modest lives and attending to what behooves their clerical state, they themselves would live with more restraint. If the cardinals could look on a pope contemplating, not what conduces to pomp and luxury and vanity, but to eternal salvation, they would not fall so
headlong into vice. And if, on the other hand, emperors, kings, 6
and the other secular princes would stay content with their own lands and not invade those of others, if they would not oppress their subjects with unjust burdens, if they would not turn aside from divine or natural or common human law, if they would lead

continenterque viverent, caeteri mortales suorum principum mores prosecuti aequo iure omnes pacifice degerent totque ac tantis vitiorum morbis non deperirent.

7 Videre per te iam potes, Antoni carissime, quo te, iuvenem nostrae urbis omnium disertissimum, senex ego forsan non indisertus, ut ipse tibi magis quam mihi videor, scribendo perduxerim: ad meam sententiam audiendam. Siquidem ad haec hominum temporumque supra narrata vitia exigenda et mores optimos imbuendos et virtutes ac scientias honestandas et civiliter libereque vivendum si concilium apostatae acclamarent, non, ut clarius luce patet, ad explenda odia, ad iniurias ulciscendas, ad maiores opes comparandas, ingentes Deo gratias agerem et ad concilium appellantes
8 non improbarem. Sed tam honesta, tam utilis, tam necessaria synodus cum indigeat tuto loco, tempore oportuno, maturo consilio, commoditatibus multis tam saecularium quam spiritualium principum, gratia, invidia, ira, odio, spe, metu pessimis consultoribus reiectis ac fraterna dilectione, iustitia, pace, fide concordiaque receptis consultoribus optimis, cumque omnia longe absint, perperam de concilio agitur, bello et armis undique circumstrepentibus.

9 Quod si me forte roges quid agendum existimem, ne serpat in tempus longius ac multas gentes populosque inficiat tanti morbi contagio, quo me filo, si Daedaleum labyrinthum ingredior, explicem non invenio. Hoc tamen in mea insipientia libere ac simpliciter tecum loquor. Ante omnia utrique humiliter convertamur ad Dominum oremusque supplicibus votis pro summo Pontifice nostro Iulio et unitate Ecclesiae, ut adsit propitius et benignus et in tanta peccatorum colluvie tamque obstinatis multorum animis ad nefanda flagitia avertat iustam iram suam ab hoc nostro ingrato

just and temperate lives, other mortals would adopt their leaders' morals; they would all live peaceably under a uniform justice and would not be undone by the vast and terrible maladies of vice.

You can see for yourself, dear Antonio, where I, an old man 7
perhaps not entirely devoid of eloquence (this is your view rather than mine), have led you—the most skilful speaker of all the young men in our city—with this dissertation: to pay attention to my feelings on the matter. If those apostates who are clamoring for a Council were doing so with a view to driving out the vices of mankind and our age just mentioned, inculcating good morals, honoring virtues and learning, living life in civility and freedom, and not rather, as is clearer than daylight, with the aim of giving vent to hatred, avenging injuries, and accumulating greater wealth, I should give God great thanks and not criticize those appealing to
a Council. But such an honorable, useful, and necessary meeting 8
would require a safe place to meet, a suitable time, mature deliberation, much goodwill on the part of princes both secular and spiritual, the rejection of those worst of all counselors: favoritism, envy, anger, hatred, vain expectation, and fear, and the acceptance of those excellent counselors, brotherly love, justice, peace, good faith, and concord; and since all those requirements are a long way from being met, it is wrong to discuss a Council when we are surrounded by the clamor of war and arms on all sides.

But if you were to ask me what I think should be done to stop 9
the contagion of this dreadful disease from spreading ever further over time and infecting many nations and peoples, I do not find the thread to extricate myself once I've entered this labyrinth of Daedalus. In my ignorance, however, I'll tell you this freely and frankly. Before anything else, let us both turn in humility to the Lord and with humble entreaty pray for our Pope Julius and for the unity of the Church, that God may look kindly and propitiously on us, and that amid such mire of sin and with many souls so intent on dreadful crimes, he may avert his just anger from

populo, libertati ecclesiasticae derogantì, et insanabiles desperatos-
que morbos nostros solus et verus et misericors medicus sapientis-
10 simusque magister ad sanitatem perducat. Praeterea, si parvos homines licet aequare magnis, ego minimus omnium si is essem qui
nunc est maximus Pontifex, votis rite nuncupatis ad Patrem Deum,
lustrata Urbe cum toto Romano clero missaque solemniter decan-
tata, ad reges ac principes Ecclesiae reconciliandos intenderem cumque paucis bonis et sanctis et prudentibus viris et ad animarum
salutem tendentibus consultarem de pacis honestae conditionibus.
Cum quibus in domo Domini ambulantibus et ea quae ad pacem
Hierusalem pertinent consulentibus, remotis adulatoribus cuncta
ad gratiam nihil ad veritatem loquentibus, spem certam concipe-
rem Dominum Iesum Christum, Deum pacis et dilectionis, in
medio semper eorum positum qui essent, ut ipse dixit, in suo nomine congregati, tutum ac salutare consilium vicario suo et spon-
11 sae suae Ecclesiae allaturum. Neque vero putarem Aloisium, Gallorum regem, a suis degeneraturum maioribus, qui Christianissimi
nuncupati nunquam scismaticis adhaesere, sed eiectos veros Pon-
tifices Leonem, Zachariam, Stephanum, Calistum, Innocentium,
Alexandrum, Pascalem Romanae sedi restituere. Neque etiam cre-
derem Christianissimum Regem gratis contra Ecclesiam Dei armis
decernere, sed metu cogente status Italici conservandi; quod si
Christi vicarium intelligeret communem optare pacem saeculo et
Ecclesiae, et ipse quae sunt Dei restitueret Deo, Bononia Ferraria-
que cedentibus et cervicem et genua inclinantibus.

12 Accepisti de re tota meum consilium. Specta nunc, si placet,
novam tragaediam. Ageretur si fabula in theatro sederentque in
dextris orchestrae gradibus cardinales et Pontifex, in sinistris Aloisius rex cum gallis baronibus prodirentque in scaenam actu primo

these ungrateful people of ours that infringe the liberty of the Church; and that as the one true and merciful healer and wisest master he brings our incurable ailments, now despaired of, back to health. And further, if one may set small men on the level of great 10
ones, if I, least of all men, were now the present pope, I should have dutiful prayers addressed to God the Father, a procession of the entire Roman clergy around the city of Rome, a solemn mass sung, and then press for the reconciliation of kings and princes with the Church. With a few good, devout, sagacious men, and ones intent on the salvation of souls, I should deliberate on the conditions of an honorable peace. Together with those who walk in the house of the Lord and take thought for the peace of Jerusalem, and after banishing those flatterers whose every utterance is aimed at gaining favor and not at truth, I should conceive a sure and certain hope that our Lord Jesus Christ, God of peace and love, ever present, as he said Himself, in the midst of those who are assembled in His name, will bring safe and salutary counsel to His Vicar and His Spouse, the Church. Nor indeed would I sup- 11
pose that Louis, the king of France, will fall short of his ancestors, who were hailed as "Most Christian Kings" and have never sided with schismatics, but actually restored to their seat at Rome those true popes who had been deposed, Leo, Zacharias, Stephen, Callistus, Innocent, Alexander, Paschal.[45] Nor would I believe either that the Most Christian King would gratuitously take arms against the Church of God, but only under the impress of fear, for the preservation of the political situation of Italy. If he realized that the Vicar of Christ wanted peace for Church and state alike, he too would render unto God what belongs to God, and Bologna and Ferrara would yield and bend neck and knee before the pope.

Here you have my advice on the entire matter. But now, if you 12
please, contemplate a new tragedy. Suppose the play takes place in the theater and on the right steps of the orchestra sit the cardinals and pope, on the left King Louis with the French nobility. In the

personati apostatae iacientes convicia in Pontificem, secundo in
actu personati theologi severe damnantes apostatas Regemque
fideliter admonentes, actu tertio e velario in scaenam egrederetur
honesto matronae pudicissimae habitu sancta Ecclesia tristi facie,
passis crinibus, palmis ad aethera versis, voce acuta, modis flebili-
13 bus eiulans: 'o caelum, o terra, o mare, o superi! Ego patriarcha-
rum prophetarumque vocibus figurata mater fidelium, ego imma-
culati Agni desponsa sanguine, ego cruore martyrum, floribus
confessorum, liliis virginum decorata, ego imperatorum ac regum
devotione ditata maximis premor a filiis meis angustiis. Quis me
praeterea consolabitur miseram? Quis medebitur meo crudeli vulneri? Pro me tuenda certabant olim boni Christiani principes, pro
me ornanda bella gerebant gentes et nationes. Nunc me reges armis infesti premunt, nunc me populi iniquis honeribus opprimunt.
Quis igitur dabit aquam capiti meo et oculis meis fontem lachri-
marum?'

14 Si, inquam, talis ageretur tragaedia atque ita flebiliter lamenta-
retur Ecclesia, non ne prodiret in scaenam actu quarto, pro sponsa
Dei, insignis prudentia sanctitateque vitae senex totis commotis
ad pietatem visceribus dicens: 'quid matri vestrae respondetis,
apostatae? An brevi interituri mortales homines Deo militantem
Ecclesiam ad consummationem saeculi duraturam audetis superbe
scindere atque Ossam Pindo more Gigantum superaddentes in
caelum scandere, post paulo caelesti fulmine intra caeca Luciferi
Tartara, nisi vos tanti sceleris vere paeniteat, detrudendi? Sed et
vos alios saeculares Christianos principes furor ne mentis an ira
Dei ad tantam impellit insaniam, ut ferrum in matris viscera
convertatis et plures annos hostiliter devastatam Italiam funditus
15 evertatis? Ingens profecto furor, superbia et avaritia et crudelis

first act those playing the part of schismatics come onto the stage, hurling abuse at the pope; in the second those playing the theologians severely condemn the schismatics and give the king some loyal advice; in the third, from behind a screen Holy Church, in the decorous dress of a modest matron, comes out onto the stage, sad of face, her hair loosed, palms turned upwards to the sky, wail-
ing in a sharp voice and tearful tones, "O heaven, o earth, o sea, o 13
gods above! The mother of the faithful prefigured by the patriarchs and prophets, the spouse betrothed by the blood of the Immaculate Lamb, adorned by the gore of martyrs, the flowers of confessors, the lilies of virgins, I that have been enriched by the devotion of kings and emperors am now most bitterly oppressed at the hands of my sons. Who will console me in my wretchedness? Who will heal my cruel wound? Good Christian princes once competed to protect me, to embellish me peoples and nations went to war. Now hostile kings harass me with arms, now peoples oppress me with unjust burdens. Oh that my head were waters, and mine eyes a fountain of tears!"[46]

If, I say, such a tragedy were being shown and the Church were 14
making these tearful lamentations, should we not have entering the stage on the Bride of Christ's behalf an old man notable for wisdom and sanctity of life, his heart all moved to pity, with these words: "What reply do you make, apostates, to your mother? Or do you, as mortal men soon set to die, dare in your pride to tear apart the Church fighting for God, which will endure till the end of the world? Do you dare like giants to pile Ossa on Pindus and scale the heights of heaven, though shortly destined to be cast down into the blind depths of Tartarus by a divine thunderbolt, unless you truly repent of your terrible crime? And you other secular princes of Christendom, is it mental derangement or God's anger that drives you to such a pitch of madness that you turn your sword on your mother's vitals and bring the Italy that you
have for many years devastated as an enemy to utter ruin? Surely 15

immanitas clericos laicosque exagitat et iusta ira Dei contra vos terram iudicantes et iustitiam non servantes. Te vero ante alios omnis decet, o summe Pontifex, pastor ac rector Christianorum fidelium et navis Ecclesiae moderator, tot undique saevientibus fluctibus tempestati cedere ac, si quo caepisti cursu quo constitueras pervenire nequiveris, mutata velificatione eum portum ingredi quem potueris. Tutissimus autem et honestissimus portus erit, amplustriis armamentisque navis abiectis, tempestati non te amplius credere, odia etiam iusta in adversarios ponere, oblivisci acceptarum iniuriarum, libenter[5] ignoscere paenitentibus, metum adimere omnibus, datam servare fidem cunctis potentibus.

16 'Tu quoque, Aloisi rex Christianissime, quid optas addi tibi ulterius in tanta Felicitate ac victoriis? Tua est longo maiorum stemmate tota trans Alpis Gallia. Tua quoque cis Alpis bello et armis parta est tota Gallia. Tua facta est Genua assuetaque malo tota Liguria. Tua est superbis devictis Venetis ingens gloria. Fines tibi, quocunque progrediare, habendi sunt. Hi quanto latius extendentur quantoque tuum imperium fuerit auctius, tanto tibi plures infestiores hostes paraveris et maioribus curis solicitudinibusque ur-
17 geberis. Fortuna quidem ipsa, virtute tua et magnitudine animi tibi multum propitia, quia instabilis et levis est multum tibi quoque timenda est. Quare iam debes victricia tua lilia non Marti Bellonaeque, sed Christo ac matri beatissimae Virgini sacra suspendere. Qui sicut pro salute humani generis ligno crucis affixus pacem suam reliquit omnibus gentibus, sic tu divino exemplo admonitus pacem tuam relinque Ecclesiae atque Italiae.'

it is vast fury, and pride, and avarice, and cruel inhumanity that lashes the clergy and laity, and just is the anger of God against you who sit in judgment on the earth and do not follow justice. Amid such a raging flood, it behooves you above all, supreme pontiff, shepherd and guide of the Christian faithful and governor of the ship of the Church, to yield to the storm, and if you cannot reach your desired goal on the course you started on, to change sail and enter the harbor that you can. The most secure and honorable port, once you have rid yourself of the ship's ornaments and gear, will lie in not entrusting yourself to the storm any longer, in setting aside hatred toward your opponents, even though justified, forgetting the injuries you have received, gladly forgiving the repentant, removing the causes of everyone's fear, keeping the promises given to all the powerful.

"Louis, most Christian king, in all your great success and victo- 16
ries, what do you wish to acquire further? All Gaul beyond the Alps is yours by long descent from your ancestors. Yours too is Gaul this side of the Alps, won by arms and warfare. Genoa has been made yours and all Liguria, accustomed now to misfortune. Your great glory is to have conquered the haughty Venetians.[47] Your borders are reckoned to be wherever you advance. But the further these extend and the larger your realm becomes, the more determined will be the enemies you find and the greater the cares
and worries that will oppress you. Fortune herself, though very 17
favorable toward you for your prowess and magnanimity, you must also greatly fear as unstable and fickle. For that reason you must dedicate your lilies of victory not to Mars or Bellona but to Christ and his blessed virgin mother. Just as He was nailed to the wood of the cross for the salvation of humankind and so bequeathed His peace to every race, so you must heed the divine example, and bequeath your peace to Italy and the Church."

18 Ad haec Sathan excitus ab inferis quinto explendo actu ignitis oculis, vultu torvo, ore ignivomo, intortis collo sibilantibus viperis, 'quid' inquit 'delire senex, addictos mihi deterres apostatas? Quid mihi pergratos lacessis principes? Quid ita pusillanimiter hortaris admonesque Pontificem? Quid bello tentas turpiter avertere regem Galliae? Quid tu quoque semper adversa mihi lamentaris Ecclesia? An regnum frustra meum conaris scindere? Fortius est ac vali-
19 dius cunctis humanis viribus. Mea sunt vivis innavigabilia Stygia. Mea inaccessibilia sunt Averna. Mea sunt horribilia Tartara. Mihi militant plurimi vita functi, bello invicti duces et imperatores et reges cum ferocissimorum equitum turmis innumeris peditumque robustissimorum cohortibus. Quanto autem quisque vestrum, o principes, o Rex, o Pontifex, in pugnam atque in mortem ibit ferocior, tanto mihi occumbens pugnando carior et in regno meo erit sublimior.

Quare agite, intrepidi ferro decernite, signa
signis, arma armis, pectora pectoribus
conferte.

Spectator ipse fortitudinis vestrae, rex inferorum Sathan, adero et quenque vestrum pro meritis honorabo.'

Peracta est fabula, Antoni. Vale.

Florentiae, Idibus Decembribus MDXI.

At this, to complete the fifth act, Satan rose from the underworld and with eyes aflame, grim of face, mouth vomiting fire, hissing vipers wrapped around his neck, saying: "Why, crazed old man, do you frighten off the apostates devoted to me? Why attack the princes I love so well? Why do you give such weak-minded counsel and advice to the pope? Why do you try shamefully to divert the king of France from war? And you too, the Church ever hostile to me, why do you lament? Are you trying in vain to tear down my kingdom? It is stronger and mightier than any human 18
powers. Mine are the waters of Styx that the living cannot sail. 19
Mine is inaccessible Avernus, mine horrible Tartarus. Fighting for me are legions of the dead, commanders and generals and kings unconquered in battle, with their squads of ferocious horsemen and cohorts of stoutest infantry. The more fiercely every one of you, princes, kings, and pope, drives into battle and death, the sweeter will his annihilation in combat be to me, and the higher his rank shall be in my realm.

> Wherefore advance, fearlessly fight with steel, standard
> against standard, arms against arms, breast against breast
> clash.[48]

The onlooker of your bravery, I myself, Satan the king of the underworld, shall be with you and shall honor each of you according to your merits."

The play is done, Antonio. Farewell.

Florence, December 13, 1511.

: 10 :

Bartholomaeus Fontius Thomae Soderino Ianvictorii filio

1 Laetor, mi Thoma, te consulere valitudini corporis vivereque honesto in ocio nunc venando, nunc legendo aliquid vel scribendo. Quod ita esse perspexi cum ex iocundissimis tuis litteris, tum ex capreolo ac lepore ad me missis. Quos equidem istic tecum cepisse mallem et caenitasse non sine multis suavissimis optatissimisque colloquiis; verum ingentia frigora et altae nives meum tibi promissum adventum distulerunt in anni tempus mitius ac benignius.
2 Quare, vere prope iam appetente, vel in isto Signano vel in nostro Mensulano agro vacui solicitudinibus et molestiis conferendo, disceptando, legendo et discentis fungemur munere et docentis. Interea nostri memor intende firmitati corporis et animi atque vitae integritati, Phaebo ac dulcisonis Musis ut decet quotidie salutatis. Vale.

Florentiae, VIII Cal. Februarias MDXI.

: 11 :

Bartholomaeus Fontius Laurentio Puccio Iulii secundi Pont. max. datario

1 Sixtus quartus Pontifex maximus Petrophilippo Pandolphino, viro clarissimo, patronatum concessit plebis Sancti Ioannis Baptistae de Montemurlo, Pistoriensis diocesis. A quo ego vigesimo ab hoc

: 10 :

Bartolomeo Fonzio to Tommaso Soderini, son of Giovan Vittorio[49]

I'm happy, dear Tommaso, that you're taking care of your health and that you're leading a life of respectable ease, now engaged in the chase, now in some reading or writing. This I've learned from your delightful letter and from the roebuck and hare you sent me. I only wish I could have caught them with you and dined on them amid agreeable and much longed-for conversation; but the deep frosts and heavy snowfall have put off the visit to you that I promised until some milder and more welcoming season of the year. 1
And so, with spring now approaching, free of cares and disturbance, we'll play the roles of master and pupil in talk, discussion and reading, either at your villa in Signa or at mine at Mensola.[50] In the meantime, think of me and pay close attention to your bodily and spiritual health, and to pure living, paying your respects every day, as you should, to Apollo and the sweet-sounding Muses. Farewell. 2

Florence, January 25, 1512.

: 11 :

Bartolomeo Fonzio to Lorenzo Pucci, Datary of Pope Julius II[51]

Pope Sixtus IV gave the nobleman Pierfilippo Pandolfini the patronage of the parish of S. Giovanni Battista di Montemurlo in the diocese of Pistoia. He chose me as parish priest twenty years 1

vertente anno in plebanum electus et canonice a Pistoriensi episcopo confirmatus exopto, mortalitatis memor beneficiique accepti non immemor, resignare praedictam plebem Petriphilippi nepoti Ioanni Pandolphino, Francisci filio, reservato mihi regimine et proventibus aureos numos quadraginta non excedentibus, ut ea per me redeat ad patronum legitimum nullaque spetialis expectativa me defuncto praeveniat.

2 Est autem Franciscus, Petriphilippi filius, excellentis ingenii atque animi dotibus insignitus et optimis ac suavissimis moribus praeditus et eleganti eruditione nostro studio et diligentia perpolitus et magnarum variarumque rerum experientia et consilio civium nostrorum omnium nulli secundus. Quare decens et aequum est concedere hoc muneris eius filio, egregiae indolis puero sponte ad sacerdotium animato, tametsi annum degit aetatis circiter decimum. Quod si propter aetatem adeo teneram reverendae Dominationis tuae modestia putabit operae pretium ut Franciscus Victorius, Florentinorum legatus, vel privato vel publico nomine id supplicet a beatissimo Papa Iulio, supplicabit amanter et diligenter.

3 Nos vero non dubitamus gratiosissimum beneficentissimumque Pontificem quod suppliciter petimus concessurum et pro felici memoria beatissimi Sixti patrui et pro perpetua in eum observantia Petriphilippi et pro magna expectatione ac gratia Francisci filii, tota mente animoque affecti erga Romanam Ecclesiam et Pontificem. Quibus addo etiam memet ipsum, in dubiis ac periculosis temporibus et voce et scriptis acerrimum defensorem pontificiae magnitudinis et ecclesiasticae potestatis. Caeterum Dominatio tua reverendissima hoc sacerdotio expedito non me tantum (semper enim Pucciae gentilitati addictus fui), sed etiam Franciscum Pandolphinum tibi ac tuis in omnem eventum devinxeris. Vale.

Florentiae, IIII Cal. Febr. 1513.

ago now, in which post I was duly confirmed by the bishop of Pistoia.[52] I wish now to resign the said office to Giovanni Pandolfini, grandson of Pierfilippo and son of Francesco, reserving for myself an income not exceeding forty gold florins per annum, so that it may return to its legitimate patron through me and that when I die no personal expectative may forestall him in it.

Pierfilippo's son Francesco is notable for his great intellectual and moral gifts: he is endowed with an excellent and affable character, highly polished in elegant learning under my careful teaching, and second to none of our citizens in his counsel and experience on a range of great matters. It is therefore fair and fitting to grant this office to his son, a boy of outstanding character and inclined toward the priesthood of his own volition, though he is only some ten years old. If on account of his tender years your Reverence in your modesty thinks it worth while for Francesco Vettori, the Florentine ambassador, to supplicate Pope Julius for this benefice, in public or in private, he will make supplication in a loyal and diligent fashion.[53] 2

We for our part do not doubt that the most gracious and beneficent pope will grant what we humbly seek, both on account of the happy memory of his uncle, the blessed Sixtus, and of the constant reverence that Pierfilippo has shown him and the great expectations and favorable impression that have been formed of his son Francesco, who is dedicated heart and soul to the Church of Rome and the pontiff. To which I may add myself, in doubtful and dangerous times a fierce defender in speech and writing of papal majesty and ecclesiastical power. By arranging this benefice your reverend Lordship will secure the devotion to you and yours in every eventuality not just of me (for I have ever been a supporter of the Pucci), but of Francesco Pandolfini too. Farewell. 3

Florence, January 29, 1513.[54]

: 12 :

Bartholomaeus Fontius Bernardo Oricellario s.

1 Dantes Populeschus tuo nomine ad me pertulit sermonem cum Pontano Neapoli habitum, quem maxime sequereris auctorem in historia Gallica describenda. Cui ego eruditissimo viro, quem loquentem inducis, non invenio quid possim demere aut addere. Quid enim, ut Lucretii verbis utar, contendat hirundo cygnis? Aut quid tremulis facere artubus haedi consimile in cursu possint ac fortis equi vis? Quoniam tamen neque volo neque debeo negare quicquam Danti perhumaniter ita pro te petenti, paucis referam non quid alii de scribendo imitandove senserint, sed quid ego adolescens a magistro perceperim.

2 Cum audirem Bernardum Nuthium Ciceronis rhetoricos libros interpretantem cum Horatianis *Epistolis* adverteremque eum dicendo ac scribendo non excellere, caepi mecum cogitare frustra ne me caeterosque condiscipulos hortaretur veteres imitari auctores et rhetoricam artem mandare memoriae, quando ipse, qui omnem aetatem in praeceptis huiusmodi et imitatione consumpserat, parum ex arte loqueretur et scriberet aliorumque dicta nimis aperte
3 suis insereret. Itaque in his carminibus explicandis,

o imitatores, servum pecus, ut mihi saepe
bilem, saepe iocum vestri movere tumultus!
Libera per vacuum posui vestigia princeps,
non aliena meo pressi pede. Qui sibi fidit,
dux regit examen,

: 12 :

Bartolomeo Fonzio to Bernardo Rucellai, greetings.

Dante Popoleschi has brought me in your name the account of the discussion held at Naples with Pontano, whom you should take as your model in writing the French history.[55] I can find nothing to add to or take away from that very erudite man you introduce as a speaker. Why, to use the words of Lucretius, should a swallow vie with swans? Or what could a kid with its shaking limbs do in running to match the vigor of a strong horse?[56] Yet since I should not deny anything to Dante when he so kindly puts this request on your behalf, and certainly have no wish to do so, I'll tell you briefly not what others think on the subject of writing and imitation, but what I myself learned from my teacher in my youth. 1

When I used to hear Bernardo Nuti's lectures on the rhetorical books of Cicero,[57] as well as on the *Epistles* of Horace, and noticed that he was not himself specially good at speaking and writing, I began to wonder whether there was any point in his encouraging me and my fellow pupils to imitate the ancient authors and commit the art of rhetoric to memory, given that he himself had spent all his life learning rules of this sort and in imitation, and yet his speech and writing was scarcely artful, and his insertion of what 2
others had said in his own works altogether too obvious. And so 3
when he came to comment on these verses:

Imitators, you servile flock, how often your antics
have made me wild with rage, how often you've made me
  laugh!
My own boss, I trod freely over virgin territory,
not following in anyone's footsteps. If you trust yourself,
you'll rule over the herd and lead them,[58]

cum ostendisset imitatorem ad alienum praescriptum ut servum vivere, statim dimisso ludo cum in pomerium venissemus, ubi fere quotidie vel solus deambulare vel me uno tantum comite consueverat, 'das ne mihi' inquam 'praeceptor humanissime, veniam ut solito liberius tecum loquar?'; 'age' inquit 'ex animo dic quod sen-
4 tis.' Tunc ego: 'te monente atque hortante rhetoricis incumbo praeceptionibus et eos auctores imitor, quorum te esse aemulum ostendisti. Verum enimvero memoriter multa artis praecepta continens multosque selectos meliorum scriptorum locos, cum aliquid elegantius dicere aut scribere mediter, intentus dicendo aut scribendo praeceptorum[6] omnium obliviscor; quorum si tunc reminisci voluero, illa etiam quae natura duce ultro se offerebant simul dila-
5 buntur et effluunt. Quod autem in me discente experior, in te quoque docente animadverto, qui demonstrandae imitationis et artis omnium, quos adhuc audierim, scientissimus parum, ni forte fallor, ex arte loqueris et, imitari veteres in scribendo cum niteris, Celso illi videris persimilis, quem damnasti hos versus Horatianos interpretans:

quid mihi Celsus agit? monitus multumque monendus,
privatas ut quaerat opes et tangere vitet
scripta Palatinus quaecunque recepit Apollo,
ne, si forte suas repetitum venerit olim
grex avium plumas, moveat cornicula risum
furtivis nudata coloribus.

Quibus carminibus congruenti fabella cornicis admonemur[7] aliena scripta nobis non vendicare ne, si unusquisque sua repetat, nihil venustatis et ornamenti remaneat.'

6 Tunc ille arridens ait: 'delector equidem tuo ferventi ingenio, cui adhaerebit, ut video, facilius eloquentia legendo et audiendo atque

he made the point that the imitator lives like a slave at the bidding of others. As soon as school had finished, when we had come to the edge of town where he habitually took a walk nearly every day, by himself or with just me for company, I said to him, "Would you mind if I spoke with you rather more openly than usual, dear teacher?" "Go ahead," he said, "say what's on your mind." Then I 4
said, "On your advice and encouragement I devote myself to the precepts of rhetoric and I imitate the authors you have said you wish to emulate. But at the same time, though I have many of the rules of the art and chosen passages of the best authors by heart, when I'm trying to say or write something with a more elegant turn of phrase, in my concentration on speaking or writing I completely forget all the rules. If I then make the effort to remember them, the matter which came to me spontaneously and naturally slips away and disappears. And what I experience as a learner I 5
notice happens with you too as a teacher: though you are the most knowledgeable of any teacher I've yet had for exposition of imitation and rhetoric, unless I'm mistaken, your speech hardly conforms to their rules. When you're trying to imitate the ancients in your writing, you seem very like the Celsus that you condemned in explicating these verses of Horace:[59]

> What is Celsus up to? He needs constant reminding
> to look for resources within himself, and to keep his hands off
> the writings received by Apollo in the Palatine temple;
> or else, when the flock of birds return to claim their plumage,
> the poor little crow will be stripped of the colors he stole
> and exposed to laughter.

In these lines we are warned by the apposite fable of the crow not to claim others' writings for ourselves, in case everyone reclaimed their own work and no charm or distinction remained."

At this he smiled and said: "I'm delighted by your passionate 6
intellect, which, as I see it, will pick up eloquence more easily by

scribendo, quam praecepta rhetorica consectando. Nam etsi artificium imitatioque non obest, non multum tamen ei confert cui vis illa desit praestantis ingenii, qua me dote carere cum adolescens adverterem,[8] studio, cura, labore, diligentia mirabiliter contendi artificio et imitatione naturae incommodum elevare. Itaque vere sentio esse neminem qui simul possit bene dicere aut scribere atque, hoc cum facit, dicendi vel scribendi vel imitandi praecepta cogitare: saepe enim intentus utrunque facere, sensi effugere quae
7 volebam ostendere. Ars vero ipsa cum sit notandis eloquentium dictis scriptisque adinventa, non facit ipsa eloquentes, sed contra fit ab hominibus eloquentibus; quas artis praeceptiones sive antea didicissent, sive potius nunquam attigissent, ne cogitabant quidem cum loquerentur. Sicut igitur infantes non fiunt artificio ullo fantes, sed loquentium audiendis locutionibus, sic adolescentes nulla eloquendi arte percepta, sed eloquentibus audiendis atque legendis eloquentiam assequuntur.'

8 Hic ego: 'rem igitur perquam gratissimam feceris quibus itineribus quibusve optimis recolendis auctoribus ad eam pervenire valeam si ostenderis.' Ad haec ille: 'nulla est via brevior ac facilior quam virtutis amore ut ardeas et honesto desiderio gloriae, quam eloquentes magnam dum vivunt, maximam post obitum consequuntur. Hoc si cordi tenaciter inhaerebit, per te ipsum scriptores omnis ad eloquentiam perducentis attentissime relegens tuopteque ingenio cuncta inveniens et disponens, nihil erit, mihi crede, tam arduum, tam laboriosum, tam asperum quod tibi non planum ac
9 lene fiat et periocundum in arcem eloquentiae ascendenti. Quo cum perveneris, in altum sublatus aethera, caeteris brevi perituris rebus despectis omnibus, te ipsum in primis, deinde creata omnia, postremo factorem omnium divinae mentis oculo contemplaberis.

reading, listening and writing than by following the precepts of rhetoric. For even if systematic rules and imitation don't get in the way, they can make little contribution if the force of a lively intellect is absent in the first place. When in my youth I realized that I lacked the gift, I tried to compensate for that natural disadvantage by the application of system and imitation, with an enormous outlay of energy, care, hard work and assiduousness. So I really do think that no one can speak or write well and, at the same time as doing so, be thinking of the rules of speaking or writing or imitation: I often found that while I was trying to do both, what I
wanted to get across escaped me. The system, though it was de- 7
vised by noting down the sayings and writings of the eloquent, does not in itself make men eloquent, but on the contrary, it is made by eloquent men. Whether they had earlier learned such rules or had never come across them, they never thought of them when they were speaking. Just as infants learn to speak not by any system of rules but by speaking and hearing others speak, so adolescents become eloquent not by absorbing any theory of eloquence but by listening to and reading eloquent authors."

At this point I said: "I'd be very grateful, then, if you'd tell me 8
the ways in which I might become eloquent, and what are the best authors to cultivate with a view to that end." He replied: "There's no briefer or easier way than a burning love of virtue and a noble thirst for glory, something that eloquent men win in large measure while they live, and absolutely after death. If you keep this always at the forefront of your mind, attentively rereading for yourself all the authors that may guide you to eloquence, finding out and arranging in your own mind all that they write, believe me, you will find nothing so hard, laborious or difficult that it will not become plain sailing and enjoyable as you make the ascent to the citadel of
eloquence. And when you reach it, lifted high aloft in the upper 9
air, despising all other things soon destined to perish, you will see with the eye of the divine mind in the first place yourself, then all

Quae bene perspecta singula et, quoad eius fieri poterit, intellecta
significare aliis cum volueris, frequenter ac multum cogitabis quid
deceat. Non enim semper eodem modo et ordine neque iisdem
sententiis aut verbis utendum est: nam locorum, temporum, personarum et cuiusque fortunae auctoritas, honoris gradusque ratio
10 est habenda. Quae omnia qui servaverit ac res magnas copiose,
parvas acute, mediocres temperate narraverit, in primo illo amplo
et ornato dicendi genere, cui omnia orationis ornamenta conveniunt, collocabitur. In tenui sermo purus erit, planus, dilucidus et
acutus et crebris sententiis expolitus. In mediocri aliquid erit suavius et validius ac robustius. Quisquis in horum aliquo trium
praestiterit disertus tantum habebitur. Qui vero excellet in omnibus et de quacunque re dixerit ut decebit, nec gravia minute nec
mediocria ieiune nec tenuia languide, rebus orationem semper ae-
11 qualem adhibens, merito vocabitur eloquens. Elucebunt autem in
eius dictis, ut stellae in caelo, multa insignia lumina, quando ute-
tur vel similiter incoantibus verbis vel desinentibus, quando vel
commutabit verba vel iterabit, quando sursum versus revertetur
gradatim, quando sine coniunctionibus dissolvetur, quando casus
eiusdem nominis commutabit, quando etiam semet ipsum cor-
rexerit, quando cur aliquid praetereat demonstrarit. Sed enim haec
et plura alia verborum et sententiarum insignia ultro se offerent
scribendo, audiendo, legendo exercitatis. Nam sicut in litteris ocu-
lus quid sequatur, ita prospicit animus in incisis, in membris, in
12 circuitibus. Quae structura verborum sicut iocundam numerosam-
que reddit orationem, sic verbis hiantibus et dissonanter composi-

creation, and finally the creator of all things. Having thoroughly
examined these things one by one and understood them as far as
possible, should you wish to communicate them to others, you will
have to ponder long and often as to how best to do so. It is not the
case that you always have to use the same method and order, or
the same words and sentiments. Account must be taken of place,
time, persons, and the fortunes of the individual concerned, his
prestige and social position. Someone who keeps to all this, and 10
treats important matters at length, small matters acutely, and matters of moderate interest with restraint, will find himself at home
with that prime style of composition—ample and decorous—to
which all manner of prose ornament is becoming. In the modest
style, the language should be pure, straightforward, lucid and
sharp, and have a polish imparted by frequent use of maxims. In
the middle style there'll be something sweeter, stronger, more ro-
bust. Someone that distinguishes himself in any of these three
styles will be reckoned just a good speaker. But he who excels in all
of them, and speaks fittingly on any sort of subject, not fussily
about matters of weight, or aridly about moderate matters or
slackly about minor matters, but always matching his speech to
the importance of the matter—he will rightly be hailed as eloquent. There should be a good many highlights, like stars in the 11
sky, shining forth in his discourse;[60] as when he uses words beginning or ending in the same way, or when he changes his words or
repeats them, when he proceeds slowly to a climax, when he
speaks disconnectedly, without conjunctions, when he repeats a
noun with change of case, when he actually corrects himself or
shows why he is passing over something. For these and many
other adornments of word and phrase come naturally to those
practiced in writing, listening and reading. For just as the eye ob-
serves what is coming up in a sequence of letters, so does the mind
foresee what will follow in clauses, sentences and periods. Such 12
verbal structures make speech pleasant and rhythmical, just as

tis purgatae aures vel potius audientium animi nuntiis auribus
offenduntur. Voces etenim sentiunt sentiendoque eas dimetiuntur
et breviores longioresque iudicant, delectantur moderatis, laedun-
tur immodicis. Attamen ut oratio debet astringi numeris, ita etiam
debet carere versibus, poematis evitata similitudine. Fit autem ex
verbis propriis, translatis, novis, priscis, facilitatem decoremque
afferentibus compositio lucida, suavis concinnitas, numerosa cano-
ritas.

13 'De eloquendo nimis pauca pro rei magnitudine accepisti, de
imitatione pauciora cognosce. Adiuvabit quam maxime doctum
imitatorem non oratoria solum, sed etiam historica et poetica frequens accurataque lectio cum variarum magnarumque rerum cognitione, tum perpolita et nitida et eleganti locutione. Sed primum
omnium quisque metiri debet ingenii sui vires et ad quid facilius
commodiusque praestandum natura ducitur. Hic nanque historiae
describendae, ille poemati decantando, alius perorando natus est
14 aptior. Ad quod ergo natura trahitur studiose incumbat ac quod
opus aggressus fuerit, inveniendo, disponendo ad amussim perfi-
ciat. Suscipere magni est animi, invenire summi ingenii, ornare
decentis eloquii, perficere elimati iudicii. Poeta natura, historicus
arte, orator utrisque perficitur; exercitatio communis est omnibus.
Tanta vero inter hos est in eloquendo similitudo, ut aeque in ver-
15 bis, in sententiis, in figuris, in ornamentis conveniant. Delectare
proprium est poetae, docere historici, movere ac vi trahere orato-
ris, prodesse quidem omnibus est commune. Populorum quoque

sensitive ears (or rather the minds of the audience, alerted by the ears) are repelled by disconnected words or words inharmoniously arranged. The ears hear the sounds and, as they do so, measure them, judging some too short or too long, taking pleasure in those with due measure and being offended by immoderate ones. Yet just as speech should be restrained in its rhythms, so it should not form verses, so as to avoid the appearance of poetry. Clarity of structure, pleasant melodiousness and rhythmic harmony depend on the words proper to it, words used metaphorically, new words, old words, all bringing their fluency and grace.

"There you have some thoughts on public eloquence, fewer in- 13
deed than that large subject demands; here now are fewer still on the subject of imitation. The learned imitator will be greatly helped by frequent close reading not just of oratory but of history and poetry too, with the knowledge they bring of varied and important subjects and their polished, refined and elegant style. But the first requirement is for each person to assess his own intellectual powers and discover what he is fitted by nature to produce most easily and conveniently. This man, for example, will be naturally better suited for the writing of history, that one for poetic composition, another for public speaking. Let him therefore de- 14
vote his best efforts to what he is drawn to by nature, and let him bring to perfection any piece of work that he takes on with 'invention' and 'disposition.'[61] To undertake an enterprise needs largeness of imagination; discovery is the mark of a great mind; embellishment the mark of a seemly eloquence; and bringing to completion the mark of refined taste. A poet is brought to perfection by nature, a historian by art, an orator by both together; practice is common to all three. There is in fact such similarity between their styles of eloquence that they have vocabulary, concepts, figures of speech and embellishments in common with one another. The 15
special characteristic of the poet is to delight and of the historian to instruct, of the orator to move and convince, although each of

illustrium maximorumque principum gesta et praeterita omnia nosse tempora quanquam convenit omnibus, tamen maxime proprium est historici, cuius insuper est munus regiones et loca et pugnas ornate describere, adhortationes concionesque interserere, causas, consilia, acta, dicta, eventa vere fideliterque narrare, non gratia, non odio, non spe, non metu laudare quenquam vel carpere, nusquam a vero discedere, nihil occulere, nihil mentiri ac fingere.

16 Caeterum in poetis maxime imitandus Virgilius, in oratoribus Tullius, in historicis Livius, siquidem tres hi complexi pro rerum ac personarum varietate illa tria dicendi genera decorumque in cunctis servantes, ut omnium eminentissimi, ita etiam sunt imitatione dignissimi. Proximi qui sunt his accurate legendi et in eorum virtutibus imitandi. Sed quoniam ingenii est exigui et inertis aliorum inventis acquiescere nihilque maius et splendidius addere nec eniti superare quem aemuletur atque ad palmam currenti quoniam turpe est non pertransire vel saltem adaequare celeriorem, satius ac tutius et laudabilius esse puto ingenioso scriptori sibi ipsi fidere et vestigiis alterius non insistere.'

17 De dicendo et imitando habes, Bernarde optime et animo meo carissime, Nuthianum iudicium, quod probabis si placuerit aut in Pontanico permanebis si contra senseris. Utcunque[9] sit, esse putabo verius quod tu censueris, quando te antiquis excellentibusque scriptoribus non minorem, novis longe sublimiorem quam rectissime iudico. Vale feliciter nec diutius patere eloquentiam, qua nostra civitas per multa saecula floruit, consenescere; cui nisi lan-

them aims to be in some way beneficial. Knowledge of the deeds of famous nations and great princes, and all the ages of the past, though it is appropriate to all of them, is the special province of the historian, whose further task it is to give splendid descriptions of regions, places, battles, to intersperse rallying speeches and public meetings, to narrate truly and faithfully the causes of things, the accompanying deliberations, what was said or done or happened, and to praise or criticize persons without favoritism, hatred, hope, or fear, and never to depart from the truth, to cover up
nothing, lie about nothing, make nothing up. Among the poets, 16
Vergil is chiefly to be imitated, among the orators Cicero, in history Livy, since these three embrace those three levels of writing according as the character of persons or events varied, and they preserve the proper measure in all of them. In surpassing all the rest, accordingly, they are the ones most worth imitating. Those who come closest to them are to be read with attention and their peculiar virtues imitated. But since only a weak and feeble talent is content with what others have found out, and adds nothing greater or more brilliant of his own, and does not strive to surpass those that he emulates, and since it is shameful, in running to win, not to try to overtake or at least draw level with the fastest, it is better, safer and more laudable for a talented writer to trust in himself and not tread in another's footsteps."

There, Bernardo, best and dearest of friends, you have Nuti's 17
views on public speaking and imitation. You'll approve it if that's what seems best, or you may stick with Pontano's opinion if you take the opposite line. Whichever it is, I shall think your judgment is sound, since I reckon in all justice that you are not inferior to those excellent writers of old, and far superior to modern ones. Farewell, and do not permit the eloquence which has flourished in our city for so many centuries to continue to wither away, for if in its frail state it is not attended to quickly, it will soon be at death's

guenti medeatur celeriter, ad interitum cito verget. Hoc qui te melius efficere possit non video, auctoritate et consilio praestantissimi medici.

Florentiae, Cal. Martiis 1513.

: 13 :

Bartholomaeus Fontius Petrofrancisco Medici s.

Paulus Ghiaccetus, praestantissimus civis et vobis Medicibus coniunctissimus, nunc si viveret, eius filius Robertus, Ghiacceti plebanus, commendatione mea non indigeret: nam plurimum per se posset mutua necessitudine, benivolentia, gratia a proavo Paulo, cuius ego descripsi vitam, cum Cosmo et Laurentio, Medicibus fratribus, incoata. Verum enimvero tali parente orbatum commendo tibi ut per te pateat ei aditus ad beatissimum Leonem Medicem, summis votis totius Christianitatis, divina gratia electum in optimum maximumque Pontificem; cui Robertus placere et obsequi et humiliter inservire vehementer optat, quem tibi etiam atque etiam summopere commendo. Vale feliciter nostri memor.

Florentiae, Idibus Martiis 1512.

door. I do not see that anyone could accomplish this better than you, with all the authority and judgment of an outstanding physician.

Florence, March 1, 1513.

: 13 :

Bartolomeo Fonzio to Pierfrancesco de' Medici, greetings.[62]

If Paolo da Ghiacceto, that excellent citizen and close ally of you Medici, were still alive, his son Roberto, the parish priest of Ghiacceto, would need no recommendation of mine, for in himself he would carry great weight in virtue of the reciprocal friendship, warmth and favor initiated by his ancestor Paolo (whose life I wrote)[63] with the Medici brothers, Cosimo and Lorenzo. But now that he is deprived of a father like that, I commend him to you so that through your offices he may gain access to the Holy Father, Leo de' Medici, by divine favor elected pope with the wholehearted support of all of Christendom. Roberto earnestly desires to please, obey and serve him in all humility, and I commend him to you with all my heart. Farewell and keep me in your thoughts.

Florence, March 15, 1513.

: 14 :

Bartholomaeus Fontius Iacopo Salviato s.

Pauli Ghiacceti, viri optimi tuique amantissimi ac Medicibus coniunctissimi, Robertus filius optat per te adscribi in familiaritatem[10] beatissimi Leonis decimi, humanis votis divinitus electi in Pontificem maximum. Quare per meum in te amorem, quem tuis egregiis animi, corporis fortunaeque dotibus iampridem tibi totum arripuisti, maximopere tibi eum commendo. Ipse quidem Ghiacceti plebanus est, genere, forma, ingenio, moribus non spernendus; cuius Paulus pater si viveret, nihil tam magnum peteret quod non consequeretur ab indulgentissimo felicissimoque Pontifice. Satis autem in praesens Roberto est eius Beatitudini humiliter ac fideliter inservire. Vale feliciter.

Flor., Idibus Martiis.

: 14 :

Bartolomeo Fonzio to Jacopo Salviati, greetings.[64]

Roberto, the son of Paolo da Ghiacceto, that excellent man so devoted to you and so closely allied to the Medici, wishes through your offices to be taken into the *familia* of the blessed Leo X, by human desire and divine guidance elected supreme pontiff. So I wholeheartedly commend him to you for the love I bear you, love that your outstanding gifts of mind, body and circumstance have long seized entire from me. He is the priest at Ghiacceto, in ancestry, appearance, intellect and character by no means to be despised. If his father Paolo were alive, there would be no request he could make of that most indulgent and successful pope that he would not obtain. It is for the present enough for Roberto to be able humbly to serve His Beatitude. Farewell.

Florence, March 15.

Note on the Text and Translation

The two most important witnesses to Fonzio's *Epistolarum libri* are Bologna, Biblioteca Universitaria MS 2382 (= **B**), datable to the middle of the 1490s, entirely in Fonzio's hand and containing the first redaction of the letter collection made about 1495. Four leaves of the original thirty-five have been lost, but in origin it had a total of forty-three letters without division into books: the letter of dedication to Amerigo Corsini (January 25, 1496), followed by the letters now designated 1.1–24 and 2.1–18, embracing a period from May–June 1467 to March 1494. The loss of the four pages of text involves the loss of the dedication to Corsini, epp. 2.12–15 and parts of 2.11 and 16. The other manuscript is Florence, Biblioteca Nazionale Centrale, Palatino V. Capponi 77 (= **F**), the unique witness to the entire letter collection: all the letters that were once present in B are here found entire, but with the text in a number of places revised and modified by Fonzio, and with the addition of a further seventeen missives from the end of the quattrocento to 1513. They thus amount to a total of sixty letters, here divided into three books. F was copied shortly after Fonzio's death by his friend Francesco Baroncini, who had as his direct exemplar Fonzio's original autograph as it was left on his desk; the work of transcription was finished on January 3, 1514.

There are also isolated witnesses that transmit individual letters before they entered these canonical collections: Venice, Biblioteca Marciana XII 135 (4100) (= **M**), in which ep. 1.17 is found in Fonzio's autograph as it was originally sent to Battista Guarini at the end of July 1472; two manuscripts, Oxford, Bodleian Library, Lat. misc. d. 85 (autograph, from the period 1472–89, = **O**) and Florence, Biblioteca Medicea Laurenziana, Ashburnham 1174 (end of s. XV, copied in part by Francesco Pandolfini, = **A**), contain the original version of ep. 2.7; Wolfenbüttel, Herzog August Bibliothek, 43 Aug. 2° (= **W**), the luxurious manuscript written in Fonzio's own hand for presentation to Matthias Corvinus at the beginning of 1489, contains among other things the first version of ep. 2.11 and the *Epistola de mensuris et ponderibus* in its oldest version, as sent to Francesco Sassetti: this curious tract later entered the *epistolario* in revised form as 3.8, now addressed to Francesco Ricci. Specimens of F, B, W, and O may be seen in Tavv. I–IV of the 2008 edition.

Two letters have a printed tradition outside the collections. The *editio princeps* of Giovanni Pico della Mirandola's works, published at Bologna in 1496 (*BMC* VI 843; indicated in this edition by the siglum *i*), includes 2.14 on Pico's *Heptaplus* in its original version as sent to Roberto Salviati. The *editio princeps* of Fonzio's commentary on Persius, printed at Florence in 1477 (*GW* 10170; *BMC* VI 621), also publishes the letter *de mensuris et ponderibus* in its original version addressed to Sassetti.

The present Latin text is closely based on my critical edition published in Messina in 2008, which follows Fonzio's final revision of the collection seen in F. The only conscious alterations are the capitalization of adjectives formed from proper names (*Florentinus, Quinqueecclesiensis,* etc.) and of indications of date (*Non. Martias, Idibus Octobribus,* etc.), in accordance with Anglophone convention. The orthography presented here is otherwise that established in detail in my critical edition (pp. cxii–cxxii). For a full report of the manuscripts, the interested reader is referred to that edition; here only a restricted selection of variants has been given in the Notes to the Text, largely with a view to giving a flavor of the tightening up (and tidying up) that went on as Fonzio worked to bring his *epistolario* to its final form.

The dating of the letters calls for some comment. Many of the letters (thirty-eight of the sixty) are given an explicit date, always in the Roman form with calends, nones, and ides, with the exception of 2.21, "Flor., die XX iunii 1503." The letters are generally dated in the "Florentine style," also known as the "style of the Incarnation," with the year beginning on March 25, so that January 1 to March 24 in Florentine style are dated a year behind the year now commonly observed (Jan. 1, 1480 F.S. = Jan. 1, 1481 in common style). Occasionally, however, Fonzio can be shown to have used the "Nativity style," in which the year began on December 25 (thus largely corresponding to the modern style, except for the days December 25–31, which were dated a year *in advance* of the common year). This style is found in missives from Rome, 2.4–6, and in the later letters, 3.11–12. Undated letters, common in the first book, of course have to be approximately dated from the contents, or from their position within the chronological sequence of the *epistolario*, taking as termini the closest preceding and following dated letters. Detailed justifications of these (for the most part, broad) datings are again given in my critical edition.

Sigla

A Florence, Biblioteca Medicea Laurenziana, Ashburnham 1174
B Bologna, Biblioteca Universitaria MS 2382
F Florence, Biblioteca Nazionale Centrale, Palatino V. Capponi 77
M Venice, Biblioteca Marciana XII 135 (4100)
O Oxford, Bodleian Library, Lat. misc. d. 85
W Wolfenbüttel, Herzog August Bibliothek, 43 Aug. 2°
i Johannes Picus de Mirandula, *Opera*. Bologna: Benedictus Hectoris, 1496

ALESSANDRO DANELONI

Professor Daneloni's first volume of his *editio maior* (Messina, 2008) provides a lengthy introduction, a Latin text and apparatus of all three books, an Italian translation of the same, and an exhaustive commentary on Book 1 of the letters. Commentary on Books 2 and 3 will follow in due course. For the English translation, I have adhered to the Latin of the critical edition while keeping an eye on the Italian translation, from which, it turns out, I have very seldom significantly diverged. In compiling the Notes to the Translation I have dredged the *mare magnum* of Daneloni's commentary of Book 1 to supply what I take to be the minimum a reader of English will need to understand the text (this is referred to in the Notes to Book 1 as *Commento,* i.e., pp. 155–504 of *Fontii Epistolarum Libri,* vol. I). For Books 2 and 3 I have endeavored with Daneloni's assistance to supply notes on a similar scale, with a slight bias throughout toward providing references to English-language works. But for these books in the future, and for Book 1 now, the reader interested in going further will find sure assistance in the *editio maior,* in relation to which this one stands very much as an *editio minor;* we are very grateful to the Centro Interdipartimentale di Studi Umanistici at Messina, and its president, Professor Vincenzo Fera, for making the edition available for adaptation to the I Tatti format. We are indebted, like all other contributors to this series, to Professor James Hankins, in the first place for suggesting and encouraging this edition, and, at a later stage, for his careful editing of the volume.

MARTIN DAVIES

Notes to the Text

LIBER PRIMUS

1. accedit quod graviter et iniquis animis multi ferunt *B*

2. s. *B* (= salutem, *perhaps rightly*)

3. s. *B*

4. hunc — unum] in hunc unum animae dimidium meae totam *B*

5. ob — discessionem] nihil autem potest intercessisse nisi Petri Cennini discessio *B*

6. tota — intestinis] cum quod omnis Italia intestinis dissensionibus est armata, tum quod princeps in ea nullus favet liberalibus disciplinis *B* ("both because all of Italy is in arms owing to internal discord, and because there is no prince in the land who shows favor to liberal disciplines")

7. ad te misi] perendie ad te misi *B*

8. qui — affectibus] qui ritu ferarum viventes nullis affectibus *M*

9. permanemus. Itaque] permanemus. Pugnae vero, seditiones, discordiae unde nobis praeterquam a corpore oriuntur? Omnia enim fere bella aut aliis a nobis aut nobis ab aliis propter opes et divitias inferuntur, quibus corporis tantum causa inhiantes, caetera omnia recta atque honesta despicimus. Caeterum *M* ("But from what source other than the body do battles and acts of sedition and discord arise? Nearly all wars are waged against others by ourselves or by others against ourselves for wealth and resources, which are desired because of the body alone, while all other right and honorable things we despise.")

10. ad vesperam] in diem crastinam *M*

11. qui semel — restituatur] cum quis semel occiderit et de se splendida Minos arbitria fecerit, non genere, non facundia, non pietate restituatur *M* ("since once someone has died and Minos has passed shining judg-

ment upon him, neither descent nor eloquence nor piety will restore him")

12. praesta liberis—egent] praesta discipulis tuis et cunctis Latini nominis, qui doctrina et ingenio tuo egent, praesta natis, amicis, cognatis, affinibus, qui una mecum tanto tuo dolore maerent *M*

13. inanibus querelis depositis] rationi obtemperans, ab inanibus querelis desistens *M*

14. Flor., XXV iulii 1472 *M*

15. cogitare statuique] cogitare. Verum, cum fieri humaniores litteras domi pauci et earum studiosos parvo in pretio esse cernerem, statui *B*

16. ad Hestensem—contuli] praeter Hestensem Borsium, Ferrariae ducem, ad quem tenderem non cernebam *B*

17. *Following* fregit, *Fonzio deleted the following passage found in the earlier redaction in B:* His ergo tantis ac tam magnis amicis orbatus viris, amissis his ornamentis vitaeque meae firmissimis fundamentis, quo me amplius verterem ignorarem, nisi Francisci Saxetti, amicissimi hominis, et domo et rebus familiarius uterer. *See Notes to the Translation.*

LIBER SECUNDUS

1. professor publicus] ad legendum publice *B*

2. contemplationi rerum coniungeretur] minime a contemplatione rerum disiungeretur *B*

3. regi Pannonio] regi *W*

4. Tadeus Ugholettus vir disertus et eruditus *W*

5. ego certe non in postremis *W*

6. hoc tenue—1488] Tadeum cum quibusdam meis opusculis ad te misi, quem non longo post tempore subsequentur maiora nostra in Valerium Flaccum nomini tuo dedicata volumina et tua celsitudine digniora. Interim hunc, oro, benignus excipe inter aliosque auctores in ista bibliotheca totius orbis terrarum nobilissima Fontium tuum repone. *W.* ("I have sent the *Tadeus* to you with some of my minor works, on which will follow my larger volumes on Valerius Flaccus dedicated to your person and

worthier of your highness. In the meantime, please accept this one and place your Fonzio among the other authors in that library of yours, the noblest in the world.")

7. fore. In quo ambigo] fore. Ex quo vero tua benignitate quod maxime optabam sum consequutus, et tibi pro tali munere ago gratias et illi vehementer gratulor quod tantum opus ab omni Christianitate concelebrandum ediderit, in quo equidem ambigo *i* ("And so thanks to your kindness I have got what I most wanted, and I give thanks to you for such a gift as this and also warmly congratulate him on publishing such a great work for all Christendom to celebrate, in which I don't know [. . .]")

8. Budae—misi] Budae nuper orationem a me habitam ad Mathiam Corvinum regem iam primum omnium ad te misi *i*

9. Vale—MCCCCLXXXIX] Vale et me, ut facis, mutuo dilige *i*

10. quos *B*

11. *B ends at this point.*

LIBER TERTIUS

1. *Omitted in F*

2. *Omitted in F*

3. *Omitted in F*

4. nautes *F*

5. libere *F*

6. perceptorum *F*

7. admovemur *F*

8. ad veterem *F*

9. utrumque *F*

10. familiariem *F*

Notes to the Translation

ABBREVIATIONS

BMC	*A Catalogue of Books Printed in the Fifteenth Century now in the British Museum*, VI (Bologna, Florence etc.) (London, 1930; repr. with corrections, 1963).
Commento	*Bartholomaei Fontii Epistolarum libri*, I, ed. Alessandro Daneloni (Messina, 2008), "Commento al Libro I," 155–504.
DBI	*Dizionario biografico degli italiani* (Rome, 1960–).
Eubel	Konrad Eubel, *Hierarchia Catholica Medii Aevi*, 2nd ed., 8 vols. (Monasterii, 1913–78).
GW	*Gesamtkatalog der Wiegendrucke* (Leipzig, 1925–).
IGI	*Indice generale degli incunaboli delle biblioteche d'Italia*, compiled by T. M. Guarnaschelli and E. Valenziani [et al.], 6 vols. (Rome, 1943–81).
RIS	*Rerum italicarum scriptores*, ed. L. A. Muratori, 25 vols. (Milan, 1723–51).

BOOK I

1. This letter to Amerigo Corsini continued to serve as dedication and preface of Fonzio's collection from its original version of 1495 to the final one of 1513. Corsini (1442–1501) was a merchant with wide cultural interests, a pupil of Landino, close to Ficino. He was earlier devoted to the Medici, writing a three-book Latin poem on Cosimo il Vecchio's life, but took a prominent role in Florentine politics as a follower of Savonarola after their expulsion in 1494.

2. Fonzio was actually forty-eight at the time of writing (b. August 26, 1447), but in wishing to stress the significant "jubilee" of fifty years (like his model, Poggio, *Lettere*, I, 99–101), he speaks in round figures.

3. Puccio di Antonio Pucci (1451–94), a civil lawyer later employed by the Medicean regime. He was at this point a student of law in Bologna. The letter is datable to end of May–beginning of June 1467.

4. An earlier, lost letter of Fonzio will have recommended to Pucci his fellow law student Battista Nelli (b. 1443).

5. The upheavals here recounted were the culmination of a long period of political tension in Florence following the death of Cosimo il Vecchio in August 1464. The "conspiracy" against Cosimo's weak son Piero de' Medici had failed and the leaders named below were exiled in September 1466. Their further attempts to have themselves reinstalled in Florence with the aid of the Venetians and their condottiere Bartolomeo Colleoni likewise ended in failure, after the period of acute anxiety revealed in this letter.

6. This *Dieci di Balìa,* an emergency war commission, was created on May 4, 1467.

7. Della Stufa returned from his successful embassy to Bologna (where Pucci was) on May 24, 1467, and this letter must follow shortly on that return. The Florentines, in alliance with the Milanese and Neapolitans and under the leadership of Federico da Montefeltro, Duke of Urbino, went on to defeat the enemy forces under Colleoni at Molinella on July 25.

8. Pucci's father, Antonio, was *capitaneus* (administrator of justice) in the subject town of Pisa from March to September 1467.

9. Pietro Cennini (1444–84), one of Fonzio's closest friends since their schooldays under Bernardo Nuti (see 3.12.2 n.); a notary by profession, he was also a notable copyist of manuscripts and editor of texts, including the first book (Servius) printed in Florence. See Marco Palma's life of him in *DBI*; Ullman, *Origin and Development*, 123–26, and other bibliography cited in *Commento*, 202, as well as Berta Maracchi Biagiarelli, "Editori di incunabuli fiorentini," in *Contributi alla storia del libro italiano. Miscellanea in onore di Lamberto Donati* (Florence, 1969), 211–20, at 212–14.

10. Diogenes the Cynic, echoing a passage from a letter ascribed to him which had been translated into Latin by Francesco Griffolini (Pseudo-Diogenes Cynicus, *Epistolae*, Florence 1487 [*GW* 8396], sig. a8v).

11. Pietro Fanni, or Vanni, was a Florentine priest (evidently away from Florence at the time) who had been schooled alongside Fonzio and Cennini (1.18.1 below), a friend and correspondent of Ficino. Two poems in Fonzio's collection *Saxettus* are addressed to him.

12. Fonzio's desire to hear the teaching of Argyropoulos (1415–87), who lectured on philosophy at the Florentine Studio from 1456 to 1471 (and again from 1477 till his death), assures us that this visit to Ferrara took place before his lengthy stay there from ca. July 1469 until Borso's death on August 19, 1471, and therefore that this letter falls in the period ca. June 1467 to June 1469. Fonzio's lecture notes on the course that Argyropoulos held on Aristotle's *Posterior Analytics* survive in Florence, Biblioteca Riccardiana, MS Ricc. 152, likewise from this period.

13. A member of one of the leading Florentine families, loyal Medicean, owner of a large humanist library. Five *volgare* letters of Fonzio to him survive (*Commento*, 219).

14. Fonzio's Latin treatise on penitence in the form of a dialogue between himself and Donato Acciaiuoli was composed 1468–69 and printed in Florence in 1488 (*GW* 10171). See the discussion in Trinkaus, *In Our Image and Likeness*, 626–33. The sideswipe at the barbarousness of style and treatment by monks was by now commonplace with the humanists.

15. The books must have been defined in earlier, lost correspondence. Gaddi was perhaps in Rome, where books of humanistic interest were more widely available.

16. The problems besetting Cennini, alluded to in the next letter as well, are nowhere explained, but seem from later correspondence (epp. 1.8–9) to have been of a financial nature.

17. Donato Acciaiuoli (1428–78) was a leading figure in the political and cultural life of Quattrocento Florence: commentator on Aristotle's *Ethics* and *Politics*, translator from Greek into Latin, and (of Bruni's *History of Florence*) from Latin into *volgare*, frequent ambassador for the Republic (dying unexpectedly on his way to France on one such embassy), the leading interlocutor in Fonzio's *De paenitentia* (see 1.4.1 n.).

18. Fanni had been appointed priest of the parish church, S. Leonardo, at Cerreto Guidi in the lower Arno Valley near Empoli, a post he still held in a document of 1482 (*Commento*, 238).

19. Farkas was a Hungarian student at Florence in 1468–69.

20. As secretary to Ridolfi, the Florentine ambassador to Naples. The letter must be datable to shortly after June 1, 1469, when the embassy departed.

21. Presumably at the intervention of Acciaiuoli, as in 1.9 above.

22. A Hungarian humanist and cleric who had been partly schooled in Italy and frequently traveled between the two countries. Fonzio had by this stage returned from Ferrara, where his hopes of advancement had been disappointed with the death of Borso d'Este; finding the situation at Florence also unpromising, he now seeks a position in Hungary. The letter is datable to September–November 1471.

23. A conspiracy of nobles to unseat Matthias Corvinus had resulted in reconciliation of the king with its leader János Vitéz, archbishop of Esztergom and Garázda's patron, formally concluded on December 19, 1471, as appears further from the next letter. The present letter probably dates from early December.

24. Fonzio will have become acquainted with the humanist teacher during his stay at Ferrara, where Battista Guarini (1434–1503) taught humanities at the university, succeeding to the post held by his famous father, Guarino da Verona, on the latter's death in 1460.

25. A trip in spring 1472 in the company of his patron Francesco Sassetti.

26. Fonzio originally wrote in B *perendie . . . misi*, under the impression that *perendie* means "two days ago" instead of "the day after tomorrow."

27. This introduces a description of the antiquities of Rome modeled on, and amply borrowing from, Poggio's *De varietate fortunae*, Book I (*Opera* II reproduces the Paris 1723 text; see also the modern edition by Coarelli and Boriaud cited in the Bibliography).

28. The Pons Fabricius, the oldest bridge in Rome (62 BC).

29. In fact the temple of Saturn.

30. The name Marcus Aurelius recorded on an inscription on the arch of Septimius Severus in the Roman Forum refers to his son Caracalla, not to the emperor of that name (whose column in Piazza Colonna is here named "Antonine"). The arch of Titus in the Forum, posthumously erected to his memory by his brother Domitian in AD 81, is given equally to Vespasian, their father.

31. The tomb-pyramid of Cestius (late first century BC) is now incorporated in the Aurelian Walls by the Porta San Paolo (the ancient *Porta Ostiense*).

32. Brought to Rome from Egypt in AD 37, it was first erected in the Circus of Nero on the Vatican hill, now (since 1586) the centerpiece of St. Peter's Square.

33. The so-called Castor and Pollux, the Dioscuri or "Horse-tamers," now in Piazza del Quirinale, then at the baths of Constantine on the Quirinal (not Esquiline). Their identification as works of the famous Greek sculptors was encouraged by inscriptions attached to them.

34. The tomb of Antius Lupus had been destroyed already by the end of the sixteenth century, but the circular mausoleum of Caecilia Metella (late first century BC) remains the most impressive monument of the Via Appia.

35. Fonzio copied these and many other inscriptions, as well as archaeological drawings, into various sylloges, of which one survives imperfectly in Oxford, Bodleian Library, MS Lat. misc. d. 85 (see 2.7 n. below), while others have extant apographs.

36. The "Antonine" baths are those of Caracalla by the Aventine, the baths of Diocletian those near the modern railway station (which takes its name, Termini, from these *thermae*).

37. The following paragraph, including the frequent mistaken identifications, is based entirely on Poggio's *De varietate.*

38. After ostensible reconciliation (see 1.13.1 n. above), Matthias Corvinus early in 1472 turned on the ringleaders of the attempted coup against him, János Vitéz, archbishop of Esztergom, and his nephew the poet and humanist (and good friend of Guarini) Janus Pannonius. Pannonius died

as he tried to escape on March 27, and Vitéz, after a spell of imprisonment, died on August 9, soon after his release. No more is heard of Fonzio's relations with Péter Garázda (see 1.12, 14, and 15 above), though he survived to follow a modest Church career in Hungary.

39. A letter of consolation in good classical style, though notably without a parade of *exempla* of fortitude, which Guarini had said he did not want (see next note), on the death of his wife, Bettina. She had been married to him since about 1456 and died in April or May of 1472. Many of the themes touched on by Fonzio derive from the pseudo-Plutarchan *Consolatio ad Apollonium* in the 1463 Latin translation by Alamanno Rinuccini (unpublished: there is a modern edition and English translation of the Plutarch letter in the Loeb series by F. C. Babbitt: Plutarch, *Moralia*, II [London 1928], 105–211). There is a good deal of variation, most of it trivial but some effecting considerable tightening up of the prose, in this letter as collected by Fonzio and the original autograph missive (M).

40. Taking up a passage of Guarini's letter to Niccolò Bendidio of June 22, 1472 (responding to a lost consolatory letter of the latter), where he declined to play the impassive Stoic sage (Battista Guarini, *Opuscula*, ed. L. Piacente [Bari, 1995], 252).

41. The river of death in Hades, suggested to Fonzio by the *Consolatio ad Apollonium* 106E and Horace, *Odes* 2.14 (*Eheu fugaces*).

42. This letter is a fictitious missive composed in the mid-1490s, on the model of Niccolò Perotti's letter *De ratione studiorum suorum* of 1454–55, to supply autobiographical information and reflection on the course of his life so far.

43. Fonzio's lament for his ten barren years (1461–71) is overdrawn. There is evidence, quite apart from that apparent in the preceding seventeen letters, that he attended university courses, wrote manuscripts for the bookseller Vespasiano da Bisticci, and acted as a notary in this period (see *Commento*, 347–48).

44. The death of both his parents in his fifteenth year places those unhappy events between August 26, 1461, and August 25, 1462. Thereafter

Fonzio had to provide for his younger siblings: three brothers, Mauro, Niccolò, and Giovanni, and a sister, Brigida.

45. Fonzio was at Ferrara from July to September 1469 until the death of Duke Borso d'Este on August 19, 1471. Early in that period he dedicated a vernacular translation of the *Letter of Aristeas* on the Septuagint to the duke (the autograph dedication copy is Vatican City, Biblioteca Apostolica Vaticana, MS Ross. 407), but otherwise little is known of his stay there.

46. See epp. 1.12–13 and notes. Fonzio had become acquainted with Garázda in the autumn-winter of 1471–72. At this point Fonzio cut from an earlier redaction a passage of heartfelt thanks for the patronage of Francesco Sassetti, director of the Medici bank, in the early 1470s ("Deprived of such great men, with the loss of these ornaments and solid foundations of my life, I should not have known where to turn had I not been able to avail myself of the home and fortune of that most amiable man Francesco Sassetti"). This was probably done for rhetorical reasons, to point up the contrast between his earlier misfortunes and the revival inspired in him by Donato Acciaiuoli (*Commento*, 363–68).

47. On Acciaiuoli, see ep. 1.9 n. above. The fact that the two embassies of Acciaiuoli (to settle the age-old border disputes between the Florentine subjects of Foiano and the Sienese subject town of Lucignano) are documented in the archives as taking place in November 1472 and January 1473 is one of a number of indications that the present letter, dated August 26, 1472, was never a real missive (*Commento*, 370–72).

48. Leonardo Bruni (1370–1444) and Poggio (1380–1459) were the two leading Florentine humanists of the first half of the Quattrocento, both of them historians of Florence and chancellors of the city. The contemporary Bartolomeo Scala (1430–97) was the incumbent chancellor, a creature of the Medici and likewise a historian of Florence, though his history remained unfinished. All had risen from modest beginnings.

49. For *De paenitentia* (1468–69), see ep. 1.4.1 n. The present letter was never a real missive to Fanni, but a reworking in letter form of a portion of *De paenitentia* from an older redaction of the treatise which is now lost; see *Commento*, 395–400.

50. These considerations derive ultimately from Plato, *Phaedrus* 245c–246a via Cicero, *Dream of Scipio* 27–28 (= *On the Republic* 6.27–28), *Tusculan Disputations* 1.53–54, and (Fonzio's probable source) Macrobius, *Commentary on the Dream of Scipio* 2.13.1–5.

51. On Pietro Dolfin (1444–1525), a Venetian patrician and one of the most powerful and cultured churchman of the time, see R. Zaccaria's life in *DBI*, 40 (1991), 565–71. He was elected general of his order (the Camaldulensian branch of the Benedictines) only in December 1480, so there must be some mild disorder in the arrangement of letters here, the next being dated January 30, 1480.

52. Fonzio's brother Mauro entered the order at the Camaldulensian house of S. Maria degli Angeli in Florence in January 1479, becoming priest a year later (*Commento*, 422).

53. Calderini (1445–ca. 1494), a pupil of Landino and friend of Ficino, was at this time an employee of the Medici bank in France.

54. This personage is very likely the chamberlain of King Louis XI, Guy de Beauclair, to whom Fonzio had earlier sent a copy of Apuleius's *Golden Ass* (or *Metamorphoses*), and now sends a copy of Bartolomeo Platina's cookbook, *De honesta voluptate*.

55. A friendly reproof to the Neoplatonic philosopher Marsilio Ficino (1433–99), the "prince of Platonists," as Fonzio calls him, for the excessively rhythmic quality of his prose, often verging on verse. The letter is in answer to Ficino's ep. 3.3 (*Opera et quae hactenus extitere et quae in lucem nunc primum prodiere omnia*, 2 vols. [Basel, 1576; repr. Turin, 1962], 723–24), which is datable to 1476–77, and must therefore be misplaced here among letters of the early 1480s, either by Fonzio's oversight or to provide a contrast to the bad-tempered polemic against Poliziano in the next letter (*Commento*, 452–53).

56. Angelo Ambrogini da Montepulciano, known from his birthplace as Poliziano (1454–94), the leading classical scholar and vernacular poet of the age. Fonzio's letter-invective marks the definitive rupture in their relations, which had earlier and for a long time been good, owing to Poliziano's constant attacks on him (and others) when they were fellow teachers at the Florentine Studio from the beginning of the 1480s.

57. A preparation of the purgative herb was the traditional cure for madness from ancient times. Poggio advises its use on Valla in his invectives of thirty years before (*Opera* II, 879, 884; *Commento*, 475–77).

58. Poliziano's account of the botched conspiracy against the Medici which led to the death of Lorenzo il Magnifico's brother Giuliano in Florence Cathedral in April 1478, composed in the summer of that year and printed soon afterward (*IGI* 7954–56).

59. Matthew 11:29 and James 4:6 (both citations drawn from Jerome, ep. 76.1).

BOOK II

1. There is no record of Fonzio's correspondent Giovanni Rosso outside this letter: see Black, *Education and Society*, 437.

2. Chalcondyles (1423–1511) was one of the best-known Byzantine scholars in Italy, professor of Greek at Padua (1463–75), at Florence (1476–91), and finally at Milan till his death. A mediocre scholar, he was close to Fonzio but a bitter enemy of Poliziano, his colleague at the Studio, who attacked him in his academic prolusions. Chalcondyles edited the *editio princeps* of Homer published at Florence in 1488, and several later editions of Greek authors (Isocrates in 1493; his own Greek grammar, the *Erotemata*, in 1494; the *Suda* in 1499). See the life by A. Petrucci (s.v. Calcondila) in *DBI*, 16 (1973), 542–47.

3. Giovanni Acciaiuoli (1460–1527), the son of Pietro and Leonarda di Dietisalvi Neroni, was very active in Florentine political life; an adversary of the Medici, he held various magistracies and diplomatic posts, especially in the post-Medicean period 1496–1513.

4. Brenta (1454–84) had studied at Padua under Chalcondyles, leaving to become Cardinal Oliviero Carafa's secretary in Rome, where he taught humanities at the Studium Urbis from 1475 until his early death.

5. Lorenzo "il Magnifico" (1448–92), leader of the oligarchic regime founded by his grandfather Cosimo il Vecchio, the ruler of Florence in all but name.

6. Alluding to the opening words of the *Odyssey*. The following lines mention some of Ulysses' adventures before his eventual return to Ithaca.

7. With a well-worn pun on *florentissimam*, "flourishing," and his home in Florence, *Florentia*.

8. The list derives from Diodorus Siculus, *Bibliotheca historica* 1.96, the first five books of which were translated into Latin by Poggio in 1449.

9. Rucellai (1448–1514), a leading literary and political personage in Florence in the second half of the Quattrocento and early Cinquecento. The husband since 1466 of Nannina de' Medici, Lorenzo il Magnifico's sister, he was among the most influential figures of the Medicean regime, holding numerous magistracies and diplomatic missions on behalf of the republic. His political fortunes survived the fall of the Medici in 1494, though he found himself in strong opposition to Savonarola and Pier Soderini, the *Gonfaloniere* for life, in succession, both of them far from his oligarchic ideal. He was the owner of the gardens (*Orti Oricellari*) where famous literary gatherings, frequented by Machiavelli, took place in the early sixteenth century. His cultural interests tended toward history, as in his writings *Bellum Mediolanense*, *De bello Pisano*, an *Oratio de auxilio Tifernatibus adferendo*, and especially his major work, *De bello Italico*, on which see ep. 3.6 n. He also wrote an important antiquarian work, *De urbe Roma* (see Weiss, *Renaissance Discovery*, 78–81).

10. Rucellai's first embassy to Milan, when he was Florentine orator from February 1482 to October 1483; see Rita Maria Comanducci, *Il carteggio di Bernardo Rucellai* (Florence, 1996), 4–28.

11. Giovanni Battista Zeno, nominated cardinal by Paul II on November 21, 1468, died May 7, 1501: see Eubel II, 15–16.

12. Amphiaraus, king of Argos, foresaw his death in the expedition of the Seven against Thebes, which duly came to pass despite his efforts to avoid going. The best-known account was in the *Thebaid* of Statius, esp. 7.690–823 and 8.

13. A contemporary tells us the sermon was on penitence: Giacomo Gherardi, *Diarium Romanum*, in *RIS* XXIII, col. 194, where Fonzio is named as the cardinal's secretary; see Daneloni, "Secondo elenco," 361 n. 3.

14. On this little-known pupil of Fonzio, Giraldo Giraldi, who was evidently instructed to arrange his return to Florence, see Verde, *Studio fiorentino*, II (1973), 86–87; Di Benedetto, "Fonzio e Landino su Orazio," 452 n. 52.

15. The Florentine Ugolino Verino (1438–1516) was one of the major Latin poets of the Quattrocento and a great friend of Fonzio; besides collections of elegies and epigrams, he wrote an epic on Charlemagne in fifteen books, the *Carlias*.

16. Literally the "greatly swollen Euripus," the strait prone to storms and strong tides that separates Euboea from mainland Greece.

17. Francesco Sassetti (1421–90) was general manager of the Medici bank from 1463 till his death. In the 1470s he became the patron of Fonzio, who acted as his librarian and was tutor of his sons in the period before his appointment at the Florentine Studio. See de la Mare, "The Library of Francesco Sassetti," with earlier bibliography, and on Fonzio esp. 165–66, 170.

18. The remarkable story of the Roman girl found on the Appian Way is recorded in many sources besides Fonzio, most of them gathered in the standard treatment of Hülsen, "Die Auffindung der römischen Leiche." Many of them took the body to be that of Tulliola, Cicero's daughter. For the original version of this letter to Sassetti, see Daneloni's *editio maior* of the *Epistolarum Libri*, Appendice, 151–52. This primitive redaction is found in Fonzio's autograph epigraphic collection, Oxford, Bodleian Library, MS Lat. misc. d. 85, fols. 159v–161v, where it is accompanied by a good drawing of the corpse and its coffin (reproduced above, p. xviii). Much of the manuscript (on which see Saxl, "The Classical Inscription") is currently visible online at http://bodley30.bodley.ox.ac.uk:8180/luna/servlet/view/all/who/Bartolomeo+Fonzio.

19. Pierfilippo Pandolfini (1437–97), a member of the famous Florentine family and well schooled in literature and the humanities, was a pupil of Johannes Argyropoulos and a long-standing friend of Fonzio (see epp. 2.4.8, 2.5.7–8); he undertook many diplomatic missions on behalf of Florence.

20. The Latin version of Pseudo-Phocylides, *Sententiae* (a late Hellenistic moralizing poem in Greek by an Alexandrian Jew) made by Fonzio has not survived.

21. For Dolfin, see ep. 1.20 n.

22. Don Mauro is Fonzio's younger brother, recorded in 1.20 as having come under the protection of the general of the Camaldulensian Order. The parish is the church of San Miniato at Popigliano, a couple of miles north of Prato and not far from Fonzio's own (later) benefice at Montemurlo. The mother house of the order was at Camaldoli in the Casentino, the wooded area of the upper Arno Valley.

23. That is, the aristocratic governing body of the Italianate city-state of Ragusa on the Dalmatian coast, now Dubrovnik.

24. Taddeo Ugoletti, humanist and professor of rhetoric at Reggio Emilia, worked at the Hungarian court from 1480 to 1490 as tutor to King Matthias's son Johannes (János) Corvinus and as the person charged with seeking out books for the royal library. In 1488 he was at Florence, where he formed friendly relations with both Poliziano and Fonzio: see Branca, *Poliziano e l'umanesimo della parola*, 125–33.

25. *Tadeus vel de locis Persianis* was a brief treatise investigating the text and interpretation of some problematic passages in the *Satires* of Persius, included in a manuscript, Wolfenbüttel, Herzog August Bibliothek, Cod. Guelf. 43 Aug. 2°, which was written by Fonzio for presentation to Corvinus in 1488 (see "Note on the Text and Translation" for this manuscript's part in the transmission of the letters). See Milde, *Wolfenbütteler Corvinen*, 18–19; it had only one late printing (Frankfurt, 1621, from this manuscript), alongside other works of Fonzio.

26. The addressee of the next letter, q.v.

27. János Móré, treasurer of the court of King Matthias Corvinus, identified as the recipient of this letter by Pajorin, "L'opera di Naldo Naldi," 328 n. 71.

28. Salviati (1459–1523), a scholar with strong philosophical interests, friend of Alamanno Rinuccini and Giovanni Pico della Mirandola. In 1489 he sponsored and edited the publication of Pico's *Heptaplus*, an allegorical interpretation of the Genesis account of creation (*IGI* 7737; *BMC*

VI 662). In 1492 he entered the Dominican order at San Marco in Florence as a supporter of Savonarola. See Verde, *Studio fiorentino*, III.2, 863.

29. Guillaume de Rochefort (1433–92) undertook important diplomatic missions to Italy for the dukes of Burgundy in the 1460s and '70s, subsequently becoming chancellor of France under Charles VIII. With strong interests in antiquity and ancient literature, he was one of the first patrons of the new learning in France; at Paris he was at the center of a small group of French and Italian humanists which included Robert Gaguin, Girolamo Balbo, and Fausto Andrelini. See Saxl, "The Classical Inscription," 37–41.

30. Federico (1472–91), another of the sons of Francesco Sassetti (younger brother of Cosimo mentioned in the preceding letter), was a priest and a favorite pupil of Fonzio.

31. Pontano (1429–1503), whose academic name was Gioviano, was one of the most important humanists of the fifteenth century: a fine poet and expert philologist, from the 1440s onward closely tied to the Aragonese court of Naples, where he assumed an ever more important role, especially under Ferdinando I (called Ferrante, reigned 1458–94). Many of his poetical works survive, among them *Amores, Eclogae, De amore coniugali, Hendecasyllabi, Eridanorum libri, Tumuli,* and *Urania,* as well as prose treatises on scholarly and ethical subjects, e.g., *De aspiratione, De sermone, De prudentia, De immanitate, De magnanimitate,* and various literary dialogues (*Asinus, Charon, Antonius, Aegidius, Actius*); there is also a history, the *De bello Neapolitano*.

32. Ferdinando I of Aragon died on January 25, 1494; his eldest son, Alfonso II, Duke of Calabria, succeeded him.

33. Brandolini (ca. 1465–1517), a humanist and scholar of Florentine origin, had long been resident at Naples, where he frequented Pontano's Academy, and then from 1495 at Rome, where he was also *cubicularius* of Julius II and later (1513), on the nomination of Leo X, professor of rhetoric at the Studium Urbis. See G. Ballistreri in *DBI*, 14 (1972), 40–42.

34. Pietro di Tommaso Soderini (1452–1522), a member of one of the most powerful families in Florence, was very active in the political life of the city at the end of the fifteenth century; he was elected *Gonfaloniere di*

Giustizia ("Standard-Bearer of Justice," the titular head of the Florentine government) for life on September 22, 1502, and remained in the post until 1512, when the Medici returned to power.

35. Fonzio draws on Livy's detailed account of this episode (205–204 BC), *Histories* 29.10.4–11, 29.14.5–14. Publius Cornelius Scipio Nasica was actually the son of Gnaeus, not Gaius.

36. Francesco Soderini (1453–1524), the brother of Pietro, a scholar and jurist (he was also professor of law at the University of Pisa) and intimate friend of Marsilio Ficino. From the beginning of the 1470s he pursued a brilliant ecclesiastical career, culminating in his nomination as cardinal by Alexander VI on May 31, 1503 (Eubel II, 26).

BOOK III

1. Pandolfini (1470–1520) was the son of Pierfilippo (ep. 2.8 n.) and a friend and pupil of Fonzio, who at his death bequeathed him his library and made him literary executor of his writings; one of the *Ufficiali* of the Florentine Studio, he held many diplomatic and political posts, among them resident ambassador at the court of the French king from 1505 to 1507.

2. 1 Thessalonians 4:13–15.

3. John 11:38.

4. Paolo di Zanobi da Ghiacceto the younger, one of Fonzio's dearest friends, a Florentine politician of some importance at the close of the Quattrocento (one of the *Signori* in July–August 1486, several times an ambassador, *Capitano del popolo* at Arezzo for July–December 1499). He evidently died in the opening years of the sixteenth century. He was the grandson of the important politician Paolo di Zanobi da Ghiacceto the elder (d. 1449), whose life Fonzio wrote (see further on ep. 3.13 below).

5. Giovanni di Pierfilippo Pandolfini, Francesco's brother, d. 1537. Very little is known of him; his ownership inscription is found in a fifteenth-century arithmetical treatise (Florence, Biblioteca Riccardiana, MS Ricc. 2991).

6. Fonzio was parish priest of San Giovanni Battista di Montemurlo in the diocese of Pistoia from 1492 (see ep. 3.11).

7. Giovanni Nesi (1456–after 1522), Florentine humanist, once close to Marsilio Ficino and a student at his private gymnasium or academy, later became a supporter of Savonarola, in defense of whom he composed his best-known work, the *Oraculum de novo saeculo*. He also wrote a treatise, *De moribus*, which records his devotion to Donato Acciaiuoli.

8. Bruni, *Opere letterarie e politiche*, ed. Paolo Viti (Turin, 1996), 444. Bruni's biography, written in 1415–16, was entitled *Cicero Novus*, the "New Cicero," reflecting his intention to overhaul and replace Plutarch's life.

9. Actually a direct quotation of the *Oration against Piso* 6, on which Asconius comments (see the Oxford Classical Text of this author, ed. A. C. Clark [1907], p. 6). The tribune was Q. Caecilius Metellus Nepos, brother of the Metellus Celer to whom Cicero wrote the letter on which Nesi seeks enlightenment (*Fam.* 5.2.7).

10. Without any indication of the addressee, this short letter (transmitted only by F) clearly remained unfinished in Fonzio's study; death prevented him from adding the person's name. It evidently accompanied a poem in praise of the addressee, equally lost to us.

11. The identity of "Spica" is unknown.

12. So the Authorized Version of Matthew 8:4. Fonzio actually wrote *ostendit*, "showed," for the Vulgate *praecepit*, "commanded," an inadvertent repetition of the verb earlier in the sentence.

13. The technical term for a "given sentence," i.e., a penalty that follows automatically from contravention of canon law.

14. Cinozzi was a Dominican friar at the Florentine convent of San Marco; one of Savonarola's most fervent and radical supporters, he was the author in early 1499 of a *volgare* commentary on Psalm 5, "Verba mea auribus percipe," in which he launched a strong attack on Florence and Pope Alexander VI. The violence of his writing aroused a furious reaction in Florence and he was punished by loss of privileges and transfer to the convent of SS. Annunziata at San Gimignano; see Polizzotto, *Elect Nation*, 173–77.

15. I.e., part of the extensive early pseudo-Clementine literature (ascribed to Pope Clement I, *fl.* AD 96), incorporated in the *Recognitiones* in the Latin translation of Rufinus (4–5C). For the passage discussed here by Fonzio, see *Die Pseudoklementinen, II: Rekognitionen in Rufins Übersetzung,* ed. B. Rehm and F. Paschke (Berlin, 1965), 134–37.

16. Augustine is quoting 2 Thessalonians 2:9–10 (not quite accurately: he read *mendacii* for the Vulgate *mendacibus*), here in the Authorized Version.

17. Augustine, *City of God Against the Pagans* 20.19 (in the translation of R. W. Dyson published by Cambridge University Press), alluding to Job 1:16ff. Fonzio next cites the late medieval theologians Jean Gerson (chancellor of the University of Paris, 1363–1429) and Nicholas of Lyra (ca. 1270–1349), the Franciscan author of the *Postillae in S. Scripturam,* the first printed commentary on the Bible.

18. Gerson, *Oeuvres complètes,* ed. P. Glorieux, vol. III (Paris, 1962), 42.

19. *Biblia latina cum postillis Nicolai de Lyra* (Strasbourg, 1492), sig. ll7r n. l.

20. A Franciscan theologian, ca. 1447–1520, originally from Bosnia (born Juraj Dragišić), who was adopted by the Salviati of Florence. His *De natura angelica* was published at Florence in 1499 (*GW* 3843, *BMC* VI 654, *IGI* 1475). See G. Ernst and P. Zambelli, "Dragišić, Juraj," in *DBI,* 42 (Rome, 1992), 644–51, and the works of C. Vasoli there referred to.

21. *Decretum* D. 15, c. 3, 29; D. 16, c. 3. The *Decretum* was the basic textbook of canon law in the Middle Ages, compiled by Gratian and perhaps other authors in the first half of the twelfth century. It formed the first of the six books making up the *Corpus iuris canonici.*

22. See Dante, *Convivio* 2.4.1–5, 2.5.4–18; *Paradiso* 2.127–44, 29.43–45.

23. Gerson, *Oeuvres complètes,* X (1973), 97.

24. For Rucellai, see ep. 2.5 n. He was the author of *De bello Italico* here referred to, the first attempt to evaluate the significance of Charles VIII's invasion of Italy, which was completed shortly after September 1511; see Pellegrini, *L'umanista Bernardo Rucellai;* Mauro de Nichilo, "L'*Actius* del Pontano e una lettera di Bernardo Rucellai," *Studi medievali e umanistici* 4

(2006): 253–317; William McCuaig, "Bernardo Rucellai and Sallust," *Rinascimento,* n.s. 22 (1982): 75–98.

25. The battle in the Neapolitan port refers to the victory of Ferdinand II (Ferrandino), which allowed him to reconquer the city from the French at the beginning of 1496, though he was to die later that year.

26. Dante Popoleschi was a common friend of Fonzio and Bernardo Rucellai, frequenting the meetings at the Orti Oricellari; he was responsible for a *volgare* translation of Caesar's *Commentarii de bello Gallico* which was printed in 1518.

27. At the time of this letter Rucellai was away from Florence, probably at Venice as the last stage of his voluntary exile (from 1505 onward, including a sojourn in France) from a political situation at home with which he was profoundly unhappy. He returned about 1510–11: Pellegrini, *L'umanista Bernardo Rucellai,* 18–20.

28. Gianfrancesco Zeffi (d. 1546), a notable figure on the cultural scene of the early Cinquecento, poet, humanist, and faithful client of Pierfrancesco de' Medici (see next note).

29. Pierfrancesco (II) de' Medici (1487–1525), son of Lorenzo "il Popolano," an important political actor in early sixteenth-century Florence; he was reconciled with the major branch of the Medici (that of Lorenzo il Magnifico) about 1512.

30. The jeering words, slightly rearranged, of the goatherd Melanthius to the disguised Odysseus at *Odyssey* 17.218.

31. This letter is a retouched version of one originally sent to Francesco Sassetti on January 1, 1473, the text of which is printed in Daneloni's *editio maior* of the *Epistolarum Libri,* Appendice, 147–50. Francesco Ricci is an unknown.

32. From a fancied resemblance between *mensura* and *membra.*

33. The second clause quotes without acknowledgment Isidore, *Etymologiae* 15.15.1.

34. An etymology (*passus* ~ *patesco*) proposed by Nonius Marcellus 370.19M, commenting on a fragment of Ennius.

35. *Oration for Milo* 74.

36. Columella 5.1.4.

37. A *iugerum*, conventionally translated as "acre," was actually about two thirds of that area, 240 by 120 Roman feet, as Fonzio says. It derives from *iugum*, "yoke" (Pliny, *Natural History* 18.9).

38. Vitruvius 3.1.8.

39. Persius 5.76.

40. Persius 5.191.

41. *Natural History* 35.136 (where the true figure, corrupt in the MSS, is 6000 sesterces).

42. Curtius Rufus, *Historiae Alexandri Magni* 9.8; Herodotus 2.180 (used by Fonzio in Lorenzo Valla's translation).

43. Antonio Pucci (1485–1544), scholar and philosopher, had a substantial ecclesiastical career, becoming bishop of Pistoia in 1518 and later cardinal (1531). Fonzio was probably among his earliest teachers.

44. For a general view of the clash between Julius II and King Louis XII of France in its various phases, throughout 1510 and 1511 in particular, leading to the summoning of a schismatic council at Pisa by the latter, Pastor's *History of the Popes* is still useful (VI, 352–92, 405–15). A modern treatment of the Holy League and its war against Louis, in whose hands the papal feuds of Bologna and Ferrara now were (§11), is found in Shaw, *Julius II*, ch. 10, "Il Papa terribile."

45. The popes listed here are probably to be identified as Leo III (795–816), Zacharias (741–52), Stephen II (752–57), Callistus II (1119–24), Innocent II (1130–43), Alexander III (1159–81), and Paschal I (817–24).

46. Jeremiah 9:1.

47. Notably at the battle of Agnadello, May 14, 1509, when the Venetian forces were humiliated by the French, and "they lost in one day what it had taken them 800 years of toil to acquire" (Machiavelli, *Il Principe*, 12).

48. Verses probably of Fonzio's own composition.

49. Giovan Vittorio Soderini (1460–1528), brother of the more famous Pietro and Francesco, was also a politician of some influence at the turn of the Quattrocento; his son Tommaso (1493–1562) was a pupil of Fonzio

and had a modest political career in Florence in the turbulent times of the first half of the Cinquecento.

50. The two villas were each a few miles outside Florence, Fonzio's to the northeast, near Settignano, Soderini's along the Arno to the west.

51. Lorenzo Pucci (1458–1531), uncle of Antonio Pucci (the addressee of ep. 3.9), jurist and professor of law at the University of Pisa. He was a close associate of Lorenzo il Magnifico at Florence. Later he pursued a notable ecclesiastical career at Rome, where he enjoyed the favor of Innocent VIII and Alexander VI. Julius II chose him as his datary in 1511; Leo X created him cardinal on September 23, 1513.

52. Fonzio received the benefice of the parish of San Giovanni Battista di Montemurlo from March 1, 1492, as appears from a notarial document in Florence, Archivio di Stato, *Notarile antecosimiano*, 20262 (unnumbered leaf), first noted by de la Mare, "New Research on Humanistic Scribes," vol. I, 446 n. 192 (with the old shelfmark T. 503). He was buried there by his own wish in October 1513 (Caroti and Zamponi, *Lo scrittoio di Bartolomeo Fonzio*, 16).

53. Francesco Vettori (1474–1539), an eminent politician of wide literary culture, was the Florentine ambassador at Rome from January 1513 to May 1515 (in this period Vettori had a most interesting correspondence with Niccolò Machiavelli, being the recipient, among other things, of the famous letter *De principatibus* of December 10, 1513).

54. Julius was in fact on his deathbed at this time, dying on February 20, 1513.

55. For Rucellai's *De bello Italico*, the Sallustian history of the French invasions, see note on ep. 3.6. On his relations with Pontano, see the letter of Rucellai to Roberto Acciaiuoli published in de Nichilo, "L'*Actius* del Pontano e una lettera di Bernardo Rucellai," *Studi medievali e umanistici* 4 (2006): 253–317, at 311–17, earlier printed in P. Burman's *Sylloges epistolarum a viris illustribus scriptarum tomi quinque*, 5 vols. (Leiden, 1727), II, 200–202. Online at www.uni-mannheim.de/mateo/cera/autoren/burman_cera.html.

56. Lucretius 3.6–8.

57. Fonzio attended Bernardo Nuti's grammar school till the age of fifteen, as we learn from ep. 1.18.3 above. On Nuti and his teaching, see Marchesi, *Bartolomeo della Fonte*, 16–19; Elisabetta Guerrieri, "Bernardus Ser Francisci de Nutis," in *Compendium Auctorum Latinorum Medii Aevi*, II, fasc. 3 (Florence, 2006), 318.

58. Horace, *Epistles* 1.19.19–23.

59. Ibid., 1.3.15–20.

60. The following ornaments are closely based on Cicero's *Orator* 135.

61. Technical terms of rhetoric: *inventio* is the "discovery" of the matter, ideas and arguments concerning the subject to be treated, *dispositio* the "arrangement" of the raw materials of *inventio*, ordering the facts and arguments.

62. Pierfrancesco di Lorenzo di Pierfrancesco (mentioned before at 3.7.3, with n.), of the branch of the Medici called "popolani," was among those who took part in the procession at Leo X's coronation.

63. Fonzio alludes to his biography of Paolo di Zanobi da Ghiacceto the elder (1390–1449), the *Vita Pauli Ghiacceti*, which is preserved in two autograph manuscripts, among others: the dedication copy to the family of Cattani da Ghiacceto (Florence, Biblioteca Nazionale Centrale, Nuovi Acquisti 980) and Wolfenbüttel, Herzog August Bibliothek, Cod. Guelf. 43 Aug. 2°, written for presentation to Corvinus in 1488 (see "Note on the Text and Translation" and ep. 2.11 n.), as well as an incunable edition of the same year: Fontius, *Orationes, Vita Pauli Ghiacceti, De paenitentia* (Florence, 1488 = *GW* 10171); on the date (after Nov. 7, 1487), see Mercuri, "L'editio princeps delle *Orationes*." See also Daneloni, "Bartholomaeus Fontius," 750. For the younger Paolo da Ghiacceto, see ep. 3.1.5 n.

64. Jacopo di Giovanni Salviati (1461–1533), a former pupil of Poliziano and follower of Savonarola, afterward active on the Florentine political scene in the first thirty years of the sixteenth century, was married to Lucrezia, the daughter of Lorenzo il Magnifico, and so was brother-in-law of Giovanni de' Medici, later Pope Leo X.

Bibliography

EDITIONS

Bartholomaeus Fontius. *Epistolarum libri III*, ed. László Juhász. Budapest, 1931. The first publication of Fonzio's letter collection, but very imperfect.

Bartholomaei Fontii Epistolarum libri, vol. I, ed. Alessandro Daneloni. Messina, 2008.

STUDIES

Black, Robert. *Education and Society in Florentine Tuscany: Teachers, Pupils and Schools, c. 1250–1500*. Leiden, 2007.

Branca, Vittore. *Poliziano e l'umanesimo della parola*. Turin, 1983.

Caroti, Stefano, and Stefano Zamponi. *Lo scrittoio di Bartolomeo Fonzio, umanista fiorentino*. Milan, 1974.

Daneloni, Alessandro. "Bartholomaeus Fontius." In *Compendium Auctorum Latinorum Medii Aevi*, vol. I, fasc. 6, 747–50. Florence, 2003.

——. "Un secondo elenco delle opere di Bartolomeo Fonzio." *Studi medievali e umanistici* 4 (2006): 351–62.

de la Mare, A. C. "The Library of Francesco Sassetti (1421–90)." In *Cultural Aspects of the Italian Renaissance: Essays in Honour of Paul Oskar Kristeller*, ed. C. H. Clough, 160–201. Manchester, 1976.

——. "New Research on Humanistic Scribes in Florence." In A. Garzelli, *Miniatura fiorentina del Rinascimento (1440–1525): Un primo censimento*. 2 vols. Florence, 1985.

Di Benedetto, Filippo. "Fonzio e Landino su Orazio." In *Tradizione classica e letteratura umanistica: Per Alessandro Perosa*, 437–53. 2 vols., continuously paginated. Rome, 1985.

Hülsen, Christian. "Die Auffindung der römischen Leiche vom Jahre 1485." *Mittheilungen des Instituts für Österreichische Geschichtsforschung* 4 (1883): 433–49.

Marchesi, Concetto. *Bartolomeo della Fonte (Bartholomaeus Fontius): Contributo alla storia degli studi classici in Firenze nella seconda metà del Quattrocento*. Catania, 1900.

Mercuri, Simona. "La *Oratio in laudem oratoriae facultatis* di Bartolomeo della Fonte: Testo e commento." *Interpres* 23 (2004): 54–84.

———. "L'editio princeps delle *Orationes* di Bartolomeo Fonzio: una nuova datazione." *Schede umanistiche* 18, no. 2 (2004): 29–33.

Milde, Wolfgang. *Die Wolfenbütteler Corvinen*. Wolfenbüttel, 1995.

Pajorin, Klára. "L'opera di Naldo Naldi sulla biblioteca di Mattia Corvino e la biblioteca umanistica ideale." In *L'Europa del libro nell'età dell'Umanesimo*. Atti del XIV Convegno Internazionale (Chianciano, Firenze, Pienza 16–19 luglio 2002), ed. L. Secchi Tarugi, 317–30. Florence, 2004.

Palma, Marco. "Cennini, Pietro." In *DBI*, 23, 572–75. Rome, 1979.

Pastor, Ludwig von. *History of the Popes*, ed. F. I. Antrobus, vol. VI. London, 1898.

Pellegrini, Guglielmo. *L'umanista Bernardo Rucellai e le sue opere storiche*. Livorno, 1921.

Poggio Bracciolini. *Lettere*, ed. H. Harth. 3 vols. Florence, 1984–87.

———. *Opera omnia*, ed. R. Fubini, 4 vols. Turin, 1964–69.

———. *Les ruines de Rome: De varietate fortunae, Livre I*, ed. P. Coarelli and J.-Y. Boriaud. Paris, 1999.

Polizzotto, Lorenzo. *The Elect Nation: The Savonarolan Movement in Florence, 1494–1545*. Oxford, 1994.

Resta, Gianvito. "Andronico Callisto, Bartolomeo Fonzio e la prima traduzione umanistica di Apollonio Rodio." In *Studi in onore di Anthos Ardizzoni*, ed. E. Livrea and G. A. Privitera, 1055–1131. Rome, 1978.

Saxl, Fritz. "The Classical Inscription in Renaissance Art and Politics: Bartholomaeus Fontius: Liber monumentorum Romanae urbis et aliorum locorum." *Journal of the Warburg and Courtauld Institutes* 4 (1940–41): 19–46.

Shaw, Christine. *Julius II: The Warrior Pope*. Oxford, 1993.

Trinkaus, Charles. "A Humanist's Image of Humanism: The Inaugural Orations of Bartolommeo della Fonte." *Studies in the Renaissance* 7 (1960): 90–147.

——. *In Our Image and Likeness: Humanity and Divinity in Italian Humanist Thought*. 2 vols. London, 1970.

——. "The Unknown Quattrocento Poetics of Bartolommeo della Fonte." *Studies in the Renaissance* 13 (1966): 40–122.

Ullman, B. L. *The Origin and Development of Humanistic Script*. Rome, 1960.

Verde, Armando. *Lo Studio fiorentino (1473–1503): Ricerche e documenti*. 6 vols. Florence, 1973–2010.

Weiss, Roberto. *The Renaissance Discovery of Classical Antiquity*. 2nd ed. Oxford, 1988.

Zaccaria, Raffaella. "Della Fonte (Fonzio), Bartolomeo." In *DBI*, 36, 808–14. Rome, 1988.

Index of Correspondents

General Index